The Two Pillars of the Market

STUDIES IN THEOLOGY
SOCIETY AND CULTURE

Volume 7

PETER LANG
Oxford • Bern • Berlin • Bruxelles • Frankfurt am Main • New York • Wien

Jean Lee

The Two Pillars of the Market

A Paradigm for Dialogue between Theology and Economics

PETER LANG
Oxford • Bern • Berlin • Bruxelles • Frankfurt am Main • New York • Wien

Bibliographic information published by Die Deutsche Nationalbibliothek.
Die Deutsche Nationalbibliothek lists this publication in the Deutsche Nationalbibliografie; detailed bibliographic data is available on the Internet at http://dnb.d-nb.de.

A catalogue record for this book is available from the British Library.

Library of Congress Cataloging-in-Publication Data:

Lee, Jean, 1965-
The two pillars of the market : a paradigm for dialogue between theology and economics / Jean Lee.
p. cm.
Includes bibliographical references (p.) and index.
ISBN 978-3-0343-0700-0 (alk. paper)
1. Economics--Religious aspects--Christianity. 2. Covenants--Religious aspects--Christianity. 3. Contracts. I. Title.
BR115.E3L36 2011
261.8'5--dc22
2011004699

Cover image by May Soong.

ISSN 1662-9930
ISBN 978-3-0343-0700-0

Hochfeldstrasse 32, CH-3012 Bern, Switzerland
info@peterlang.com, www.peterlang.com, www.peterlang.net

Printed in Germany

Contents

Preface

This is the formulation of a theological response to the modern economic market. It presents a Two Pillars paradigm for the economic market, whereby covenant and contract serve together as the two 'pillars' that uphold economic order. The modern market is derived and developed upon the legal contract that supports and governs economic activities. Non-contractible assertions in the market remain background presuppositions, of which enactment depends largely on the individual economic agent. In the Two Pillars paradigm, the theological covenant and the legal contract are equally significant assertions that interact and complement each other to uphold a well-balanced economic market. They are both essential in deriving a market that promotes genuine human relationship, freedom and economic justice.

In this book, the covenant foundation of society and its economic significance are rediscovered and examined. The universality and relevance of the covenant concept for economic order is explored, and the covenant compared and contrasted with the contract to show their distinctiveness, significance and interaction in the market. The Two Pillars paradigm is then presented and illustrated through the example of long-term employment arrangements to demonstrate its practicability and potential use as a dialogical framework to examine other economic relationships. Finally, market fundamentals including market motif, limits, assumptions, morality and regulations are explored in dialogue with the Two Pillars response to economics.

This book should appeal to a wider audience beyond the ecclesiastical community, placing it in the arena of public theology. It draws upon the thoughts of economists to examine the Two Pillars paradigm in a wider context. The result is an interdisciplinary study offering a theological-based paradigm that addresses the situation of the modern market in a fundamental and practical way.

This book began life in 2007, when I started to work on the interface between theology and economics. I am indebted to Professor Carver Yu of CGST ('China Graduate School of Theology') for encouraging me to embark on this route, and to CGST for their prayers and financial support throughout my years of research in Edinburgh, where this book was written. In the beautiful historic city of Edinburgh, I learnt from renowned scholars at the University of Edinburgh including Professor David Fergusson of the Divinity School, and Professor Jonathan Thomas of the School of Economics. In addition, I am thankful to Professor Thomas Torrance and Professor Michael Purcell for reviewing and commenting on my work. I am also indebted to the THECE ('Theologically Hopeful Ethnic Chinese in Edinburgh') community for many evenings of intellectual exchanges and sharing of project experiences. In January 2009, an earlier idea of the paradigm in this book was presented at the Young Scholars session of the 'Adam Smith as Theologian' conference in Edinburgh, sponsored by the Templeton Foundation. I am deeply grateful to the encouragement and comments from scholars who attended the session.

PART I

The Covenant Concept in Response to Society and the Economic Order

CHAPTER 1

Introduction

This book starts from the need for a theological response to modern economics. It examines the interface between theology and economics, and offers a comprehensive theological paradigm in response to the modern market. At first sight, the disciplines of theology and economics may appear to have little in common. In fact, the two disciplines share a very fundamental common interest in the nature and activities of human persons as well as the interaction among them. Economics places priority on the satisfaction of human needs and wants through resource allocation and utility maximization. Theology is concerned with the human quest for the truth and the overall well-being of the human person. Unfortunately, the interface between the two disciplines remains relatively underexplored. This book examines the different worldviews and assumptions on human nature of the two disciplines, and proposes a paradigm for the economic market that is both theological and practical. It starts with a rediscovery of the covenant concept underlying the historical development of political society through the work of Johannes Althusius. The scriptural foundation and theology of the covenant concept are then examined to reveal its contents and relevance to economic activities. Its significance having been established, the covenant concept is analysed in comparison with the contract arrangement to derive a theological response to the existing contract-based economic market. This proposal, named the 'Two Pillars' paradigm, offers a framework for illustrative discussion and interdisciplinary dialogue between theology and economics. It also forms the general basis for further discussion of specific economic issues. I shall start my investigation with a brief review of the interface between theology and economics, and a layout of the basis of my proposed paradigm.

1.1 The Need for a Theological Response to Economics

Economic life affects individuals in far greater ways than ever before in this modern era. Participation in the economic market is an unavoidable part of human daily life. No matter how competent a person is in obtaining goods for one's own needs and desires, the dependence on other people to serve such needs is undeniable. Market transactions occur every minute of the day as an integral part of our daily life. Modern markets handle the exchange of goods and services by attaching price values to the objects of exchange. As such, the economy provides a platform for cooperative transactions that allow participants to obtain what they need for daily living by means of exchange in monetary terms. Through the economic order, human life is preserved within a mutually interdependent community of exchange. At the same time, the economic market formed under this process has priorities and inclinations within its own structure and mechanism of exchange. It contains an inclination to exclude intangible but vitally necessary items that can be 'valueless' yet invaluable to human life. Examples of these are fresh air, loving care, friendship, etc. Attempts to package 'love' into sellable services quickly reduce it to something other than genuine love. This means that participants in the economic market are served through the market, while in turn moulded and driven by market priorities and the assigned values within market exchanges. It is therefore up to market participants to establish and uphold the human values that are unquantifiable yet essential to human life. Accordingly, the task of economics is not simply to minimize scarcity or maximize efficiency, but also to help people make the most out of the material gifts of nature by creating conditions and opportunities for participants to lead the best possible life in relation and cooperation with one another. This objective transcends the satisfaction of material needs and wants, to a concern for the total well-being of the human person. A theological response to economics is needed to identify and to offer a balancing framework for healthy economic life. It offers a reflection on human nature, a worldview based on truth, and a genuine concern for the overall well-being of each human person and of humankind as a whole.

Relatively little has been done on the interface between the theology of the human person and market economics in the past. Those who attempt to integrate theology and economics have attempted to draw from a wide range of resources including biblical principles, social ethics or radical theological ideologies. The results have either been piecemeal teachings about economics, or unrealistic radical conceptions about the economy. Few attempt to approach economics from a theological point of view that emphasizes both a theological ground and realistic application. The reason for a lack of interdisciplinary work on theology and economics is partly due to the complexity of the subject, because such interface involves a wide range of factors not only concerning theology and economics, but also philosophy, politics, sociology and psychology. In addition, economics is a subject that deals with the material aspects of human life, while theology has traditionally tended to develop in the tradition of spirituality, with less focus on earthly means and ends. Nevertheless, material means and ends shape our daily lives and significantly affect human capacity for seeking the spiritual truth. The market structure dictates human relationships and imposes its own set of values and priorities on humankind. Continuous reflection upon these market assertions is therefore essential to ensure that the market and its functions serve the overall well-being of society, within their original boundaries and intended purposes. In this regard, theology has a critically important role.

Economics has a theological dimension that has not received systematic exploration in the past. Many are alert to its significance, but a proper framework and structural approach is yet to be presented. The methodology that is required to build a mutually meaningful interface among economists and theologians needs to be investigated. Since the separation of economics as a science in the late 1800s, theologians have been trying to build a bridge between theology and economics from the viewpoint of ethics and morality. Unfortunately, the term 'ethics' appears to have diminishing significance in this postmodern age. At the same time, in the mist of econometrics and scientific pursuit of the discipline, economists struggle with underlying assumptions behind their economic models. The interface between theology and economics offers a valuable bridge for the investigation of human nature, beliefs, values and choices as these relate to economic life. These are issues fundamental to human living, affecting the total well-being of the human person. Recent criticisms of the market and the reconstruction of what is called a 'divine economy' appear to mark a renewed theological interest in this interdisciplinary subject. A reconstruction strongly rooted in a theological stance is yet to find its appeal to the secular audience to whom its proclamation must be directed.

1.2 The Interface between Theology and Economics

When responding to the economic situation, early Christian scholars focus on the relationship between theology and political economy.[1] Waterman presents two possible views between economics and theology, namely 'monistic' and 'pluralistic'. Before 1890, the 'monistic' view takes theology as preceding all subjects, therefore economics as merely a branch of it. From the 1890s to the 1980s, the 'pluralistic' view allots independent status to economics, or scientific knowledge in general.[2] Theologians shift from one extreme where clerics and church assemblies meddled with economic issues, to the other extreme where analysis and facts become distinct from values and prescriptions of the discipline. From then on, as economics takes on its own course of development, Christian scholars embark on studies of selected aspects of the interface between theology and economics. These may be classified into three general areas: (i) Socio-theology – theologians' work on

1 For a collection of essays exploring the interaction between theology and economics from the earliest times to the modern day, see Ian R. Harper and Samuel Gregg, ed., *Christian Theology and Market Economics* (Cheltenham: Edward Elgar, 2008), 1–225.

2 Anthony Michael C. Waterman, 'Economists on the Relation Between Political Economy and Christian Theology: A Preliminary Survey,' *International Journal of Social Economics* 14 (1987): 46–68.

social economics and ethics; (ii) Economics of Religion – Christian economists' attempts to align faith and economics; and (iii) Divine Economy or Theological Economics – a critical approach towards economics, and a subversive theological reconstruction of economics.

In terms of socio-theology and ethics, Catholic encyclicals play a significant role in continuing to address socio-economic issues over the years. Pope John Paul II has issued a number of papers examining how economics related to socio-theological principles. The encyclicals most relevant to economic concerns begin with *Rerum Novarum* (1891), and continue to *Populorum Progressio* (1967) and *Centesimus Annus* (1991), among others. In 2009, Pope Benedict XVI issued the encyclical *Caritas In Veritate*, with a particular emphasis on the importance of truth in our understanding of charity and economics. Together, these papers put forth the Catholic Church's social doctrines on economics, addressing issues such as unemployment, capital, property rights, distribution and planning. The Catholic Church, in its tradition of responding to social issues, mainly focuses on the socio-economic aspects of societal matters in relation to economics.[3]

Over the years, numerous articles have been written on the ethical aspects of economics, many with good biblical references. There is no lack of discussion on the biblical view of economic issues such as stewardship, poverty, materialism, work, etc. In January 1990, the *Oxford Declaration on Christian Faith and Economics* was issued jointly by over one hundred theologians, economists, ethicists, development practitioners, church leaders and business managers from around the world. The declaration consists of basic issues relating to economic life from a biblical viewpoint. Christian reconstructionists, as they are sometimes called, have sought to fashion a

3 A comprehensive exploration of Catholic Social Teachings on economics is beyond the scope of this book. However, I will draw upon relevant sections of the encyclicals during my discussion, especially on concerns over moral aspects of economics. In particular, *Caritas in Veritate* is discussed in chapter 6.4. For discussions of Catholic Social Teachings on economic issues, see Philip Booth, ed., *Catholic Social Teaching and the Market Economy* (London: Institute of Economic Affairs, 2007), 27–43. This book also contains articles about Catholic Social Teachings on some specific economic issues that may be of interest to the reader.

biblical economic epistemology through matters such as theonomy, welfare, debts and the Jubilee law.[4]

In terms of early theological literature, the work and approach of John Calvin on ethics are often quoted as references in response to economic situations. The Reformation takes place at a time of inflation in the economy. While Luther goes back to a mediaeval economic order, Calvin attempts to come to terms with the realities of economic life. However, the dynamic changing context across time gives rise to new economic situations and issues in the modern world. The 'to be known' remains in our understanding of scriptural norms, and the unfolding of world events calls for continuous enquiry into God's purpose in creation. Rather than a single, ideal normative prescription, the Word of God invites us to enter the world in continuous renewal and reflection in discerning the truth. This discernment applies to the economic function, the reasons behind its function, and its consequences.[5] Without such continuous reflections, economic enquiry remains incomplete.

From economists' point of view, social and ethical concerns have also been raised. For example, Richardson calls for awareness in preventing economics from developing as a purely technical discipline. In particular, he raises concerns over a decline in integrity, a narrowing of priorities, and an emasculation of method.[6] Besides biblical approaches, many of the socio-economic discussions have historically centred upon debates about economic systems such as capitalism and socialism. Although there appears to be a consensus over a modest defence of capitalism especially with the

4 For a detailed evaluation on the views of Christian Reconstructionists, see Edd S. Nell, 'A Reformed Approach to Economics: Christian Reconstructionism,' *Journal of the Association of Christian Economists* (1993): 6–20.

5 As Sauer concludes, Christian ethics yield knowledge about economics on the 'transcendent pole of economic enquiry'. For a discussion on the ethical contribution of theology to economics, see James B. Sauer, 'Christian Faith, Economy, and Economics: What Do Christian Ethics Contribute to Understanding Economies?,' *Journal of the Association of Christian Economists* 42 (2003): 17–25.

6 J. David Richardson, 'Frontiers in Economics and Christian Scholarship,' *Christian Scholar's Review* 17, no. 4 (1988): 1–20.

decline of socialism in the modern world, it has also been pointed out that democratic capitalism does not represent the kingdom of God because it is neither a uniquely Christian system nor a system under perfect divine sovereignty.[7]

In 2005, the Association of Christian Economists gathered for a symposium on 'Economics of Religion'. Although the interface between religion and economics is seen as equally important and relevant to the study of economics, the task on hand takes on a different angle in the hands of the economists. Economics of religion is seen to be distinct from religious economics. Religious economics is social and economic reaction from the perspective of the sacred truth. Economics of religion concerns religion and its consequences from social and economic perspectives.[8] The latter approach applies economics and scientific analysis to the study of religion, in order to gain an understanding of economics through an investigation of the belief system. In 1997 the Association of Christian Economists published a special issue of the Journal of the Association of Christian Economists. The issue contains a comprehensive bibliography on Christianity and Economics largely from the viewpoint of Christian economists.[9]

Besides general and methodological concerns, Christian economists have written from a Christian perspective on the economic systems, micro- and macroeconomics, industrial organization, labour, capital, land, poverty, welfare, household, health, education, international economics and economic growth. A couple of the publications have been extensive in

7 John P. Tiemstra, 'Christianity and Economics: A Review of the Recent Literature,' *Christian Scholar's Review* 22 (1993): 227–47.

8 Laurence R. Iannaccone, 'Economics of Religion: Debating the Costs and Benefits of a New Field,' *The Economics of Religion: A Symposium* (2005): 1–9.

9 This publication aims to assist Christian economists to explore economic approaches and issues from a Christian point of view. Accordingly, the bibliography is listed by sixteen economic topics including microeconomic theory, macroeconomics, industrial organization, labour, land and natural resources, economic growth, etc. See Andy Hartropp, 'Christianity and Economics: An Annotated Bibliography by Andy Hartropp', *Journal of the Association of Christian Economists* special issue (December 1997): 1–36.

discussing major economic sub-topics. Hay's book *Economics Today: A Christian Critique* covers many areas in terms of what Christianity has to say about economics.[10] Tiemstra's work is another comprehensive survey of the economic fields from a Reformed Christian viewpoint. These studies emphasize the biblical basis of doing economics, particularly on concepts of stewardship, failure of the scientific methodology, and the nature of human interactions, families and organizations.[11] The traditional approaches by theologians and Christian economists tend to focus on the ethical aspects of economics and human life. While they present valuable insights and contributions to the interdisciplinary area, there remains a continuing need for a comprehensive theological approach.[12]

In recent years, some theologians begin to embark on a critique of modern economics and propose a subversive reconstruction of the economy. These approaches range from metaphorical assertions of the divine economy, to a radical critique and reconstruction of the economy. Loy finds economics to be the most influential of all social sciences in modern times, which has come to fulfil a religious function for men. In particular, the market has become 'a vicious cycle of ever-increasing production and consumption by pretending to offer a secular salvation'.[13] Hill argues that Adam Smith's economics is inherently theological and dependent on the

10 Donald A. Hay, *Economics Today: A Christian Critique* (Vancouver: Regent College Publishing, 2001), 1–340.

11 John P. Tiemstra, ed., *Reforming Economics: Calvinist Studies on Methods and Institutions* (New York: Edwin Mellen Press, 1990), 1–344.

12 This is by no means an exhaustive list of materials in this interdisciplinary area. For example, Latin American economists and theologians including Franz Hinkelammert, Hugo Assmann and Jung Mo Sung have published on this subject in Portuguese and German. See Joerg Rieger, *No Rising Tide: Theology, Economics and the Future* (Minneapolis: Fortress Press, 2009), 5.

13 Loy traces the development of the market as a religion that increasingly penetrates and transforms human life by commodifying the world. He asserts that the market takes on a religious dimension by attempting to satisfy our spiritual needs through our secular obsessions. This leads to environmental catastrophe and social deterioration. The solution needs to come from a struggle against the false market religion and a redirection of spiritual concerns towards religious truth. See David R. Loy,

notion of God's action in nature.[14] In 2001, Nelson's book *Economics as Religion: From Samuelson to Chicago and Beyond* finds modern economics 'the most powerful set of religious beliefs of the modern era'.[15] Functionally, economics is found to dominate modern culture as it did during the early days of Christianity. Economic progress is seen to be a new form of secular religion which has been developing since the early days when social scientists made their way from the Protestant ministry to economics and other related professions.

Following this line of critique, some theologians formulate theological reconstructions of economics. Oslington calls for a 'theological economics' by which theologians discuss theology implicit in contemporary economics. He advocates that the classical theological heritage commends itself and finds its full meaning in relation to economics.[16] Along these lines comes Milbank with the argument for a radical orthodoxy, positioning theology as a meta-discourse in postmodern terms. Taking the radical orthodoxy approach, Long published *Divine Economy*, which traces three strategies for theology to respond to economic questions. These include

---

'The Religion of the Market,' *Journal of the American Academy of Religion* 65 (1997): 275–90.

14 Hill's work contains a good overview of the hidden theology behind Adam Smith's work. Her article contains evaluations of Adam Smith's thoughts from the viewpoints of a natural theology, a 'scientific' religion, a teleology, a psychology, and an evolutionary system. See Lisa Hill, 'The Hidden Theology of Adam Smith,' *The European Journal of the History of Economic Thought* 8 (2001): 1–29.

15 Nelson's work presents a comprehensive view of the gradual penetration and domination of economics in the development of modern culture. See Robert H. Nelson, *Economics as Religion: From Samuelson to Chicago and Beyond* (Pennsylvania: Pennsylvania State University Press, 2001), xxv; and Robert H. Nelson, 'What is "Economic Theology"?,' (paper presented at the Second Abraham Kuyper Consultation on 'Theology and Economic Life: Exploring Hidden Links' Princeton Theological Seminary, Princeton, New Jersey, 22 March 2003).

16 Oslington argues that a separation of theology and economics is neither desirable nor possible. He sees theology as taking an implicit place in modern economics, and that it is necessary for orthodox Christian teachings to take primacy in economics. See Paul Oslington, 'A Theological Economics,' *International Journal of Social Economics* 27 (2000): 32–44.

the early tradition of respecting economics as an independent science, a later tradition of social-theological approach, and a third tradition that draws on ancient understandings of a functional economy. Long argues for the latter approach in asserting theology as the essential participant in economics.[17] This view requires theology to assert and inform economic debates. The concept of divine economy is further explored by Grau in a more recent publication, *Of Divine Economy: Refinancing Redemption*. Using the theological doctrine of redemption as a metaphor, economic subtexts of Christian tradition and their formation by society's economic constructions are examined. Grau points out that the proponents of liberation theology and radical orthodoxy identify neoclassical economics as a problematic outgrowth of modernity. Accordingly, her work attempts to map a 'third space' – a theology of counter-economy, between neoclassical economics and theological discourse.[18] While these critiques of the economy are theologically based and are helpful reflections, they tend to lack realistic applicability. They present assertions and ideologies that are considered a kind of 'theological imperialism', especially to the non-believing community, which forms a significant part of society and therefore a major group of economic participants, which any theological paradigm must take account of.

Another theological alternative to the economic system that has received much attention is Kathryn Tanner's *Economy of Grace*. Tanner attempts to take up a semantic linkage between money and grace within the economic structure. The economy of grace differs radically from the competitiveness and self-interest of the market economy. Under the grace of unconditional giving, God's gifts to humankind lay the foundation of the theological economy on earth. Tanner lays out the theological economy of grace by taking God as an economic concept. Accordingly, God's free giving and lack of needs are taken as the basis for economic endeavours.

17 D. Stephen Long, *Divine Economy: Theology and the Market* (London: Routledge, 2000), 1–336.

18 Marion Grau, *Of Divine Economy: Refinancing Redemption* (New York: T & T Clark, 2005), 1–255.

God's giving as Creator is universal and ever-sufficient. As a result, competition is unnecessary and we can always give freely out of our own 'fullness'.[19] Unfortunately, how this fullness and lack of need can be achieved by any given individual is unclear in Tanner's model. In principle, God is abundance and grants enough of everything for everyone's needs. Therefore we can give freely all the time. In reality, when one is faced with poverty and hunger, this principle appears to lack practicality. In fact, the principle of the creation and providential order appears to be a transcendent and overriding provision, not to be taken as a practical tool, but a collective provision that should be worked out collectively by all humankind. This means that God does create and provide, but human stewardship and the effort to strive against sinful self-interest for equality and solidarity are necessary to preserve the original purpose of creation. Taking such theological concepts and applying them directly to individual acts of giving would reduce the underlying principle to a level deceptive of its original meaning. Consequently, one ends up with practical suggestions that appear unrealistic in given circumstances. Tanner's economy of grace presents a radically different proposal based on principles that are entirely in opposition to various assumptions of current economics. Unconditional giving runs against self-interest, and non-competition against competition for profits. In her opinion, applying minor changes to the existing system appears to be a compromise more than a transformation because the resulting effect is bound to fall short of the radical ideal proposed.[20] I shall argue in chapter 3 that the theological notion for an economy of sharing and grace based on gifting is meaningful in terms of divine truth, but such an ideal economy

19 Kathryn Tanner, *Economy of Grace* (Minneapolis: Fortress Press, 2005), 1–158.

20 Weingartner finds Tanner's work engaging because she is not calling for a new economic system but a transformation of the existing one. See Robert J. Weingartner, review of *Economy of Grace*, by Kathryn Tanner, *Missiology*, 34 (2006): 262–4. Unfortunately, this argument is self-conflicting in itself because Tanner's economy of grace challenges the very fundamental structure and monetary exchange mechanism in the modern market. The only possibility for realizing the gifting notion asserted by the economy of grace is a subversive abandoning of the exchange concept and transformation of the monetary notion as the basis of value measurement.

can only be realized in the end of time when all creation is renewed and restored to perfection in the kingdom of God.

1.3 Theological Concepts as Heuristic Tools for Economic Life

Along the continuing quest for a theological response to economic life, Meeks' *God the Economist* is taken by some theologians as the best work to appear in many years on the theological end of the chain of knowledge about economic life.[21] Meeks employs *oikonomia* as a metaphor for the household, of the divine agency within creation. This reconstruction then stands in critical dialogue with neoclassical economics, pushing towards a broader scope of the term 'economy'. He thinks that the problem with the market is that God has been taken out of the economics arena, such that the plenipotent being became functionalistic and then nihilistic. The concepts of God as the promiser and covenanter no longer reside in daily economic life. To reintroduce the concept, Meeks presents God in the metaphor of the economist with respect to His work as the Torah keeper, as the Creator, of creating human persons in His image, and of the resurrection.[22] God's sovereignty over His household is also revealed in the death and resurrection of Jesus. Scarcity should not be an assumption of God's household because of the freedom and dominance over the means to livelihood by the householder. Accordingly, Meeks calls for a broader meaning of property and property rights to include all those who are called to be God's economist and disciple.

21 J. Philip Wogaman, review of *God the Economist: The Doctrine of God and Political Economy*, *Theology Today*, 47 (1990): 201–2.

22 M. Douglas Meeks, *God the Economist: The Doctrine of God and Political Economy* (Minneapolis: Fortress Press, 1989), 83–92.

Meeks sees work as a central theological issue because of the relationships of authority and subordination that it contains. This falls into his concern of domination and exploitation within human relationships. He points out that work should not be degraded to suffering or valued as the ordering and self-justification of life. Instead, it is the revelation of one's inner self, in parallel to God's work and His rest. God redeems the household from dehumanizing work through redemption from the power of death and sin. Work is therefore a right that leads to personal dignity and inclusion in the community, rather than a commodity to be defined by efficiency. It serves the communal needs of the person so that one may belong to, share in and contribute to the community. Similarly, human needs are distorted by sin and require the realization of divine sovereignty and divine infinity to set us free. Meeks asserts that God is willing to provide for everyone. Although shortages are not illusions, they are attributable to human insatiability rather than the economists' definition of scarcity. In God's household, it is an economy that gives to all access to life and life abundant.[23]

Meeks' work offers some insightful metaphors through the use of theological concepts as heuristic tools. Unfortunately, his discussion lacks a workable framework through which Christians may respond to contemporary economic principles and powers. The political democracy that Meeks affirms often leads to economic distortions in his theological analysis. Meeks criticizes a reliance on market forces as mechanistic and unintended. This is indeed the case but the market has a lot more to offer than Meeks presents. Although the market is built on free choice and individual interests, it is also a combination of what each individual jointly makes out to be. While Meeks is correct in pointing out that freedom is not merely free choice, this argument needs to be further explored.[24]

Meeks finds vast similarities between the economic languages of debt, trust, fiduciary, redemption, confidence, etc., with the biblical uses of the

23 Ibid., 127–55.

24 The concept of freedom as a covenant characteristic and how it relates to economic life are discussed in chapter 3.4.

same words. He therefore goes on to correlate God and economy through the term *oikos*.[25] However, such rhetorical uses of the words do not necessarily support a correlation between the actual issues to hand. Whether the household of God represents the meaning of the economy willed by God on earth is yet to be argued. In addition, Meeks finds that the economy of the church has been corrupted by contemporary market logic such that justice and stewardship have been set aside. While it is true that Christians are to seek the realization of the kingdom of God 'on earth as it is in heaven', does this mean that favourable circumstances must exist for exhibition of such justice and stewardship on earth? Biblical teachings do not appear to presuppose a 'workable' environment. Rather, the church is to stand against the tides of the secular waves to witness its justice and stewardship for Christ. While market logic may be distorted and deficient in itself, it does not claim to exhibit justice in distribution, or to act as a way of organizing human behaviour. The market's formation is based upon natural exhibition of human behaviour and circumstance, not vice versa. To this end, Meeks' understanding of the market requires some modification.

Metaphors and theological concepts are helpful in illustrating theological truth, but the concepts deployed need to be relevant and practicable for economic life. To derive a theological response to economic relationships, it is necessary to start by questioning the market presuppositions concerning human nature and the way human relationships are structured and driven in the market. This can then be compared and contrasted with the theological stance on human nature and relationships. My findings reveal the significance of the covenant way of living that the believing community has long held. The significance of the covenant lies in its relevant application not only as a theory or theology, but as a practical reality of relational order and fundamental structure for society and human life. It is not merely a theological metaphor but a relational concept and way of life deeply rooted in scriptural narratives. The covenant concept has been the basic paradigm for relationships and community life since the times of the Old Testament. It embraces the morality, responsibility and commitment

25 Meeks, *God the Economist: The Doctrine of God and Political Economy*, 33–7.

to economic order that have been eroded as the market economy develops. Covenant encompasses sacred promise, oath, contract, bond or troth. The richness and universality of the covenant concept are embedded in the special disclosures of God – 'in the covenant with Moses that forms Israel, in the new covenant in Jesus Christ that forms the church, and in those wonderful and rare friendships, marriages, and work teams or voluntary associations we sometimes experience'.[26] As Stackhouse points out, 'it was in the very nature of God, and thus of those made in the image of God, to be covenantal'.[27]

The covenant as a theological concept has been subject to a number of explorations from different angles throughout theological scholarship. It has formed the basis of biblical studies, theological frameworks, as well as sociological concerns. In particular, Weir identifies the distinction between the covenant concept, covenant theology and federal theology. The *covenant concept* itself is a broad series of theological thoughts based on scriptural narratives. This concept is used as a framework to derive a system of theology that is known as *covenant theology*. *Federal theology* places the covenant at the core of an entire theological system starting from a prelapsarian covenant with the first Adam, to the postlapsarian covenant with the second Adam Jesus Christ.[28] In Europe, federal theology was developed in the sixteenth century by Reformed Protestant theologians who struggled for church reformation and political liberty.[29] They see the biblical covenant concept not only as a metaphor but as a means of shaping reality.

26 Max L. Stackhouse, *Covenant and Commitments: Faith, Family, and Economic Life* (Louisville: Westminster John Knox Press, 1997), 145.

27 Ibid., 150.

28 David A. Weir, *The Origins of the Federal Theology in Sixteenth-Century Reformation Thought* (Oxford: Clarendon Press, 1990), 3.

29 In particular, federal theology was taught and developed further by Johannes Althusius and his colleagues during the sixteenth century at the University of Herborn into a system of social-federal covenant that became the foundation of common sovereignty and governance. See Thomas O. Hueglin, *Early Modern Concepts for a Late Modern World: Althusius on Community and Federalism* (Waterloo: Wilfrid Laurier University Press, 1999), 57–8. Chapter 2 of this book examines the development and application of the covenant concept to society in further detail.

Accordingly, they applied the federal or covenantal principle to political society, leading to the gradual development of a federal political structure and the various types of modern federalism.

In this book, I identify the covenant as a concept that reveals the intended way of human community life and relational order embedded in the creation and providence of God. It is God's chosen way of relating with Israel, later on renewed through the relational order established by the redemptive work of Christ. As such, it is also the authentic way of relating among human persons, and serves as the foundation of human relationships in community and the wider society. The covenant is therefore applied in this book as an ethical-practical concept, rather than in the form of a covenant theology or a doctrinal concern. The covenant concept is revealed through scriptural narratives, explored through covenant or federal theology, grounded within the doctrine of creation, and part of a Christian theological worldview. Theology has much to contribute in terms of the appropriate definition, characteristics, content and application of the covenant concept. The covenant concept itself is not limited to a theology or a particular doctrine. It is a fundamental way of being that is contained in a theological anthropology about authentic human relationships. Accordingly, covenant characteristics must be identified and enacted in human life and economic activities for the benefit of human well-being. These characteristics are inherent in the goodness of human persons since their creation by the Divine. In analysing the covenant concept, comparing it to the modern contract-based market arrangements, and exploring the place of covenantal elements in economic activities, we rediscover the route to a well-balanced economic market for the total well-being of the whole person.

A number of scholars have applied the covenant concept to various spheres of human life. Allen puts it in a straight forward manner. He sees covenantal relationships to involve a sense of faith and belonging with respect to a moral community. Within this moral community, each person is uniquely valuable while at the same time participates by entrusting oneself to the others. Accordingly, participants in the covenant community are mutually responsible to each other.[30] Sacks describes the act of covenant as one requiring both parties to respect each other's integrity as free agents. The key element here is not power or history, but a verbal declaration that is mutually binding. Covenant binds the parties involved under an open-ended bond of mutuality and loyalty.[31] Horton identifies the specific praxis throughout redemptive history of the covenant as the culture of the people of God. The believing community incorporates the covenant as part of its own cultic culture, through which it interprets the secular world.[32] Although the covenant concept has been widely discussed as a relational concept and in the form of covenant or federal theology, it has not been examined in the context of a comprehensive approach to economic life. This book fulfils this important task through an appropriate deployment of the covenant concept in a comprehensive paradigm that offers a universal framework to economic life. As the divine way of relational order, the covenantal economic life extends into the end of time, when the people of God shall be redeemed and reside in common allegiance to the Creator within the economy or household of the Triune God. It is the mission of the believing community to articulate and practise this covenantal way so that economic life can be humanized and restored to its original truth intended by the Creator.

30 Allen's application of the covenant concept emphasizes the moral and relational aspects of community life. See Joseph L. Allen, *Love and Conflict: A Covenantal Model of Christian Ethics* (Nashville: Abingdon Press, 1984), 17.

31 As a Jewish Rabbi, Sacks advocates the covenant concept as a fundamental basis of societal, political and human living. See Jonathan Sacks, *The Home We Build Together: Recreating Society* (London: Continuum, 2007), 109.

32 Horton extends the covenant concept to examine its basis and implications in salvation, redemption and eschatology. See Michael S. Horton, *Covenant and Eschatology: The Divine Drama* (Louisville: Westminster John Knox Press, 2002), 13.

1.4 Towards a Theological Paradigm for the Market

Humanization of life is the rediscovery and enactment of the truth and goodness within human nature that is embedded in creation. Such truth and goodness reside in the authenticity of humankind as originally created by God in its perfect form. In the beginning God sees 'goodness' (טוב) in His creation, where all things created are pleasing to His eyes. Human sin leads to a dehumanization of human life, causing distortion and distress to the original intention of creation. A theology of economics neither stops at a theological reflection on economics, nor is it merely a social ethical view of economics. It offers a theological worldview that starts from truth and authenticity, deriving a framework for examining the economic activities that make up a vital part of human life. It is a public theology that responds to contemporary economic situations, calling for reflective examinations and a return to the truth and goodness of creation. The knowledge of God and divine acts shape not only the morality of Christian life, but offer universal truths that are highly relevant to secular life. The God of creation sets no boundaries between secular and spiritual as the Creator embraces and upholds the whole cosmos. In the economic arena, material needs and desires cannot be separated from spiritual needs and the quest for authenticity in human living. These include the need for relationship with others from the level of intimacy to casual social encounters. In this regard, a person acts and in turn reacts in association with others. The economic market is a platform for exchange relationships and cooperative measures. As economic agents participate and act within the market, market norms are formed within the boundaries of contractual arrangements. These norms, together with the underlying assumptions of the market, in turn shape and steer the participants within it.

In this study, I derive a theological response to the market economy by examining the covenant concept in contrast and comparison with the contract arrangement that makes up economic market exchanges. Since society and economic activities have undergone drastic changes throughout history, I shall focus on the modern context rather than on the alternative forms of economic structures in the past. While I draw upon certain historical roots in discussing the development of concepts and formation of the modern economic order, my primary concern is to formulate a workable and relevant economic paradigm for the modern market. Accordingly, detailed historical explorations and study of alternative forms of economic structures are beyond the scope of this book. The book explores the following questions: What are the foundation and assumptions of the modern economic market? What do theological insights offer in terms of responding to the need for a market that promotes the well-being of the whole person? How does the covenant concept contribute to and interact with the contract in the modern contract-based market? I argue for a Two Pillars paradigm asserting that both contract and covenant concepts are essential to a harmonious functioning of the economy on earth. A purely contract-based market deteriorates to an egocentric individualism while a completely covenantal society resides in eschatological hope. The two concepts need to act and interact in complementary ways with each other to uphold a well-balanced economic market. Accordingly, I define and apply the concepts of covenant and contract within a theological paradigm in response to the economic market in a relevant and realistic way.

This book is interdisciplinary in scope but primarily theological in nature. It affirms the importance of the discipline of economics while at the same time presents theological truth and insights concerning the unquantifiable, human characteristics that are easily overlooked in economic analysis. Accordingly, this study is directed towards an audience from the disciplines of both theology and economics, as well as the wider public interested and participating in economic activities. Theology offers a view of human nature that reminds humankind of the relational nature of human activities as well as the distorted sinfulness of human desires. It also offers a worldview based on creation that responds to the economic concerns of the modern times. Rather than taking the traditional socio-ethical approach that offers a narrower response to particular economic issues or principles, I work towards a more fundamental and comprehensive framework. At the same time, I avoid the overwhelming assertions of a subversive theological reconstruction that tends to remain an ideology.

This book is divided into two parts. Part I starts the formulation of a theological response to the economic market by identifying the covenant concept as the foundation of society and the economic order. Its goal is to derive a theological concept that is both relevant and practical to economic activities. Starting from a historical study on the development of the polity, the theological covenant is identified as the underlying concept for the development of federalism. Chapter 2 studies the covenant concept as the basis of early federalism through the work of Johannes Althusius. It shows the historical significance of the covenant concept in the development of political society and the economic order, and argues for a rediscovery of covenant roots, awareness, understanding and enactment in the modern market. Chapter 3 follows with a discussion on the significance of human nature on economic activities, and the place of the covenant concept as an essential part of human nature under the doctrine of creation. It introduces the covenant as a concept deeply rooted in scriptural narratives and highly relevant to relational, societal and economic order. The result is a call for the need to rediscover covenant characteristics in society, and to find a way for covenant characteristics to penetrate the existing economic market.

Part II of this book presents and illustrates the Two Pillars paradigm that results from the theological formulation in Part I. The covenant concept is rediscovered and reintroduced in the modern market as an essential pillar that upholds economic life in a complementary way to the contractual arrangement. Chapter 4 presents the Two Pillars paradigm as a realistic alternative for a paradigm shift of the economic market. It contains a conceptual analysis of the contract and covenant concepts. The Two Pillars paradigm is then presented in respect of its impact on productivity and possessions in the market. To demonstrate the Two Pillars paradigm and the interaction between covenant and contract within this framework, chapter 5 examines its application to long-term employment arrangements. This specific illustration further clarifies the interaction and complementary nature of covenant and contract when applied simultaneously to economic arrangements. Chapter 6 then places the Two Pillars paradigm in dialogue with the work of various economists. It identifies the boundaries and limitations of market models, and points towards continuous reflection and renewal of the underlying motif and assumptions of economic life.

Chapter 7 contains a final summary of my findings and conclusion. For the believing community, this book rediscovers the significance of the covenant as a scriptural and theological resource relevant to economic and community life. It reiterates the importance of covenant awareness and shows how covenantal living can be practicable and enacted in the contract-based modern market. For the non-believing community, it offers 'covenant' as a distinct and practicable theological concept that carries rich insights relevant to economic life. It contains an apologetic call for the rediscovery of and reflection upon the essential covenant characteristics that must interact with the contractual arrangements for the well-being of the whole person. To retain a proper focus for this study, the discussion of political order and civil society is limited to that of the application of the covenant, with an intention of identifying the implications related to a covenantal economic order. Discussion of the contract and its development is limited to those aspects that are relevant to development of the economic market. Areas relating to the development of political order such as the social contract, civil society, political contractual arrangements, or development of later forms of federalism, are beyond the scope of this study.

This book takes an ethical-practical approach.[33] It involves exploring application of the covenant concept to the economic order in critique of the contract-based market order. A conceptual analysis of the covenant concept in comparison and contrast to the contractual approach will be included to derive the Two Pillars paradigm that emphasizes the importance of simultaneously applying covenant and contract to economic activities. I will interact with the work of economists Adam Smith, Amartya Sen, Gary Becker and others; as well as theologians Johannes Althusius, Karl Barth, Herman Bavinck, Jürgen Moltmann and others. For a discussion of the covenant concept and its application to economic life, I will engage with the work of Jonathan Sacks, Max Stackhouse, Eric Mount, among others. I will also draw upon the work of legal scholars and sociologists.

33 This approach is described in Herman Bavinck, *Reformed Dogmatics, vol. 1: Prolegomena* (Grand Rapids: Baker Academic, 2003), 536. It is discussed in further details in chapter 2.1 of this book.

The philosopher and economist Smith is selected for his pioneering role in economics, and for a study of his moral philosophy that serves as presupposition to the Smithian economic system and modern day economics. Amartya and Becker are Nobel Prize Winners in economics with rather different views and approaches towards the market. Althusius is selected for his application of the covenant concept to a system of political and economic order. A specific example of the practical insights presented using the Two Pillars theological framework will be demonstrated through interaction with the modern economic concept of relational contracts as applied to long-term employment situations.

My argument for a theologically based ethical-practical paradigm to economic order is grounded upon a conviction in the doctrine of creation. Exploration of the economic order must originate from creation because of its relational nature, and the fundamental cosmic nature of its material content. The existence of humankind depends on the cosmic creation in the absolute sense. One cannot survive in the world without this cosmic creation. This is also the reason why economics appears as a paradoxical problem that is both unimportant to spiritual reflections yet highly significant to human concerns. Our ontological existence depends upon it. Its significance is captured in the assertion that creation 'is an incontestable and unshakeable sign of the real grace of God addressed to him that the cosmos is a home prepared to satisfy his own and his fellow-creatures' needs, to nourish him and them, and in this way, when existence has been given to them, to assure their continuation as the presupposition of the activity assigned to them'.[34] Therefore creation is a divine blessing freely given to humankind, granting the possibility for us to become God's covenant partners.

Applying the covenant idea to society and polity is not a new idea, but the use of the covenant concept in deriving a comprehensive market paradigm has not been fully explored in the past. As I shall demonstrate in chapter 2, the covenant concept serves as the foundation in the early formulation of the federal political structure. The economic structure

34 Karl Barth, *Church Dogmatics* (Edinburgh: T. & T. Clark, 1958), III/1: 207.

is part of this political order in society. Being a fundamental element of relational order, the covenant does not stop at a structural level. Covenant characteristics need to penetrate every aspect of societal living to cultivate the norms necessary for authentic human living. This authenticity resides in the original intention of creation by the divine Creator. Accordingly, a detailed exploration of the covenant in respect of economic relationship is vital for our understanding of the missing authenticity in modern economic life. The use of the covenant concept in parallel with the contractual basis of the modern market reveals a new paradigm that contributes to our understanding of what the economic market should be and how a well-balanced market can be formulated. The following chapter starts my formulation of a theological response to the modern economic market from the rediscovery of the covenant concept fundamental to the historical development of political society.

CHAPTER 2

The Covenantal Federalism of Johannes Althusius

This chapter studies the historical roots of political society and rediscovers the significance of covenant as a fundamental concept underlying the development of society and as the basis of federalism. Economic activities denote the cooperation and interaction of individuals in society to satisfy the material needs and wants of each other. In the modern era, this is done primarily through increasingly global and complex markets that govern the economic order. Such economic order in turn falls under the political society that determines and governs it. Accordingly, the structural foundation of the polity lays the context and fundamentals for the political and economic activities within it.

The work of seventeenth-century Reformed theologian and philosopher Johannes Althusius is selected for this study because he pioneered the application of covenant and federal theology to the development of the polity. To the seventeenth-century theologians, theology is not merely an intellectual pursuit but a reality that penetrates all aspects of human life. The covenantal way of relating is thus taken as a reality that offers insights into the actual formation of society and political structure. Althusius' work shows that the economic order is embedded within a universal, covenantal polity that has become the foundation of federalism. Accordingly, the covenant concept is rediscovered as a relevant, practicable and essential notion known to underlie the formation of the Western society. This covenantal polity becomes the context of the economic activities within it. The place of the economic order in Althusius' polity is examined through a comparison of the covenant concept with notions of contractual arrangements developing around his time. The result is a rediscovery of the covenant concept as a significant theological notion essential for proper functioning of the economic order.

2.1 An Ethical-Practical Approach to Covenant Theology

In modern society, the contractual structure is backed up by law, enforced through the legal system, and clarified in written documentation. The contract is used daily in written and unwritten forms as a readily understood means of transactional exchange. In contrast, the covenant that remains in the background or as an underlying subconscious assumption is not easily identifiable. Where it is considered, its origin and meaning can easily be distorted or rendered similar to that of the contract. This lack of conscious awareness and enactment of the covenant concepts tilts the balance of the economic market towards an unhealthy over-reliance on the contract. Examining the application of the covenant concept and its implications for economic order helps to rediscover and clarify the meaning and reality of the covenant concept in society. The development of covenant theology in history brought about a strand of covenant theology known as federal theology, which in turn developed into fundamental notions of federalism for a covenant-based polity.

The argument in this book follows the ethical-practical theological approach identified by reformed theologian Herman Bavinck.[1] It is devel-

1 Bavinck asserts that human persons live before philosophizing. The way that human persons connect to the world and each other affect their capacity to receive the truth as revealed to them. Accordingly, he identifies four groups of theological approaches during the development of theological methods from an apologetic point of view. These are historical-apologetic, speculative, religious-empirical, and ethical-psychological. The historical-apologetic approach sought historical proofs for the truth of revelation. Examples include natural theology, the history-of-religion movement, scientific theology and the historical-critical method. The speculative approach, such as the mediating theology of Schleiermacher, emphasizes the dominance and autonomy of the subject. The religious-empirical approach infers religious content from experience and epistemology. The ethical-psychological approach accents ethical self-assertion with a religious-ethical power addressed to the human conscience. Within this last group of approaches, the ethical-practical method sees Christianity as a spiritual and moral religion focusing on redemption and the kingdom of God. See Bavinck, *Reformed Dogmatics, vol. 1: Prolegomena*, 497–559.

oped based on the emphasis of ethical self-assertion. Because of the universal nature of economic relationships, the theological response to economic order must be able to speak to both believers and non-believers. It is the formulation of a public theology that speaks to authentic human nature as well as the needs and desires of the human person. The ethical-practical method does not start with the Christian doctrine or historical fact, but a religious-ethical power within the human heart and conscience. It leaves space for diversity in the process and decision of religious inclinations, but demands from human persons an antecedent moral state, a capacity for the good, and the need for redemption. This approach does not take theology as a state of the subject to be justified to the human intellect or to be analysed, but as 'an objective historical power corresponding to the moral needs of human beings and finds its proof and justification in those needs'.[2] Rediscovery of federal and covenantal origins for the polity represents a rediscovery of the objective historical intentions for the covenant to serve as an essential foundation of society and the economic order.

Historically, covenant theology has taken covenant as the core organizing theme of Christian theology. In the sixteenth and seventeenth centuries, covenant (*foedus*) developed as a core dogmatic concept in federal theology by Ulrich Zwingli. From the middle of the sixteenth century, views of the covenant as an alliance with God began to emerge. Theologians distinguished between the covenant of works (*foedus operum*) or covenant of nature (*foedus naturae*) before the Fall, and the covenant of grace (*foedus gratiae*) in Christ. In the *Summa doctrinae de foedere et testamento Dei* by federal theologian Johannes Cocceius, the covenant is identified with the nature of God himself, while the covenant of grace refers to the eternal redemption through the Son in the Father. Salvation history is therefore considered to be characterized by God's act in the covenant of works and grace. During that time, controversial discussions continued around Cocceius' approach and John Calvin's doctrine of predestination.[3]

2 Ibid., 552.

3 Stackhouse points out that federal theology evolved from the creedal-doctrinal side of the Calvinist-influenced movement. Others involved in this development includes

In the eighteenth and nineteenth centuries, debates among Reformed theologians have increasingly showed that this segregation of the covenant into works and grace is problematic.[4] Because of the richness and variations in application of the covenant concept to different relationships and contexts, attempts to use the covenant as a core anchor for a system of dogmatic theology give rise to many controversial debates concerning double covenants and predestination. While such discussions contribute to theological understanding, they attenuate the scope of covenant theology by only insisting on its place as a doctrinal concern. Covenant theology is better reconceived as involving both the doctrinal relationship between God and humankind, as well as the relational order of societal living among human persons. Its application to economic order is an ethical-practical concern beyond doctrinal implications that capitalizes upon the intended covenantal way of life prescribed in the order of creation.

Every theological method has its own shortcomings. The ethical-practical approach faces drawbacks when used apologetically.[5] It presupposes the significance of the moral needs of human persons and that those needs correspond to spiritual desires. Unfortunately, human nature does not necessarily incline towards the truth. The gospel contains messages that are contradictory to the natural liking of human nature. Thus there is always danger for the truth to be deformed to suit human tastes. A solid theological understanding must be developed to ensure the covenant concept retains its theological root and meaning when placed in the public

---

Ames in England, Ussher in Ireland and Witsius in Holland. Later on, critiques of covenantal thought associate federal theology with a dogmatic scholasticism. For more details on development of the covenantal confessions and critiques, see Max L. Stackhouse, 'The Moral Meanings of Covenant,' *Annual of the Society of Christian Ethics* (1996): 249–64.

4 A detailed discussion of the history and content of covenant and federal theologies is beyond the scope of this book. For a discussion of the dogmatic aspects of the covenant, see Hans Hübner, 'Covenant,' in *The Encyclopedia of Christianity*, ed. Erwin Fahlbusch, Jan Milic Lochman, John Mibiti, Jaroslav Pelikan and Lukas Vischer (Grand Rapids: Eerdmans, 1999), 713.

5 For more details on the limitations of the ethical-practical approach, see Bavinck, *Reformed Dogmatics, vol. 1: Prolegomena*, 551–9.

spectrum. I shall proceed to show that the federal form of political structure is deeply rooted in a covenant theology that contains implications for the economic order within the polity.

2.2 Development of Federalism from the Covenant Concept

The word for the political pattern 'federalism' comes from the word *foedus*, the Latin word for 'covenant'. These words were often used interchangeably in the sixteenth and seventeenth centuries. Karlberg finds that political covenants formed the foundation of civil order in many places under the Reformed faith, but the relationship between the theological covenant concept and the covenant as a political theory is not easily determined.[6] In spite of such complexities, the connection between covenant theology and the rise of federalism is undeniable.

Early ideas of the federalist state started to develop in the sixteenth century, when the covenant concept was applied to politics by the Monarchomachists, a group of Calvinists resisting absolutism in France. Their theory of resistance against tyranny is based on the Old Testament theology of the double covenant. In the first covenant on Mount Sinai, the Decalogue serves as the law between God and Israel. There has been no king other than the Divine. In the second covenant, Israel transfers their sovereignty to the king before God. Therefore they argue that when a king breaks the covenant, sovereignty should revert to the people. In the case of a tyrant or when the king breaks God's own covenant with His people, the people are thus bound to resist under God's will. This means that in a

6 Mark W. Karlberg, *Covenant Theology in Reformed Perspective* (Oregon: Wipf and Stock Publishers, 2000), 60.

covenantal nation, the people have the authority to act against rulers who breach the covenant.[7]

Klempa points out that although the different forms and meanings of covenant in the Bible were not recognized by theologians before the advent of modern critical study of the Bible, earlier theologians already noticed the pervasiveness of the covenant idea in the Bible. A number of them in the Reformation and post-Reformation period even constructed their dogmatic systems upon it. The two most influential theologians with regard to covenant theology in the 1500s were Caspar Olevianus and Zacharius Ursinus. Around the same time, corresponding developments of covenant theology took place with treatises written by Dudley Fenner and William Perkins in England, and Robert Rollock in Scotland. Later on, covenant theology took the name of federal theology under John Coccejus and Herman Witsius, among others.[8]

In the sixteenth to eighteenth centuries, use of the covenant in political thought took on the name of federalism. Federalism originates from the federal theology presented by Swiss reformed theologian Heinrich Bullinger in *De Testamento seu Feodere unico et aeterno* (*The One and Eternal Testament or Covenant of God*) published in 1534. It becomes a form of political pattern, while federal theologians continue their attempts to deal with both political and ecclesiastical issues. Other early exponents of the federal polity include Caspar Oelvian in Heidelberg and Johannes

7 In this regard, Moltmann asserts that the covenantal state presupposes a positive anthropology that enables a critical theology of power, i.e. a democratic process for the control of power. It supports equality and human rights, offering power to a covenant of free citizens under an anticipation of the kingdom of God. See Jürgen Moltmann, *God for a Secular Society: The Public Relevance of Theology* (London: SCM Press, 1999), 26–39.

8 William Klempa, 'The Concept of the Covenant in 16th and 17th Century Continental and British Reformed Theology,' in *A Covenant Challenge to Our Broken World*, ed. Allen O. Miller (Atlanta: Darby Printing, 1982), 130–47. In this article, Klempa finds that the root of the covenant idea is in patristic and medieval theology since the concept was first mentioned briefly in the works of Irenaeus and Augustine. Many other theologians took up the development of covenant theology during the 1500s–1600s. Their names are not listed exhaustively here.

Althusius in Herborn. This covenant-based system of political prototype is brought into New England and American through the Puritan emigration.[9] McCoy and Baker point out that 'federalism understands the relationships between God and the world and among humans as based on covenants among their members, some tacit and inherited from the past, others explicit and made or renewed in the present'.[10] Scholars find that in the Bible, the covenant shapes economic, political and familial relationships, as well as the relation between God, creation and humanity. Federal theologians affirm that God has established His covenant with all nature and humans in creation. Subsequent covenants continue, renew and respond to the original covenant by which the world was created. Accordingly, the nature of and relationships within social groups are covenantal by sovereign design. Continuous renewal of the covenant affirms that humanity is developing towards greater fulfilment within the unfolding economies of God's covenant. This is a dynamic process heading towards ultimate justice and love. Federal theologians hold a strong hope for the future in spite of their acknowledgement of human sinful nature because of this development towards original goodness that is shaped and committed through the covenant.[11] Under federalism, covenant is the basis of a political-civil society, developing from private to public associations, forming cities, provinces and commonwealth. Without covenant, society is merely a crowd or a collection of beings.[12] Federal theology soon passed from the scene, but it left a meditational role in restating the biblical covenantal concept within historical circumstances.[13]

9 Moltmann, *God for a Secular Society: The Public Relevance of Theology*, 30.

10 Charles S. McCoy and J. Wayne Baker, *Fountainhead of Federalism* (Louisville: Westminster John Knox Press, 1991), 12.

11 Ibid., 13–14.

12 Ibid., 57.

13 Gardner points out that 'not only did covenant serve as the mediator of an essentially biblical and communal concept of society; it also provided the basis for a synthesis of reason and revelation grounded in a strong doctrine of Creation. ... Covenant points to the fundamental unity of virtue and law in a concept of community, and, more especially, of political community based upon mutual trust and fidelity to a

There are fundamental confusions between the system of covenant theology and the biblical idea of the covenant concept during their development. As Weir asserts, federal theology is a specific type of covenant theology in that the covenant concept holds together every detail of the theological system, and is characterized by a covenant scheme centred on the first and second Adam. He traces the development of the covenant concept as follows:

> [T]he covenant with Adam comes out of the thought patterns and manner of argumentation of the second half of the sixteenth century. Once the prelapsarian covenant had developed into a theological commonplace, it was utilized further in the scholastic debates, disputations, and discussions of theology of the period between 1560 and 1600. Once this novel idea entered into the theological systems of the time, it quickly assumed a powerful and prominent place in the structure of Reformed dogmatics, for it was one of the bases of the theology of nature, which in turn was the framework and foundation for the theology of grace.[14]

Attempts to apply the covenant concept to systematic theology face a number of drawbacks. Covenant theologians identify two main covenants – the covenant of works and the covenant of grace. This double-covenant scheme is criticized for a lack of solid biblical basis. A greater difficulty lies in the notion of God dealing with humanity in distinct ways of works and grace. This leads to the question of two salvations. In spite of such difficulties, covenant theology has made some positive contributions. It sought to base itself on scriptural revelation and to provide an inclusive and universal understanding of salvation. More importantly, the covenant concept takes on a significant role in shaping the early forms of federal order with its evangelical interpretation and practical application. Covenant holds together the sovereignty of God and human responsibility, presenting the

---

common cause.' See E. Clinton Gardner, *Justice and Christian Ethics* (Cambridge: Cambridge University Press, 1995), 117–19.

14 Weir, *The Origins of the Federal Theology in Sixteenth-Century Reformation Thought*, 63.

rightful claims of God and human freedom.[15] The covenant is therefore an important concept alongside others in a theological system. However, it does not necessarily take a doctrinal or central role within the theological system, but provides a focal awareness of theological relationships and integrating structures.[16] In particular, the covenant concept presents the prescribed and revealed structure for practical earthly order that is relevant and applicable to all arenas of living, including political, familial and economic life.

Elazar's work offers some clarification of the complexities in terms of the application of the covenant concept to politics. He identifies a bridge from the theological covenant concept to its political definition, as follows:

> Theologically, covenant embodies the idea that relationships between God and human are based upon morally sustained compacts of mutual promise and obligation, as in the covenants with Noah, Abraham, Moses, and, for Christians, the New Testament or Covenant. Politically, covenant expresses the idea that people can create communities and civil societies through such compacts (whether religious or secular), thereby establishing enduring partnerships.[17]

For over twenty-five years, Elazar has endeavoured to show the impact of the political theology of federalism on modern federalism. Taking this work one step further, Baker connects covenant theology and federalism by suggesting several layers of political federalisms in the stream of thought from the early Protestant Reformers to the founding fathers of America. The fundamental assertion underlying these scholarly endeavours is that the covenant theology of early Protestantism lays the basis for modern

15 Klempa, 'The Concept of the Covenant in 16th and 17th Century Continental and British Reformed Theology', 137–43.

16 Horton, *Covenant and Eschatology: The Divine Drama*, 17.

17 Daniel J. Elazar and John Kincard, ed., *The Covenant Connection: From Federal Theology to Modern Federalism* (New York: Lexington, 2000), 5.

federalism. Modern political theorists then borrow the concept, embrace the covenant idea and secularize it.[18]

The covenant concept was developed and applied to society during the seventeenth century in the Netherlands, England, Scotland and America. Its scope extends from the social compacts of the early Israelites, to a broad understanding of the cosmos and the relationships within. It takes on a form of unity expressed as a divine commonwealth. It is not a family, company or democracy, but an ordering principle of loyalty to the fundamental law of reason and revelation. The ultimate covenantal society involves the maturity of free and responsible citizenships embracing and participating in its law and order.[19] Torrance points out that the ancient coronation oaths and the practice of contracts in feudal society in Scotland and France clearly indicate a long history of contractual government arrangements. The doctrine of social contract goes back to Plato's *Republic*. Contractarian forms of society start with feudalism and continue to exert significant influence in modern democracy.[20] Nevertheless, there are important differences between contracts and covenants, or contractarian communities versus covenant consociations.[21] These differences must be properly distinguished for a clear picture of the covenantal society.

18 J. Wayne Baker, 'Faces of Federalism: From Bullinger to Jefferson,' *Publius* 30, no. 4 (2000): 25. In particular, Rothman provides a useful account of the historical development and implication of the covenant concept and the contract theories in deriving the American constitution. See Rozann Rothman, 'The Impact of Covenant and Contract Theories on Conceptions of the U.S Constitution,' *Publius* 10, no. 4 (1980): 149–63.

19 Niebuhr asserts that 'covenant was the binding together in one body politic of persons who assumed through unlimited promise responsibility to and for each other and for the common laws under God.' See H. Richard Niebuhr, 'The Idea of Covenant and American Democracy,' *Church History* 23 (1954): 130–3.

20 James B. Torrance, 'The Covenant Concept in Scottish Theology and Politics and Its Legacy,' *Scottish Journal of Theology* 34 (1981): 232–3.

21 For a conceptual analysis of covenant and contract, see chapter 4.2.

2.3 Johannes Althusius and His Method

In spite of the wide applications of the covenant concept to theology and hermeneutics, the most significant use of the covenant is in its application to society. Since covenant is the way of relating among human persons by divine creation and design, it is the most authentic way for building political and economic society. This can be demonstrated through the work of seventeenth-century philosopher and Reformed theologian Johannes Althusius. Althusius is known as the intellectual 'father of federalism'. His work demonstrates application of the covenant concept to a federal or covenantal political system embracing both ecclesiastical and secular communities. Althusius' political philosophy is built upon the Reformed Calvinistic view of human nature and application of the covenant concept. His work draws on the covenant tradition of the Reformed Protestant faith as well as a range of other sources including the Bible, history and political philosophy, the Roman law, his experience with the sixteenth-century political structure, and other writers of his times. For the federalists, God's covenant is the basis of the order of creation. Being the authoritative sources of covenantal elements and conditions, divine commandments permeate nature and set out the necessary moral order. This approach stands in contrast to the rational or natural approaches to reality. Since creation is in covenant with God, society is also based on covenantal arrangements. Therefore application of the covenant concept penetrates politics, family, church, economic relations and all aspects of human relationships. Human communities are often represented by particular persons in the biblical covenants. Examples of these are Abraham representing the people of Israel, and Christ representing humanity under sufferings and redemption.[22] Based on a Reformed view of sinful humankind after the fall, federalists set limits to human power because of the necessity for checks and balances to restrain evil and to direct humankind towards goodness and justice. Under

22 See chapter 3 for a discussion of some specific biblical covenants and their implications on the economic order.

the covenant between God and His creation, God's creative acts continue in human history until the consummation of all things.[23]

Althusius (1563–1638) received his doctorate in civil and ecclesiastical law in 1586 at Basle, and published his first book *Jurisprudentia Romana* in the same year. From 1586 to 1604, Althusius was a member of the faculty of law at the Reformed Academy in Herborn. He became the rector of Herborn in 1597, and published *Civilis Conversationis Libri Duo* in 1601. In 1603, Althusius published his most successful work, the *Politica*, in which the first systematic philosophy of political federalism is developed based on the covenant concept.[24] Skinner describes the *Politica* as 'the most systematic statement of revolutionary Calvinist political thought'.[25] To explore the application of the covenant concept and Calvinistic human nature to society, I shall focus specifically on the political and economic order demonstrated in the *Politica*.

The initial publication of *Politica* attracted significant interest and secured for Althusius the position of chief magistrate of Emden, an imperial city of the new Dutch Republic. Althusius held this position for the next thirty-four years until his death. During the seventeenth century, Emden was a wealthy city known as the 'Geneva of the North'. It was engaged in religious conflict and struggle over control that was typical, and a garrison was put to arbitrate between religious opinions and decisions of the imperial authorities.[26] Emden was also a city that embraced the Reformed faith with a strong Calvinist spirit, often known as the 'alma mater' of the Dutch Reformed Church. This was the environment where Althusius tested and

23 McCoy and Baker, *Fountainhead of Federalism*, 52–4.

24 Johannes Althusius, *Politica* (Indianapolis: Liberty Fund, 1995), xi. Althusius' *Politica Methodice Digesta, Atque Exemplis Sacris et Profanis Illustrata* (Politics Methodically Digested, Illustrated with Sacred and Profane Examples) was first published in 1603; revised editions were published in 1610 and 1614. The Liberty Classics edition used in this book was translated from Latin to English with an introduction by Frederick S. Carney in 1964, and revised with a foreword by Daniel J. Elazar in 1995.

25 Quentin Skinner, *The Foundations of Modern Political Thought* (Cambridge: Cambridge University Press, 1978), II: 341.

26 Carl J. Friedrich, *The Age of the Baroque* (New York: Harper & Row, 1952), 143.

elaborated his *Politica*.[27] Revised extended versions of the *Politica* were subsequently reissued in 1610 and 1614. In 1617, he published another book on a system of juridical law based on biblical law, Roman law and various customary laws.

German historian Otto von Gierke points out that Althusius' work was largely forgotten until it was rediscovered in the nineteenth century. He identifies Althusius' *Politica* as 'the earliest attempt at a strictly systematic and complete exposition of what is called Politics'.[28] Indeed, the political framework in *Politica* turns out to be practical, logical and complete especially when viewed within the context of the 1600s.[29] The Netherlands was claiming its own independence by the end of the sixteenth century. The Dutch were consolidating victory of their revolutionary move to establish the Dutch Republic (1581–1795). Although Althusius was not Dutch, he resided in the territory and was confronted with the political scenes before him. He advocated the idea of establishing an ordered and harmonious society through mutual agreement. This notion later develops into the single social contract concept presented by Rousseau. However, Althusius' covenantal 'contract' differs from the social contract in that it resides not only between persons but also in multifaceted capacities among rulers, community and people.[30]

27 Althusius, *Politica*, xi-xii.

28 Otto von Gierke, *The Development of Political Theory* (New York: Howard Fertig, 1966), 16.

29 Gierke speculates that Althusius' significant contribution to political philosophy being overlooked may be attributable to him being German, since German literature has been given little account until the work of Samuel Pufendorf. However, Althusius' contribution is not only in politics. His work contains a synthesis of embedded concepts of community, covenant and human nature. Althusius' work is found to have influenced a number of later thinkers including Samuel Rutherford, John Milton, Baron de Montesquieu, and Jean-Jacques Rousseau. See Hueglin, *Early Modern Concepts for a Late Modern World: Althusius on Community and Federalism*, 16–17.

30 John Neville Figgis, *From Gerson to Grotius* (Cambridge: Cambridge University Press, 1916), 299–331.

Althusius organized the *Politica* according to Ramist logic, a humanist method of using syllogisms and propositions to derive clear and persuasive arguments. This is a popular method in the sixteenth and seventeenth century, also used by Protestant Reformers to help believers understand Scripture and theological arguments. Ramist logic is based on 'invention' and 'disposition'. Through invention, we determine the materials that belong to the subjects of scholarly disciplines. Through disposition, we organize the materials appropriate to the given discipline in a structured manner. As a result, logic is applied to organize not only the propositions but the entire field of study.[31] Although Ramist logic was later on refuted by modern scientists, it is highly relevant at a time when new scholarly disciplines emerge. This is because the idea of invention in Ramist logic promotes creative formulation of a new discipline, while the idea of disposition helps to organize the new discipline. Through careful assimilation of universal versus particular propositions, Althusius' work clarifies the scope for politics and law in a structured manner.

Although much of Althusius' thinking is influenced by Calvinistic concepts, his treatise presents an exclusively political system without imposing religious duties to the secular. Skinner asserts that Althusius had the ambition of emancipating politics from the confines of theology and jurisprudence.[32] In fact, the absence of theological language and religious concerns in Althusius' work allows it to possess a universal nature whereby the underlying theological presuppositions can be embraced by the secular discipline of political philosophy. A strong Reformed theological stance can be found in the *Politica* although the use of theological language is skilfully avoided. Hueglin identifies Althusius' approach in terms of the

31 Althusius, *Politica*, xiii.

32 Skinner compares Johannes Althusius with the Scottish humanist George Buchanan (1506–1582) who affirmed the political right of the people to repudiate a legitimate prince in his 1579 publication *The Right of the Kingdom in Scotland*. He sees the same approach in both Buchanan's and Althusius' work in taking politics as a discipline independent from theology and religion, yet embracing an important theological stance within the construction of political thought. For details see Skinner, *The Foundations of Modern Political Thought*, II: 338–45.

presentation of political theory as a normative theory based on the factual observations of social life. Both theory and practice are emphasized in Althusius' work. At the same time, Althusius is committed to a synthesis of Calvinism, Aristotelianism, and Germanic corporatism. Comparing Althusius' method with that of Bodin, Hueglin points out that Bodin starts from sovereignty to deduce the nature of social life, while Althusius starts from social life to determine the general principle of sovereignty. Therefore sovereignty is the dependent variable of the nature of social life.[33] This is an approach that starts from the very nature of humankind rather than attempting to fit society into presumed principles or norms.

In the preface to the third edition of *Politica* published in 1614, Althusius states that he has revised his book into a new political work and 'have returned all merely theological, juridical, and philosophical elements to their proper places, and have retained only those ... essential and homogeneous to this science and discipline'.[34] This shows his intention for *Politica* to stand independently as a complete work for a political system of universal association. Rich insights are embedded in Althusius' assimilation of theological thoughts with practical implications of the times.[35] A thorough investigation of Althusius' concepts of law, sovereignty and political structure is beyond the scope of this book. The following exploration focuses on the covenant-based ideas of consociation and symbiotics in the *Politica*, with a view of drawing out the underlying implications on economic order.

33 Hueglin, *Early Modern Concepts for a Late Modern World: Althusius on Community and Federalism*, 71–6.

34 Althusius, *Politica*, 11.

35 For example, Gooch finds the novelty of Althusius' work to be less in the subjects of popular sovereignty or social contract, than in the democratic ideas he embraces in the republican framework. In his view, this provides for a defence of the birth of democracy and independence in Holland. See George P. Gooch, *English Democratic Ideas in the Seventeenth Century* (Cambridge: Cambridge University Press, 1927), 47.

2.4 A Polity of Symbiotics and Collegia

Althusius' primary concern is the extent to which associations fulfil their purposes in society. He defines politics as 'the art of associating (*consociandi*) men for the purpose of establishing, cultivating, and conserving social life among them'.[36] This association or consociation is known as 'symbiotics'. Those who live together are known as 'symbiotes'. The symbiotes 'pledge themselves each to the other, by explicit or tacit agreement, to mutual communication of whatever is useful and necessary for the harmonious exercise of social life'.[37] Within such symbiotics, symbiotes live together happily and comfortably in a holy and just manner. Since no individual person is entirely self-sufficient by nature, everyone needs to depend on others to live a comfortable and holy life. Therefore, it is necessary for people to live harmoniously together, especially when it comes to the material codependency of goods and services. In this regard, Althusius recognizes the necessity of economic order and interdependence at the very start of his political system.

Althusius defines the polity with three principal connotations: the communication of right or citizenship, the manner of administering and regulating the commonwealth, and the form and constitution of the commonwealth by which all actions of the citizens are guided.[38] This definition is wider in scope that that of Aristotle, who understands polity only by the last of these three connotations. Within the polity, consent, agreement and communication among the citizens are critical elements of association.

> The formal cause is indeed the association brought about by contributing and communicating one with the other, in which political men institute, cultivate, maintain, and conserve the fellowship of human life through decisions about those things useful and necessary to his social life.[39]

36 Althusius, *Politica*, 17.
37 Ibid., 17.
38 Ibid., 18.
39 Ibid., 24.

Accordingly, the symbiotes work together for a comfortable, useful and happy life with piety towards God, justice within the society, and peace against other nations. The role of communication is central to realizing these as things, services and rights are brought together for fair distribution and common advantage.

Althusius is concerned not merely with associations and functions, but the community in totality. Accordingly, he builds an entire system of political association from the individual and family units to the mega political community. He asserts that 'the community is an association formed by fixed law and composed of many families and collegia living in the same place'.[40] At a time when the political realm is generally understood to belong to the monarch and the commonwealth as being polyarchical, Althusius presents a structure in which the realm belongs to the people and the administration belongs to the king. This is the concept of popular sovereignty. The rights of the realm do not reside with its individual members but are owned jointly by members of the entire association within the realm. Such a political structure is built upon a solid application of the covenant concept, whereby individuals are bound closely to one another without exception. To Althusius, this universal symbiotic communion is both ecclesiastical, involving the welfare of the soul; and secular, involving justice and the material life.[41]

When compared with other forms of politics and federal structures, Hueglin and Fenna identify Althusius' political process as bottom-up rather than top-down. Consociations are the most general and basic principle of political organizations, through which families and guilds act as building blocks of society. Interests of each consociation within the community must be represented and taken care of in the universal assembly of the commonwealth. This arrangement enables participation by the people, where Althusius' sense of 'the people' is not individual citizens but the organized bodies of interacting collective entities. Faced with notions of monarchy and shadows of feudalism during his lifetime, Althusius' work inclines towards

40 Ibid., 40.
41 Ibid., 66–75.

diversity rather than unity. Hueglin and Fenna suggest that the reason for Althusius' polity being largely neglected during his time is because of its emphasis on consensus and compromise among the consociations of popular sovereignty. This structure is dismissed as anachronistic and inefficient in his time. Nevertheless, as the modern world develops into a globalized era of pluralistic culture and religious compositions, Althusius' system becomes more and more appealing as it allows for harmonious coexistence among different interest groups.[42] Althusius' work shows that the covenant concept is fundamental to the way of human bonding, allows for diversity, and is applicable to pluralistic societies.

In Althusius' polity, different units of collegium or private association link together through the law of nations to establish an inclusive political order called a community or political association. The need for good order, proper discipline and communication of things increases with the size of the community, yet the fundamental association remains unchanged. Althusius defines political order as 'the right and power of communicating and participating in useful and necessary matters that are brought to the life of the organized body by its associated members'.[43] Citizens of the community communicate and relate in a similar manner to those within collegia, for the same purpose of self-sufficiency and symbiosis of things, services, right, and mutual benevolence. Accordingly, Althusius applies the covenantal way of association to the various spheres and levels of symbiosis in society from the basic family unit to the administrative order of public duties.

In later editions of *Politica*, Althusius includes a discussion of the ecclesiastical versus secular order of the Province. He lays out the various levels and different objectives of ecclesiastical, political and economic order as follows:

42 Empirically, consociational practices of consensus democracy have continued in countries such as Germany, the Netherlands and Switzerland, boasting a record as least as efficient to other systems. See Thomas O. Hueglin and Alan Fenna, *Comparative Federalism* (Toronto: Broadview Press, 2006), 92–6.

43 Althusius, *Politica*, 39.

> As the ecclesiastical order of the province will bring forth pious, learned, wise, and good men, so the political and secular order of the nobility will be concerned to bring forth for the province strong, militant, and brave men who are ready with arms and counsel, and are experienced in military matters. So also the order of burghers and agrarians – the commons – will strive to produce and bring forth for the fatherland merchants, farmers, and workmen who are skilled, industrious and distinguished. By the service, labor, and industry of these orders, self-sufficiency can be obtained in association and symbiosis.[44]

Althusius sees the prince or supreme magistrate as the steward and administrator of political rights that originated through the people and are returned to the people upon retirement or death of the ruler. He asserts that administration of such rights has been granted to a ruler by a 'precarium or covenant'. Within the polity, associations are bonded together by consensus and trust. Althusius describes this bond to be 'a tacit or expressed promise to communicate things, mutual services, aid, counsel and the same common law (*jura*) to the extent that the utility and necessity of universal social life in a realm shall require'.[45] The power for the people to establish the right of jurisdiction and to bind the participants to it is essential. The existence of symbiotic life depends on it. This universal association is not constituted by one member, but jointly by all the members. According to this bond, members share ownership and responsibility of the polity. Althusius' assertion of the concept of popular sovereignty is depicted in his saying that, 'the right of the realm, or right of sovereignty, does not belong to individual members, but to all members joined together and to the entire associated body of the realm'.[46]

An obligatory and binding covenant relationship is established between the people and the governing authorities, as follows:

44 Ibid., 61.
45 Ibid., 67.
46 Ibid., 70.

> There is no doubt that this covenant, or contractual mandate (*contractum mandati*) entered into with the supreme magistrate, obligates both of the contracting parties, so much so that it is permitted to neither magistrate nor subjects to revoke or dishonor it.[47]

The obligation of the magistrate comes first, when he binds himself to the mandator – body of the universal association. The obligations of the people then follow as part of the nature of the mandate, to be obedient and compliant to the magistrate and prescribed laws. Accordingly, power is circumscribed by laws and remains with the people, preventing degeneration into absolute power or tyranny.

Symbiotics and collegia are fundamental units of the covenantal society. Symbiotic associations can be either private or public. The simple or private association is a symbiosis or society initiated by a special covenant (*pactum*) among the members. It brings the members together to hold a particular interest (*quid peculiare*) in common to each other. This is the primary basis of all associations.

> The efficient causes of this simple and private association and symbiosis are individual men covenanting among themselves to communicate whatever is necessary and useful for organizing and living in private life.[48]

The act of covenanting is essential to the symbiotes. It represents the way through which individuals and groups are bound together, i.e. the way political and economic relationships are carried out in communication of mutual benefits within the society. This relationship is as close and intimate as the metaphor of the private association described as 'one person', i.e. one body with each part carrying out its designated function by nature, communicating in good order, structure and consensus. These private associations include natural symbiotic association such as family and friends, as well as civil associations organized by groups of individuals for social interests or specific purposes.[49]

47 Ibid., 121.
48 Ibid., 27.
49 Ibid., 28.

The covenantal essence of the symbiotics is clearly depicted in Althusius' definition of the consociation in the communication and commitment of the symbiotes to each other, both explicitly and implicitly. The symbiotes are committed as co-workers who communicate among themselves in cooperation and in search for a comfortable life of both body and soul. Mutual communication and contribution mark the essence of symbiotic social life, together with the benefits and responsibilities required of the participants within each particular association.[50] To Althusius, an association is initiated and maintained through a covenant among the symbiotes, setting forth their common agreement about the necessary and useful purposes to be observed by the association, and the means appropriate to fulfil these purposes. Even if no explicit covenant is in place, an implicit one is assumed in the continuing consent of those who live together in association with each other.[51]

The symbiotes form collegia. Althusius defines collegium as a civil, private association of colleagues, associates or brothers coming together for a joint profess such as duty, way of life or craft. The commercial organization or corporation in the modern sense is essentially of such nature. The framework of the modern corporate takes shape as Althusius considers the collegia to be one single legal body with separate ownership and independent mandate. Through participation in a corporate body, all colleagues are bound within a common legal structure. The colleagues are thus called into session to contribute their services to the collegia, just as the modern day individual enters in upon signing of an employment contract. Similar to the symbiotics, Althusius' collegia maintain an implicit covenant that draws the participants into a body of association, not only legally but as 'one body' in solidarity and in relation to one another.

For both the symbiotics and collegia, communication is a cooperative process whereby individuals assist one another to uphold the covenanted agreements in social life. These covenants and laws are written in each collegium's corporate book, and act to uphold the collegium of association. They

50 Ibid., 19.

51 Ibid., xvi.

involve communication pertaining to things, services, rights and mutual benevolence. For the symbiotes, communication of things brings useful and necessary goods to the symbiotic for both individual and collective advantage. Communication of services represents the labour and occupation contributed by symbiotes for social life. Communication of rights is the process by which the symbiotes live and are ruled by just laws in a common life among themselves. In order to communicate things and services among the symbioties, common laws and proper laws are prescribed. Common laws, such as governing rules, are natural and unchanging to every type of symbioses. Proper laws, such as association charters, are particular to each consociation.[52] Accordingly, the communication of things and services refers directly to the economic dealings that are to be carried out among symbiotes in a covenantal manner. The common rights and related laws provide the basis by which proper communication of goods and services can be carried out. For the collegia, things such as money, consumable items, seals or records represent mutual contributions and acquisitions according to the laws of the collegia, aim at common purposes and are owned commonly. Services such as crafts, professions or vocations are mutually determined and carried out according to the manner tacitly or explicitly agreed upon. Rights involve the liberty and equality for everyone to live and be ruled by the same laws. Mutual benevolence is the affection and love of individuals to others. Since the associations exist under harmoniously willed common utility, benevolence is nourished, sustained and conserved through public banquets, entertainment and love feasts.[53] These elements explicitly laid out in Althusius' political system closely resemble the covenantal community of the Israelites in the Bible. In particular, the manifestation of mutual benevolence through love feasts and sacraments is a unique characteristic of the Israelite covenantal commitments.

52 Ibid., 19.
53 Ibid., 34–7.

2.5 Althusius on Human Nature and Benevolence

Baker identifies Althusius as a bridge between the sixteenth-century federal thinkers, and philosophical thinkers such as Hobbes and Locke on the matter of human nature. Hobbes and Locke are of the view the 'state of nature' necessitates government and laws. While covenant theologians such as Bullinger explain this necessity through sinful human nature, Althusius presents this warning in non-theological terms.[54] In particular, because of sinful human nature after the fall, Althusius asserts that 'the pride and high spirits of man should be restrained by sure reins of reason, law, and imperium less he throw himself precipitously into ruin'.[55]

Althusius' description of the nature of the symbiotes portrays an explicit undertone of a Calvinistic theological anthropology. He states that when the human being is born, he is 'destitute of all help, naked and defenceless, as if having lost all his goods in a shipwreck'.[56] The misfortunate of fallen humankind is described vividly at the very beginning of *Politica*, in support of the human being's helplessness and need for codependence. The human person is unable to provide for all his necessities on his own. Therefore cooperation and sharing are necessary for comfortable living. The emphasis on satisfaction of human needs and wants identified by Althusius yields an underlying concern for the functioning of the economic order as part of political concerns – an important consideration often missing from political philosophy theories.

The symbiotic human nature is fundamentally covenantal and inevitably social. Through different spheres of social consociations, human persons interact, relate and seek fulfilment. Skillen points out that Althusius does not merely construct society out of contracts among individuals. Althusius accounts for the diversity of communities, associations and relationships that constitute society, with considerations for the proper laws that may

54 Baker, 'Faces of Federalism: From Bullinger to Jefferson,' 31.

55 Althusius, *Politica*, 26.

56 Ibid., 17.

differ among associations according to their unique natures.[57] Indeed, Althusius' work is an admirable demonstration of the application of fundamental theological reflections to practical living that is not only limited to the particular political concerns on hand, but a mega and universal worldview of community and functioning of humankind. Although Althusius is concerned with the ecclesiastics, he does not look to the church to mediate all the divine laws or rely entirely on grace. Instead, the Word becomes the source of life and provides the law for social life in the different spheres of association. Skillen notes that Althusius' notion of a just public life is based on God's covenant with creation, a covenant made by God 'with human creatures who were made, from the beginning, to associate in political communities according to God's laws for political symbiosis'.[58] According to this assertion, the covenant basis of society reflects God's original design for creation and the true essence of the relationships among God and human persons embedded in human nature. Since this societal structure is based on the fundamental human element of creation, it is also universal.

Medieval thinkers have generally taken the community as a hierarchy of smaller communities. Althusius takes this view further and traces the development of the family units to the city, province and state, through federal bonding.[59] A crucial presupposition of the political covenant is the

57 Skillen rejects Gierke's assertion that Althusius yields to a secularistic utilitarian notion. Instead, he asserts that 'Althusius is a believing Calvinist who recognizes God's sovereignty everywhere, who goes to the Scriptures to see how the light of revelation illumines the human world that God made'. See James W. Skillen, 'From Covenant of Grace to Equitable Public Pluralism: The Dutch Calvinist Contribution,' *Calvin Theological Journal* 31 (2006): 73–5.

58 Ibid., 76.

59 Figgis asserts here that Althusius sees one supreme authority founded on a 'contract' binding the people as a whole. At the same time, there is a second 'contract' between the governor and the people. See John Neville Figgis, 'Political Thought in the Sixteenth Century,' in *The Cambridge Modern History*, ed. A.W. Ward, G.W. Prothero and S. Leathes (Cambridge: Cambridge University Press, 1905), 767. These 'contracts' identified by Figgis are in fact 'covenants' as they are characterized by their covenantal nature.

exercise of freedom and solidarity.[60] The covenant binds these multi-levels of interconnected units together to yield a picture of Althusius' carefully worked out structure of covenantal relationships from the smallest association between two symbiotes and within the symbiotics, to that among symbiotics and with the ruler.

Carney points out that early Calvinists conceive of associations as faithful ways of life that fulfil various aspects of human living such as glorifying God and attending to the welfare of the neighbour. Accordingly, such associations are teleological. They are natural in terms of God's creation, and voluntary within the boundaries of human finiteness and sinfulness. Carney identifies Althusius as a Calvinist for whom the canon law serves as foundation of the expression of law. To the Calvinists, the law represents an objective rightness that is to be discovered and affirmed about human associational experience. It is also the natural tendency of human persons and their association to be constitutionally oriented through legal expression. They are motivated to live an associational life according to the primordial essence of particular associations. Obeying the law therefore represents a response to God's command and an understanding of divine authority. Carney differentiates the social covenant, political covenant, and religious covenant within the covenant concept. These are relationships pertaining to societal living, mode of government, and association with God. He points out that the interpreters who relate concepts in the Roman law to the early Calvinist writers are mistaken. In fact, the nature of society or associations in Calvinistic thought is rooted in the very nature of things as social endowment. Every human person must participate in these societal associations in order to be truly human.[61] Indeed the covenant is

60 Skinner asserts that 'if a multitude of individuals or families in a pre-political condition possesses the ability to covenant with a chosen ruler, this can only be because they have the capacity to exercise a single will and make decisions with a single voice.' See Quentin Skinner, *Visions of Politics* (Cambridge: Cambridge University Press, 2002), II: 389–90.

61 Carney affirms that the source of Calvinist covenant theory is the Bible, whereby the old and new covenants are understood as offers of grace to be accepted by humankind. Such covenants present themselves as relations that the human persons enter into

different from the contract in Roman private law. The social and political covenants are commitments to conform to the rules and regulations that are designed to express and fulfil the common law of the consociation. The religious covenant shares a similar social basis as that of the social and political covenants because it is the agreement of human persons to live authentic communal lives just as the agreement with God requires.

The socio-ethical element of the covenant is one of the core differences between the covenant and private contract. This aspect is presented vividly within Althusius' political philosophy. Mutual benevolence, compassion and loving-care are clearly depicted within the description of roles and ranks. Althusius asserts that administrations should have both love and ability. Ephors should act as custodians of the public welfare with great love, concern and care.[62] Communication takes on a dominant social dimension in Althusius' political system. While Althusius acknowledges uneven distribution of natural gifts and degrees of social status, he asserts that natural inequality guides humankind towards social communication and cooperation. This implies a natural concern for a high degree of social equality within the system. Hueglin finds that in Althusius' system, politics as a process of communication is not primarily a problem of power and governmental authority, but of mutual assistance, cooperation and trust. It emphasizes coordination over subordination, although it acknowledges the need for the government and its necessary role in handling social conflict.[63] The city is to establish statutes concerning the private functions of the

---

by acts of their own will. They form the agreement of an association or among the leaders of different associations, to conduct the life of their associations in accordance with the primordial essence of the entire consociation of associations, including the particular expressions of this essence as commonly adopted under the circumstance of its time and space. See Frederick S. Carney, 'Association Thought in Early Calvinism,' in *Voluntary Associations: A Study of Groups in Free Societies*, ed. D.B. Robertson (Richmond: Westminster John Knox Press, 1966), 43–52.

62 Althusius, *Politica*, 99–102.

63 Thomas O. Hueglin, 'Johannes Althusius: Medieval Constitutionalist or Modern Federalist?,' *Publius* 9, no. 4 (1979): 25.

community. Included in such statutes are important characters of mutual benevolence or accord.

> Enthusiasm for concord is the means of conserving friendship, equity, justice, peace, and honor among the citizens, and of overcoming strife ... whatever cultivates love among the citizens and conserves the common good is to be nurtured, and the causes of discord among citizens and neighbours are to be guarded against.[64]

To illustrate this, Althusius quotes the Old Testament example of Abraham and Isaac living in unity and overcoming differences together. A covenantal way of life that models the divine commandments for the Israelites in the Old Testament is clearly depicted.

The Israelites requested a king in the Old Testament. During the process when Israelite kings are chosen and anointed, the people are always involved in the approval and designation process. Althusius constructs the polity based on this hierarchical covenant concept. Rectors and administrators are constituted by the commonwealth itself on the notion that all are equal. The Supreme magistrate appointed by the people exercises not his own power but that of the realm of which he is minister. Althusius asserts that constituting the supreme magistrate is the process by which the people and the supreme magistrate faithfully extend and accept oaths from each other, entering into a covenant concerning certain laws and conditions that set forth the form and manner of imperium and subjection. This covenant or contractual mandate obligates both of the contracting parties so that neither the magistrate nor the subjects can revoke or dishonour it.[65] By applying the covenant concept and structuring the polity on its basis, Althusius addresses the problem of absolute power. He points out that absolute power destroys justice, steers attention away from utility and welfare, and leads to the indulgence of private pleasure. In an economic sense, absolute power leads to an imbalance that turns power into robbery. Althusius' polity recognizes the diversity of abilities, preferences and status of the participants, yet remains inclusive of different associations with a platform that

64 Althusius, *Politica*, 49.

65 Ibid., 95–121.

allows equality and freedom.[66] It is within such an environment that the economic order is embedded and allowed to flourish.

2.6 Economic Order Within Althusius' Polity

Economic order resides within the political structure of a society to form an essential part of community life. Althusius puts forth the federalistic concept and connects it with the medieval theory of community life. To Althusius, the smaller unit of associations within society, such as the family, is anything but economic in the functional sense.[67] Thus the material exchanges of things and services are essential and embedded in relationships that exceed mere functionalities. Althusius asserts that it is God's will to distribute earthly gifts unevenly, so that there is a need for human beings to communicate necessary and useful things. As each person serves the other and in turn receives help from others, each will find value in the other and in the self, and be bound together in friendship. In this way, no one lives alone. Our needs draw us together to form different institutions, work communities and social groups. These interrelate to form societies as well as a public body of the commonwealth. He states that 'need' induces association, and 'want' conserves life because such wants are acquired and

66 Hueglin asserts that the revolutionary element in Althusius' system is the ability to maintain a multi-tiered plural order that supports shared sovereignty among multiple communities of different nature. These communities include higher and lower corporate orders from professional organizations to territorial parties. Skillen finds that Althusius' uniqueness lies in his foresight of the process of societal differentiation, recognizing that politics is to encompass both ecclesiastical and secular arenas. This allows Althusius' system to be an inclusive political community for all people. See Hueglin, *Early Modern Concepts for a Late Modern World: Althusius on Community and Federalism*, 65; and Skillen, 'From Covenant of Grace to Equitable Public Pluralism: The Dutch Calvinist Contribution,' 73.

67 Figgis, *From Gerson to Grotius*, 234.

communicated through mutual cooperation with one another.[68] According to this codependence, human being by nature strives for association. The commonwealth by mutual aid devotes to the general good and welfare of its body.

Economic order is fundamental and vital to human survival in Althusius' communal political system of codependence. He points out that we cannot live our lives conveniently without commerce. The arrangement for procuring the material necessities of life, hence the arena for economic cooperation, is a special right that should be equitable, good, useful and adapted to place, time and persons. This is under the civil law and can be peculiar to each polity. It involves commercial regulations, monetary system, common language, public duties, and privileges and titles of nobility. The consociation is given the task of the 'care of goods', a concept termed as stewardship in biblical covenant language. The care of goods involves diligent and faithful conversation of things and services necessary and useful to the commonwealth, as well as the augmentation and extension of such things. In laying out the economic order within the consociation, Althusius essentially places commerce and market exchange activities within the boundaries of the covenant and covenantal practices. He sees communicating and exchanging goods and services with one another as a fundamental necessity and utility of life. The universal association also consists of the proper administration of taxes, public welfare, and donations. The council of the polity is therefore charged with the duty to examine, discuss and make decisions on benevolence and distributive measures.[69] Accordingly, the covenant community is administered with a view towards achieving the common good.

Althusius finds all associations essentially political in nature, making political consociations the foundation of private economic associations. He differentiates between economics and politics by identifying economics as the skill of conserving and attending to household goods and the family. In contrast, political activities are public in nature and separate

68 Althusius, *Politica*, 25.

69 Ibid., 84–91.

from household economic functions. Nevertheless, economic activities of the primary private unit of kinship serve the very fundamental unit of society and must be treated differently.

> I concede that the skill of attending to household goods, of supplying, increasing, and conserving the goods of the family, is entirely economic, and as such is correctly eliminated from politics. But altogether different from this is association among spouses and kinsmen, which is entirely political and general, and which communicates things, services, rights, and aid for living the domestic and economic life piously, justly, and beneficially.[70]

Here he draws the line between politics and economics. While economics deals with the furnishing, augmentation and conservation of household goods, politics teaches what the participants may contribute and communicate among themselves for a pious and just life. Private or particular associations that follow economic interests differ from political consociations in terms of purposes and goals. Nevertheless, these private associations such as families and collegia together form the basis for public or general associations, and are attributed to politics.

Althusius sees economic inequality as part of natural economic order intended by the Divine to promote social unity and harmony. The diversity of wealth, skills and talents are similar to lyres of diverse tones that give rise to pleasant harmony when properly tuned. He quotes Petrus Gregorius in pointing out that 'if all were truly equal, and each wished to rule others according to his own will, discord would easily arise ... equality itself would be the greatest inequality'.[71] Accordingly, diversities in professions, roles for services and leaders, etc., are essential to political and economic order. Such order is part of divine providence. The covenant concept supports a hierarchical structure of political and economic order that enables distribution based on capabilities and needs. In a perfectly covenantal community, such a hierarchical structure will not lead to exploitations and inequality

70 Ibid., 31.
71 Ibid., 26.

from the misuse of power and resources, because of perfect covenantal love and justice under divine authority.

The Jewish political scientist Daniel J. Elazar has been studying extensively the application of biblical covenants to systems of law, society, justice, and systems of economic distribution. He sees Althusius' federalism as a grand design that is general to all of politics and not only to federalism. The biblical design for humankind is federal in its basic design of interwoven webs of covenant relationships, yielding a classic biblical commonwealth of a federation of tribes. More importantly, Elazar points towards the biblical vision for the messianic end times when there will be a restoration of Israel's tribal system as well as a world confederation. The nations will come together under a common divine covenant while preserving their own unique integrity.[72] Trimiew asserts that Elazar shows the function of group rights in ancient Israel, especially in regard to economic rights. Within the biblical system of economic distribution, community and group rights play a central role. The moral foundation of Israel is the covenant of God and His people in a communal sense, rather than the moral unit of the individual in modern Western culture. The claims for public welfare and economic justice are in fact group duties and covenantal obligations. Accordingly, the misunderstanding of such obligations is the primary moral problem in modern society. A renewed understanding of the covenant concept would be useful to the proper assimilation of group economic rights versus individual political rights in modern society.[73]

72 Daniel J. Elazar, 'Althusius and Federalism as Grand Design,' available from <http://www.jcpa.org/dje/articles2/althus-fed.htm> (cited 15 February 2008).

73 Darryl M. Trimiew, 'The Renewal of Covenant and the Problem of Economic Rights: The Contributions of Daniel Elazar,' *Annual of the Society of Christian Ethics* 20 (2000): 105–9.

2.7 Covenant Versus the Social Contract and Other Critiques

The covenant concept in political thought faces certain criticisms. Walzer identifies Puritanism as the earliest form of political radicalism. He describes medieval society as composed largely of non-participating, inactive people. The Calvinists are the first to switch the focus of political thought from 'princes' to 'saints', therefore allowing justification for political actions by the believing community. Walzer asserts that the collapse of the universal sovereignty of the empire shatters politics of the philosophers, subjecting people to make private arrangements. This is when the feudal system substitutes family and kinship with formal, impersonal, legal and functional ties. Consequently, 'ordinary men lived in a narrower world, tied to family, village and feudal lord, and forgot the very idea of citizenship and the common good'.[74] According to Walzer, free persons are 'masterless'. He views Catholics as those striving to combine morality and salvation, and Protestants as those pushing morality and salvation further apart. Walzer finds that as the Lutherans experience personal faith and salvation through justification, the invisible church becomes an increasingly sharp reality to them. This gives rise to a multitude of pietistic sects that focus on cultivating personal spirituality. On the other hand, Calvinism directs believers' energies to public disciplines, therefore focusing on the visible church in an attempt to take the world and transform it. As a result, Walzer sees Protestantism either as a privately cultivated communion with God or a social religion.[75] Walzer's classifications appear to be rather simplistic because pietism certainly appears in the Calvinistic tradition, while social participation is not missing from Lutheranism. However, the more striking part of Walzer's argument lies in his assertion of the subversive nature of Calvinistic political thoughts.

74 Michael Walzer, *The Revolution of the Saints: A Study in the Origins of Radical Politics* (London: Weidenfeld and Nicolson, 1966), 4–6.

75 Ibid., 17–25.

Walzer sees Calvin's political thought as a demand for politics to be bent to serve a religious purpose within a view of politics that is excessively realistic.[76] This is due to the Calvinistic assertion that authority is recognized only in the divine Word. As such there is no discussion of the forms of authority or the law, resulting in a detached and pessimistic acknowledgement of worldly methods. He identifies Calvinism as individualistic and restraining because in 'obedience to God', everyone must wrestle with their own individual problems.[77] Walzer's opposing view to the covenant concept is clearly presented as follows:

> The covenant emphasized once again the abolition of the older connections founded upon created love, filial humility, and the merciful intercession of saints and angels. An agreement between God and man whose terms were supposedly written out in Scripture, it symbolized perfectly the artificial nature of all relations. Through the covenant men became the 'bondsmen' of God – not the children – and the image implied the voluntary recognition of an existing debt, a legal or commercial obligation.[78]

It appears that Walzer has missed the significance of relational bonds and mutual benevolence that are core elements of covenants. Instead, he seems to be commenting on purely functional and obligatory contracts. This is an unfortunate misunderstanding because as Meilaender points out, Walzer's work contains a commitment to a pluralistic world of particular

76 Gorski provides a good historical account of Calvinist revolts in sixteenth-century Geneva. He argues against Walzer's thesis because Calvinism only developed in a revolutionary direction when it had a popular base, faced monarchical opposition, and when they could draw on strong traditions of representative government. As such, he finds no automatic connection between Calvinism and revolution from the cases of revolts by the covenantors. See Philip S. Gorski, 'Calvinism and Revolution: The Walzer Thesis Reconsidered,' in *Meaning and Modernity*, ed. Richard Madsen (Berkeley: University of California Press, 2002), 78–104.

77 Walzer, *The Revolution of the Saints: A Study in the Origins of Radical Politics*, 26–55.

78 Ibid., 168.

communities and to the individuals who form these communities.[79] A proper understanding of the covenant as a relational concept may find common ground for a more constructive dialogue between Walzer's work and Calvinism. Walzer's attack on the covenant concept is also based on a rejection of the Calvinistic view of sinful human nature. In fact, modern political society is deeply rooted in covenants, but the original form of covenant-based federalism has since developed into many different types of federalism and contractual arrangements over the years. Coupled with the complexities of modern society, the confusion of what the covenant concept encompasses is further extended.

Gierke points out that Rousseau's social contract has a remarkable resemblance to the politics of Althusius in fundamental ways that have not appeared in previous scholarly work. Yet Rousseau's work is based on the older doctrine of popular sovereignty and the doctrine of the law of nature. In contrast, a stern Calvinistic spirit appears in all Althusius' work.[80] Essentially, Gierke sees Althusius as the real creator of the social contract, dissolving all public law into private law. This view is challenged by Hueglin, who asserts that public law could not have been reduced into private law when a state in the modern sense has not existed. The distinction between public and private spheres had not been made in Althusius' time. Hueglin points towards the interpretation by Joachim Fredrich in that Althusius had included all private functions within a hierarchy of groups that is more or less public in nature. A pact that can be either explicit or tacit appears fundamentally different from a social contract in the private and legal sense. Rousseau locates virtue, liberty and reason exclusively in the individual self. In contrast, the individual in Althusius' polity is at the

79 Meilaender argues that Walzer's attempt to reject universal moral claims is unsuccessful because Walzer himself offers some universally shared principles that are enriched by the particular narratives in the communities that he seeks to converse with. For example, Walzer asserts that after allowing for cultural differences, the Athenians share a moral vocabulary with the people of Mytilene and Melos, and even with us. See Gilbert Meilaender, 'A View from Somewhere: The Political Thought of Michael Walzer,' *Religious Studies Review* (1990): 197–201.

80 Gierke, *The Development of Political Theory*, 18–19.

same time private, social and political; participating in the state through federal associations that act as mediators between the universal association and the individual.[81]

Natural law has an important role in the development of the contract as a departure from the covenant concept. During Althusius' time, the new scientific focus has been the discovery of the laws of nature. This preoccupation with unveiling the regularities of universal functions has marked every political system developed during that time.[82] Karlberg finds the covenant concept in political philosophy distinctively different from the Reformed ecclesiological covenant idea, at least until the latter half of the seventeenth century. He asserts that the theological bridge connecting these two concepts is the medieval doctrine of natural law. Natural law reveals the human moral debt of obedience to God, which constitutes the foundation of the covenant of creation or covenant of works, and later on, the Mosaic covenant.[83]

As the concept of the covenant, pact or contract develops into various different forms, it becomes more and more important to differentiate between covenantal and contractual arrangements. When discussing the various forms of federal systems, Riley points out that federalism quickly reduces to the idea of an easily breakable contract because its covenantal nature is misunderstood and overlooked. 'If federal systems were to be mere treaties, and treaties mere contracts, then breach of contract of course involved the breach of treaty, and a breach of treaty released the remaining parties from their obligations.'[84] As a result of these abstractions, the essence of federal systems as a public form of order is reduced to the form of an agreement in private law.

In contrast to Althusius' political covenant between the people and the ruler, Hobbes' contract is one that makes the ruler the recipient of power.

81 Hueglin, 'Johannes Althusius: Medieval Constitutionalist or Modern Federalist?,' 18–22.

82 Friedrich, *The Age of the Baroque*, 22.

83 Karlberg, *Covenant Theology in Reformed Perspective*, 60–1.

84 Patrick Riley, 'Three 17th Century German Theorists of Federalism: Althusius, Hugo and Leibniz,' *Publius* 6, no. 3 (1976): 8–9.

The people do not enter into covenant or contract with the ruler, but are considered an aggregate of individuals subject to the ruler. Hobbes limits the concept of the contract to that of the individual with one another, which is only enforceable when the individuals surrender their liberty to a common sovereignty. This is based on Hobbes' view of human nature as being selfish and timorous. As a result, people can only be driven to obedience for self-preservation. Rousseau shares Hobbes' view of the individual being led to submission under the quest for self-preservation.[85] These notions of self-interest and self-preservation are later on elaborated by Adam Smith. Although Smith does not describe social or legal contracts directly, there is an implied contractual notion in the division of labour and the codependency process for wealth creation, for the individual to contribute and exchange goods and services for mutual interest and preservation. These concepts of the contractual arrangement differ greatly with Althusius' federal arrangement. As Moltmann points out, Hobbes' idea of the state as a Leviathan is a negative anthropology that legitimates power, authority and sovereignty based on human sinful nature. It is an anarchical justification of state power. In contrast, the covenant presents a positive anthropology of equality that legitimates power and democratic institutions for the control of power. This is a covenant of free citizens participating in the design of a commonwealth in anticipation of heavenly citizenship in the kingdom of God.[86]

Not all scholars identify Althusius as a Federalist. Although Riley acknowledges Althusius' system of universal symbiotic association united by communicative pacts, he identifies this as a system of medieval constitutionalism rather than that of modern federalism. This is because Althusius presents a hierarchy of autonomous political units rather than a federal

85 In comparison, Locke presents political relations as that of trusteeship whereby the people create the legislature to act as trustee on its behalf. In such a government, the ruler takes on duties while the people possess rights. Rousseau goes further to make the government a mere delegate of the general will. See J.W. Gough, *The Social Contract: A Critical Study of Its Development* (Oxford: Clarendon Press, 1957), 108–11 and 143–4.

86 Moltmann, *God for a Secular Society: The Public Relevance of Theology*, 38–9.

state in the modern sense. He finds no mention of international federalism, idea of a federal world-state, or leagues of sovereign powers in the work of Althusius.[87] Indeed Althusius has not developed the modern federal system, nor has he intended to do so. Rather than modern concerns with regard to federalism, confederalism, decentralization, devolution, corporatism, pluralism, etc., Althusius is primarily concerned with a polity for harmonious and covenantal living among the symbiotic participants in relation to each other. He lays the foundation of a system of symbiotic polity that contains the fundamental presuppositions of the covenant concept. This polity is federal in the true sense.[88] Although some of his late-medieval thoughts may not apply in the modern era, the covenantal foundation of Althusius' system provides timeless and valuable insights, and merits careful exploration.

Carlyle and Carlyle point out that the concept of a contract between the ruler and the people was common and important in the sixteenth century when Althusius laid out the 'contract' principle. Althusius identifies it in elective or hereditary forms in France, England, Sweden, Spain and Germany. It can also be identified in relation to the oath taken by princes on their accession.[89] In effect, Althusius' work contributes to the understanding and distinction between contract and covenant in their societal application.[90] Unfortunately, the covenant concept gradually erodes and changes

87 Riley, 'Three 17th Century German Theorists of Federalism: Althusius, Hugo and Leibniz,' 7–41.

88 As Elazar asserts, a postmodern federalism must be able to secure individuals in their rights while at the same time recognize groups as real and legitimate. Althusius is the first political philosopher who provides for this synthesis. See Althusius, *Politica*, xl.

89 R.W. Carlyle and A.J. Carlyle, *A History of Mediaeval Political Theory in the West* (London: William Blackwood & Sons, 1936), VI: 395.

90 Salmon identifies Althusius' view of contract as the most important aspect of Althusius' interpretation of French theory. 'In the thought of Althusius the combination of Calvinist views with the traditional controversies of the civilians drew out and rendered explicit those radical implications contained in contract theory.' See J.H.M. Salmon, *The French Religious Wars in English Political Thought* (Oxford: Clarendon Press, 1959), 44.

shape as contract theory develops.[91] Calvin's covenant turns into a contractualist interpretation mainly from the writings of the Monarchomachs, the Calvinist-Huguenot publicists defending themselves against the French Catholic monarchy. The covenant concept is extended to a 'double covenant' – that between God and his people, as well as that between the ruler and the people. This doctrine of double covenant becomes the core of federal theology. It aims at the lawful regulation of plural communities through mutual obligations.[92] Under the political system of Althusius, the covenant extends further to that among the people and among different groups of people. The original intention clearly exceeds a contractual interpretation.

Allen points out that the contract is a human contrivance that differs from the covenant. A political community is a special covenant that recognizes the voluntary and social aspects of the participants, with a special kind of belonging and mutual ownership of the association. A covenant is rooted in historical events and exchanges among the participants that lead to implicit promissory commitments. Therefore political obligations are never simply general, but reflect the promises, uses of power, entrustments and interactions of the political community. Under a contract, the basis for political obligation is a duty of fair play from past actions. However, the argument based on fair play is deficient since it deals only with part of the political obligation. Where a certain participant disrupts the fairness of the system, this duty no longer applies. On the other hand, the covenant offers a broader interpretation of such political obligations. Not only does fairness play a part in the participants' choices and actions,

91 The word 'covenant' originates from the Latin word '*foedus*' while the word 'contract' originates from the Latin word '*pacta*'. These were different concepts until the end of the sixteenth century, when the contractualists rendered a covenant invalid if one of the parties failed to fulfil its obligation. The words 'covenant' and 'contract' were then used interchangeably during the development of contract law. See chapter 4 for further discussions on the development of contract and contract law, and the conceptual difference between covenant and contract.

92 Hueglin, *Early Modern Concepts for a Late Modern World: Althusius on Community and Federalism*, 57–8.

the participants are also entrusted with political power over their fellow citizens. Through mutual participation, citizens accept each others' entrustment and obligate themselves even though others have not acted fairly. Accordingly, the focus in a covenantal community is on the human persons rather than the law.[93]

Social contacts are similar to the covenant in many ways. Yet they are at most, partial covenants. Within the structure of human polities, constitutions and contractual formats are necessary for setting proper constraints and procedures. Laws and written commitments are fundamental and essential even in the biblical Israelite tribes in the form of Commandments and Torah. Nevertheless, as Mount points out, 'Israel's constitution comes off less as absolute rules than as an expression of a more basic set of relationships. Identity, participation, responsibility, and respect for diversity are all present to some degree.'[94] No written rules can fully contain the essence of societal covenant. Accordingly, all constitutions are partial. Any effort to hold laws and constitutions absolute will break down. The covenantal community, including its legal rendering, must be a dynamic reflection of the participants' interactions and experiences. Only a recognition of such covenantal aspects of human community yields freedom, equality, and respect for diversities.

2.8 Rediscovery of the Covenant Foundation for Society

Althusius is the pioneer for a comprehensive system of a polity that is deeply grounded in the covenant concept. His use of non-theological language demonstrates the highly accessible and universal nature of the covenant concept as applied to societal order. The greatest contribution of Althusius

93 Allen, *Love and Conflict: A Covenantal Model of Christian Ethics*, 257–61.

94 Eric Jr. Mount, *Covenant, Community and the Common Good: An Interpretation of Christian Ethics* (Cleveland: The Pilgrim Press, 1999), 47–8.

lies in his ability to achieve this goal, making his work timeless and necessary for understanding the essence of the relational order in society as intended in the order of creation. As Elazar asserts, the Calvinist, Althusian model of the religiously homogeneous polity is unlikely to be revived in the postmodern epoch. However, we are beginning to rediscover the old understanding that all civil societies require some basic norms for survival. These norms are needed to obligate and bind the citizens, and to provide the basis for trust and communication.[95] Human beings are essentially relational by nature. The intrinsic yet essential notions of bonding, love, trust and communication are universal and fundamental to authentic living and must be restored in the postmodern political and economic society.

Althusius' form of federal political thought is deeply rooted in the Reformed theological concept of the covenant, which in turn is based on a Calvinistic view of human nature. His work shows that the covenant does not remain merely an ideological concept, but contains a highly realistic and practicable application to human life. Unfortunately, as political systems developed over the centuries, certain elements of the covenant concept become eroded and reduced to functional use. Things, services and rights are considered from the viewpoint of satisfying individual wants, rather than from a view of mutual cooperation and communal effort. Mutual benevolence has a lower priority when compared to individual advantage. The essence of covenant communities and relationships is understood more and more from a contractual point of view in the modern world. Its detrimental effects are penetrating every aspect of contemporary life, extending from politics to welfare and social life. A rediscovery of the structure, emphasis and implications of the covenant foundation is urgently called for.

We have seen that in Althusius' polity, consociations reside at different levels with differing purposes and goals. Covenants are present from the family unit, corporation, society, community, etc., up to the mega level of the nation and humanity. Such variations and divergence support the functioning of a pluralistic society, while consociations converge at a higher level to a common humanity to form the polity. Participation and exclusive

95 Althusius, *Politica*, xliii.

communities provide a sense of identity that is sought by the modern individual. At the same time, humankind strives towards a common nature and destiny, no matter how diverse individual beliefs may be. The different levels of commonality serve different common goals. Freedom and individualities are preserved while society converges to an overall covenant of the polity. Within this covenantal polity, the same covenant essence penetrates every sphere of human society, ensuring the authentic and organic functioning of the economic order. Such a covenantal society provides the guidance and boundaries for a covenantal exchange of goods and services in the economic market. This gives rise to a universal marketplace that promotes genuine human relationship, individual freedom, communal living and economic justice. In the next chapter, I shall draw upon scriptural and theological resources to examine the fundamental nature and content of the covenant concept in terms of its relevance and applicability to economic life.

CHAPTER 3

Universality, Content and Relevance of the Covenant

In the previous chapter, we found that the covenant concept has long been established by early theologians and political philosophers as a fundamental means that upholds societal order. This chapter explores the contents of the covenant concept and discusses its relevance as a theological response to the modern economic market. To formulate a theological response to economics, we need to discern the intention of authentic economic life as originally created by the Divine. Although economic life relates to the material life on earth rather than spirituality, the well-being of both the body and the soul is vital to the overall well-being of the human person. Theological concerns over spirituality cannot be segregated from decisions about daily life. Accordingly, this chapter starts with a discussion on human nature and economic activities, and proceeds to a rediscovery of the covenant concept as the original intended relational order within the doctrine of creation. In doing so, I draw upon theological interpretations and scriptural narratives to demonstrate the characteristics of the covenant concept as a relational order. Since the covenant is a rich concept that can take on different forms and can comprise a number of characteristics pertaining to society and human life in each of the scriptural narratives, I shall not exhaustively explore the contents of the covenant. My focus is on covenantal elements such as relational order, freedom, morality and personal agency that are fundamental to the economic life.[1]

The objective of formulating a theological response to economic life is not to assert a subversive view of Christian ideology, but to rediscover

1 For a detailed examination of the Biblical covenants and their implications on modern economic life, see Richard A. Horsley, *Covenant Economics: A Biblical Vision of Justice for All* (Louisville: Westminster John Knox Press, 2009), 1–180.

the truth and order of creation that enables authentic economic life. To achieve this, I examine whether and how the covenant appeals as universally applicable to economic order. After establishing its universality, I further analyse the relevance of the covenant concept over the issues of personal agency and human freedom in the market. The potential for a covenantal economy is then explored in comparison with the economy of grace or gift in order to find a proper balance between theological ideology and realism. The results point towards a rediscovery of the significance of the covenant concept for society and the economic order, and the call for reintroducing the covenant to balance the modern economic market that has become increasingly contract-based.

3.1 Human Nature Determines Economic Activities

Before we have a chance to give it any thought, we are engaged in the economic order of the market. The market influences our daily decisions and actions, shaping the life of the community. In the market, human persons interact with partners and strangers alike, contracting to exchange goods and services implicitly and explicitly. Choices are made within the market, not only with respect to goods and services, but also in terms of ethical priorities and methods of dealings. The market carries its own inclinations that interact with inert human nature to derive a structure of tendencies and priorities. It is up to the participants to become aware of the ways through which they interact within the market, whether they choose to be driven by market priorities or to become master of a market that contains humanizing values. What is the authentic way of human interaction within the economic market? The answer to this question points us towards identifying a theological anthropology relevant to economic life.[2] Although a

2 As Atherton suggests, the pursuit of human well-being in modern economics and other secular disciplines increasingly points towards questions that require a

comprehensive discussion of theological anthropology is beyond the scope of this book, basic views regarding human nature are fundamental to the formulation of the economic market. These must be considered when deriving the conditions necessary for an authentic market.

In fact, enquiries about human nature mark the birth of the discipline of economics. Moral philosopher and father of economics Adam Smith starts with a philosophical enquiry into human nature. In his early years, he holds an anxious curiosity about the design or blueprints of order that underlie the naturalistic approach implicit in his later work. To explore the universal design of the deity, Smith takes an interest in astronomy, moving on to moral philosophy during his years of professorship, before applying his inquisitive and observant method to political and economic matters.[3] Following a strand of Smithian thinking, free market advocates over the past decades have advocated a natural evolution of the economic interaction between human persons. This natural evolution under an unidentified 'invisible hand' becomes a natural development of economic activities based on human nature. While human persons form the market, the

reformulated anthropology. He identifies a faith-based anthropology in response to the post-scarcity anthropology that turns from concerns regarding economic scarcity to the well-being of human persons. See John Atherton, *Transfiguring Capitalism* (London: SCM Press, 2008), 201–15.

3 Adam Smith never completed his comprehensive work on 'history of the astronomical systems', but his interests and intentions are expressed in his correspondence with his long time intellectual companion, David Hume. For more details, see John Rae, *Life of Adam Smith* (London: Macmillan, 1895), 262–3. Smith's work includes the most influential writing *An Inquiry into the Nature and Causes of the Wealth of Nations*, moral philosophical treatise *The Theory of Moral Sentiments*, *Lectures on Jurisprudence*, *Essays on Philosophical Subjects*, *Lectures on Rhetoric and Belles Lettres*, and other miscellaneous correspondences. In 1984, the bicentenary of the *Wealth of Nations*, Adam Smith's collection has been published in six titles and two associated volumes under *The Glasgow Edition of the Works and Correspondence of Adam Smith*, in hardcover by Oxford University Press and in softcover by Liberty Fund. This remains the most comprehensive collection of his published and unpublished writings.

market left to its natural evolution in turn shapes the mindset and culture of the economic persons.

Many people know Adam Smith according to the 'Chicago school' of economics, which begins with the assumption that human persons are driven by the motive of personal utility maximization. According to this *homo economicus* argument, the Smithian view of human nature is the pursuit of self-interest under competitive conditions. This individualistic construct forms the basis for allocation of resource in the market economy.[4] Unfortunately, such an understanding of Smith's system is a misreading of his self-interest concept. Smith's vision of the liberal society comprises self-commanding individuals working together in a cohesive society, with government institutions that enforce justice and freedom. Starting from a natural description of human nature, Smith observes human behaviour and the underlying sentiments of such behaviour. He then develops a system based on his observations, and advocates that institutions enhance the opulence of the system aiming towards a society of justice and freedom.[5] This Smithian system of human nature, and its later version of egocentric self-interest, both differ from the view of human nature offered by theological anthropology.

Theological anthropology offers a view of human nature based on creation and the sinful distortion of the order of creation when the first Adam turns away from the commandment of God. It points out the dangerous tendency of dehumanization in a market that relies solely on individualistic constructs of human nature, and offers a relational view of human nature that promotes genuine economic relationships.[6] From an egocentric

4 Jerry Evensky, '"Chicago Smith" versus "Kirkaldy Smith"', *History of Political Economy* 37 (2005): 197–203.

5 See chapter 6.1 for a detailed exploration of Smith's view of human nature and self-interest.

6 Botman appropriately points out that the covenant serves a crucial role in theological anthropology. 'Covenant calls for a universal interpretation of God's initiative in preserving human dignity; it also connects human beings to one another, humanity to creation, and current generations to future generations. Covenant is the most universal and proper theological category for a theological anthropology.' See H. Russel

self-interested point of view, greed is the human motive that overwhelmingly drives human history and economic activities. There is little hope for genuine human relationships if the only concern is egocentric self-interest because virtues are assumed to be non-rewarding. Theology points out the sinfulness and finitude of humankind, and the need to rediscover the true and good nature of human persons within the order of creation. Virtues that cannot be adequately quantified and represented in economic models retain their characteristics and values in this quest for human goodness.

From a theological point of view, human persons are created in the *imago Dei* (image of God), after the likeness of God, and as creatures of God. One would not be a human person if not created in His image. Therefore the human person reflects the nature of the triune God with His will for human persons to be capable of relating to each other as well as to God Himself as covenantal partners. This relational characteristic is central to the covenant implications on economic order. Only Christ is the One not distorted by sin and maintaining all original goodness of creation. The way He relates to us is covenantal, as He comes before humankind in the fullness of His humanity as a gift. The covenantal way of relating is demonstrated in the ultimate manifestation of God's act through His Son in the narrative history of the covenant. In this same narrative history, humankind is elected and called into personal responsibility in a societal and economic order that mirrors the covenantal assertions of the Creator. The contract-based market encourages independence and disassociation of human persons by focusing on choices that benefit the self. An emphasis of the covenantal nature of authentic human interactions injects human relational qualities of trust and care into economic behaviour. It gives the economic participant a personal identity of the self and in relation to others.

Botman, 'Covenantal Anthropology: Integrating Three Contemporary Discourses of Human Dignity,' in *God and Human Dignity*, ed. R. Kendall Soulen and Linda Woodhead (Grand Rapids: Eerdmans, 2006), 82.

3.2 The Covenant Concept

The word 'covenant' originates from the Hebrew ברית, and corresponds to the Greek διαθήκη[7] and Latin *foedus*.[8] The richness of the covenant concept and its development throughout history lead to different understandings and confusion among the various definitions of covenant and contract forms. While the covenant tradition has commonalities with the development of social contract, legal contract and commercial contract, it is essential to distinguish between contract and covenant in order to grasp the essence of the two distinct ideas.[9] A *covenant* is a promise with one or more counterparties under common pursuit of shared values for long term cooperation and the well-being of the community.[10] Contracts form

7 The translation of ברית into διαθήκη is contested because διαθήκη usually means last will or testament in classical and Hellenistic Greek. However, many New Testament Scholars takes covenant as the true meaning of διαθήκη. In every reference to διαθήκη in the New Testament, God's saving work is prominent. The word is used in the Eucharist to take up the meaning of the new covenant of God with His people through the reconciliation of Jesus Christ. See Hübner, 'Covenant,' in 710–13.

8 The Latin *foedus* becomes the origin of the word 'federal', which in turn develops into 'federalism'. This implementation of the covenant concept to political society is discussed in chapter 2.

9 See chapter 4.2 for a detailed conceptual analysis of covenant versus contract.

10 Due to the complexity and richness of the covenant concept, few scholars attempt to provide a clear definition. Mount defines contract/covenant by stating that 'a contract constitutes an alliance of individuals for the satisfaction or guarantee of mutual interests; a covenant unites people with common allegiance to shared values or norms in a commitment to the long-term well-being of the community members'. His definitions tend to limit a contract to mutual interests, and a covenant to community bonding and alignment of values. However, the contractual mechanism does not guarantee mutual interests. It is subject to the threats of coercion and inequality. The development of neo-classical contract law is based on the necessity of arbitration and safeguard against such threats. On the other hand, while the covenant emphasizes communal relationships and bonding, it also contains an understanding of cooperative responsibility for the attainment of the common good. See Mount, *Covenant, Community and the Common Good: An Interpretation of Christian Ethics*, 21.

the basis of the market while covenants form the basis of community.[11] Awareness and enactment of the covenant must precede that of the contract since the covenant forms an essential and fundamental basis for society and the economic order. The Covenant-God is a God of grace whose acts must not be reduced to legalistic contractual terms. As Torrance points out, 'the fallacy of legalism in all ages – perhaps this is the tendency of the human heart in all ages – is to turn God's covenant of grace into a contract … In the Bible, the form of the covenant is such that the indicatives of grace are always prior to the obligations of law and human obedience.'[12]

Theologically, the covenant concept has been placed at the core of a conscious covenant or federal theology, which reduces this concept to dogmatic terms. In fact, the covenant concept is a broader concept that underlies the foundation of human society with practical applications beyond dogmatic concerns. It is a relational concept that reflects the *imago Dei* in terms of the intimate and multifaceted means of relating among different parties. The value of the covenant paradigm therefore resides in the ways and means of societal living. As Mount asserts, 'covenant is a distinctively, though not exclusively, Hebraic metaphor and model that locates the relational self in a community of identity, promise, and obligation with God and neighbor'.[13] The covenant is the major form of providential order that provides a model for the formation of societies derived from the Divine-human relationship. Since it is given in the possibilities of creation, it is a basic feature of human life that surpasses contractual voluntarism to retain the sense of community. The economic order, among others, is thus subject to God's will and care within the covenantal arrangement.[14]

11 Development of the legal contract and contract law, and the formation of the contract-based market are examined in chapter 4.1.

12 Torrance, 'The Covenant Concept in Scottish Theology and Politics and Its Legacy,' 230.

13 Mount, *Covenant, Community and the Common Good: An Interpretation of Christian Ethics*, 1.

14 Max L. Stackhouse, *Globalization and Grace* (New York: Continuum, 2007), 163. Stackhouse actively advocates the relevance and applicability of the covenant concept to society, family and other human relationships in his work. Unfortunately,

The covenant of humanity resides within the covenant of God. The covenant concept is based upon God's creation of human nature in covenantal interdependency. This covenantal interdependency implies that human nature is inevitably social and relational. Humankind finds its fulfilment in the family, voluntary groups, religious associations, and political entities as ordered in federal or covenantal ways.[15] Covenant is also a way of dealing with plurality, through which unique persons can be responsive to God's covenant and fit into the creative, ordering and redeeming governance of God. Although human persons have fallen into sin and have become unfaithful to the covenant, nature and humanity can be continuously renewed in the covenantal process towards consummation in God. Accordingly, virtue in society is not mere goodness, but the social achievement from covenantal interaction of human persons through which God's grace may work within the historical redeeming process.[16]

The covenant concept takes up multiple dimensions of societal life involving friendship, marriage, family, tribe, kingdom, nation, employment, teaching, law and the Divine in the Bible. Scriptural narratives reveal the multifaceted nature of the covenant concept and its characteristics. The covenantal way through which God relates to individuals such as Noah, Abraham, Moses and David in the Old Testament points towards a meta-narrative of covenantal history in the relationship between God and Israel.[17] This meta-narrative extends into the new covenant between Christ

---

he has not examined the details of applying the covenant to economic activities or the economic market.

15 McCoy and Baker, *Fountainhead of Federalism*, 59.

16 Covenant theologian Cocceius takes a view of human nature that is strongly rooted in such covenantal interdependencies. He asserts that humans are covenantal by nature. The covenant characterizes a human social context whereby the human person emerges, becomes self-aware and develops self-identity. See Ibid., 77.

17 An exhaustive examination of all covenants and their related characteristics in the Bible is not feasible within the scope of this book because of the richness of the covenant concept and its contents. Therefore I shall focus on a selection of the more prominent scriptural narratives – the Noachic, Abrahamic, Mosaic and Davidic covenants in the Old Testament, and the redemptive covenant through the work of Christ in the New Testament.

and His people in the New Testament. The covenant is thus revealed as the intended way of relational order with fundamental significance embedded in human nature, inclusive of the ethical characteristics common to humankind. Stackhouse asserts that 'the common feature of these is that each may represent an ethical outworking of the divine-human relationship, for each not only is constituted but may be measured by a God-given framework and purpose for human life'.[18] Since it is such a fundamental and rich concept, the ethical assertions of the covenant can be further explored from many angles. For example, Niebuhr uses the covenant concept as a symbol to define moral relationships in terms of the responses of the self in the community. His concept of 'responsibility' places the person within the covenantal structure rather than in the aspiration for goodness or obedience to laws and duties.[19] Similarly, Stackhouse traces the renewal of covenant to the Mosaic days and asserts that covenant renewal confers moral identity and calls each person to responsibility and public integrity.[20]

Covenant involves simultaneously a passive and an active element whereby the relationships formed are based on active and autonomous free will, yet passively bounded by extrinsic orderly moral constructs that the parties adhere to. It entails a moral and legal association that can be pluralistic, federated or hierarchical. The primitive ritual of cutting a covenant in the context of the sharing of material resources in a sacrificial

18 Stackhouse, *Covenant and Commitments: Faith, Family, and Economic Life*, 142.

19 Niebuhr defines moral agency as the response of the self to the action of others. Gardner points out that 'at the formal level Niebuhr defined responsibility as a pattern of response to prior action, interpretation of that prior action, accountability of the self for its response, and participation in an ongoing moral community. At a less abstract level, the meaning of responsibility was expressed concretely and collectively in the history of Israel as a covenant people.' See Gardner, *Justice and Christian Ethics*, 120–3.

20 Max L. Stackhouse, 'The Ten Commandments: Economic Implications,' in Max L. Stackhouse, Dennis McCann and Shirley J. Roels, ed., *On Moral Business: Classical and Contemporary Resources for Ethics in Economic Life* (Grand Rapids: Eerdmans, 1995), 62.

and celebrative rite invokes the presence or witness of God.[21] It is enacted within a framework of duties and rights that form a system of justice. A covenant is not casual but based on enduring law and purpose established by a higher authority. It shifts the focus of domination and control from within the particular dealings to the incorporation of shared duties, rights and higher meanings.

Covenant entails responsible human association rooted in human nature, with a relational rather than self-interested focus. The Calvinistic concept of the covenant differs profoundly from the secularized individualistic liberal contractarianism.[22] Human persons do not exist in neutrality but are granted the choices and responsibilities that come with life on earth.[23] To participate as a covenant partner of God is part of human nature and its necessity. Humankind does not hover infinitely over its creatureliness, but must rediscover its humanity through participation in God's covenant. This covenant order must in turn become the free choice of human participation. As the relational order of the covenant is rediscovered, it is naturally manifested in societal relationships and market interactions. Such a decision is not neutral but intentionally determined through the freedom to act. The economic person thereby takes on a covenant awareness that induces freedom in the trust and care that transcend mere contractual obligations. For the non-believer, this covenantal desire

21 Stackhouse explains the rite of the covenant as 'the recognition that what is at stake is not merely an opportune human agreement or a power ploy but the establishment of a more righteous social order than would otherwise be present, under the standards of holiness. In a covenant, something is at stake in the material sharing that is sacred, life-giving, enduring, and transcendent.' See Stackhouse, *Covenant and Commitments: Faith, Family, and Economic Life*, 140–1.

22 Jonathan Chaplin, 'Suspended Communities or Covenanted Communities? Reformed Reflections on the Social Thought of Radical Orthodoxy,' in *Radical Orthodoxy and the Reformed Tradition*, ed. James K.A. Smith and James H. Olthuis (Grand Rapids: Baker Academics, 2005), 179.

23 As Barth asserts, the human person is 'directed to and prepared for the fulfilment of his determination, his being in the grace of God, by his correspondence and similarity to this determination for the covenant with God'. See Barth, *Church Dogmatics*, III/2: 207.

remains throughout the quest for truth as a hidden need for reconciliation with the Creator. This desire is reflected in the need for relationship with fellow human persons, whether the individual is a believer or not.

After the sinful distortion of human nature, human persons exert a degree of self-interest that naturally precedes self-giving love for the other. As a result, human bonds and relationships cannot be taken for granted but need to be nurtured. As one human person is confronted with an absolutely different person who stands in the same brokenness of sin, self-contradictory acts and human finitudes repeatedly prevent authentic fellowship and cooperation. Accordingly, natural development of the economic market without protective measures for covenantal concerns gradually leads to dehumanization. Forrester asserts that sin in theological anthropology avoids overemphasis on human goodness and prevents the tendency to believe that true humanity can be fully understood through empirical observations. Accordingly, the actuality and potentiality of human nature do not reside with the social sciences but with the order of creation and eschatological reality. In a fallen, sinful world, the perfect human nature that reflects the *imago Dei* is hidden and distorted. As such, a proper functioning of economic order cannot rely entirely on empirical observations. The brokenness of the human condition means that selfishness, manipulation, legalism, exploitation, etc., continue to obscure the original intention of creation.[24]

The humanizing of the market is essential to the well-being of humankind, as human persons must act in accordance with their authentic human nature for them to be complete. Human persons are intended to be in relationship with one another. Hence a person in isolation or neutrality is inclined towards inhumanity, placing oneself in a self-contradictory state.[25] The encounter among human persons involves seeing through

24 Duncan B. Forrester, *Theological Fragments: Explorations in Unsystematic Theology* (New York: T & T Clark, 2005), 31–2.

25 Barth points out that the sin of inhumanity is not only against God but against oneself. The human person cannot accomplish new creation by sinning. He asserts that 'humanity is the determination of our being as a being in encounter with the other man'. See Barth, *Church Dogmatics*, III/2: 227, 248.

each other's eyes, reciprocity and mutual assistance. The humanity of the person depends upon the awareness that we are in necessary assistance of one another. To act humanly is to be human, and to be determined as a human person with gladness. This humanity is not an ideal or virtue, but an order of creation to be actualized.[26] The economic market is one of the platforms for actualizing this mutual dependence. An inhuman market is contradictory to the original humanizing intent of mutual assistance.

Relational order in the *imago Dei* is further revealed through the intra-relationship of the Trinity. The doctrine of the Trinity establishes that God's inner life and His ways of relating to the world involve both diversity and unity. The result is a coherent, integrated diversity that embraces a plurality of consociations. It is a conviction that the world is created by an ultimate reality that governs history, comprising inextricably bound persons in their respective vocations, forming a covenantal community that is cosmic in scope.[27] These elements embedded in the structural composition of economic life mean that the clue is a rediscovery of the intricate relationships of community that have been overlooked. The meaning and characteristics of the covenant as relational order are contained in scriptural narratives throughout the New and Old Testaments. Ecclesiastical communities involve human persons living together in covenantal relationships with a view towards God's kingdom where God's justice reigns.[28] This covenan-

26 Ibid., III/2: 263–7. A comprehensive examination of Karl Barth's theology of persons and covenant is beyond the scope of this book. Nevertheless, the *Church Dogmatics* III/2 contains a detailed exposition of the relational nature of human persons and the necessity for mutual assistance. Economic activities represent one of the important cooperative measures among human persons necessary for basic survival of humankind.

27 Max L. Stackhouse, *Public Theology and Political Economy: Christian Stewardship in Modern Society* (Grad Rapids: Eerdmans, 1987), 32. Stackhouse asserts that the social nature of the human persons, together with its spiritual and moral principles, is empirically and normatively presupposed within the structure of social relationships prior to economic activities.

28 Similar to this view, Moltmann presents a confederate theology of creation that conceives God's relationship to the world as a multilayered, multifaceted and multileveled intricate relationship of community. This is based on the Trinitarian unity

tal way of life offers a prototype for economic relationships both within and beyond the ecclesiastical community. I shall proceed to establish the universality of the covenant concept for both believers and non-believers by examining the Noachic and Abrahamic covenants.

3.3 The Noachic and Abrahamic Covenants: Universality Versus Particularity

The concepts of creation, providence, redemption and ecclesiastical order are fundamental to the origin of the covenant. However, they appear in the first instance, concepts that belong exclusively to the ecclesiastical community. In order for the covenant concept to be applicable to economics and market order, it must not be an exclusive notion. The covenantal community, while bounded together by a common and exclusive set of values, means and objectives, must at the same time remain open to participation. If God's relational covenant is only intended for an elected few and necessarily excludes the others, it cannot be applied to the economic order that serves all humankind. Therefore in the midst of theological languages and articulation of covenant economic implications, we need to establish that the covenant concept is relevant to and inclusive of all humankind. The

of the Father, Son and Spirit of the Creator. Life is communication in communion, whereby the real and living can only be known within relationships and interconnections. The purpose of life is therefore to participate and to enter into mutual relationships with one another. These interconnections build up and extent into a network of symbiotic life. Moltmann names it a 'covenant with nature' on the political level, 'the psychosomatic totality' on the medical level, and 'a community of creation' on the religious level. See Jürgen Moltmann, *God in Creation: An Ecological Doctrine of Creation* (London: SCM Press, 1985), 2–4. On the economic level, I assert that these interconnections are best described as the intention for a 'covenantal market'. It is a market order of mutual responsibility and stewardship for the cosmic creation within a community of interconnections.

paradox between particularity and universality in the covenant concept is revealed in the Abrahamic and Noachic covenants. The Noachic covenant is a universal covenant between the Divine and the whole cosmos, while the Abrahamic covenant depicts a particular covenant between God and Israel.

The word ברית (covenant) first appears in the Old Testament when God announces to Noah His decision to destroy the corrupted world. God establishes a covenant with Noah and promises to spare all that enters the ark (Gen. 6:18–19). After the flood, God establishes a covenant under the sign of the rainbow, promising not to repeat this destruction of the world as long as the earth remains (Gen. 8:22). Before the flood, humankind is so corrupted that 'every imagination of the thoughts of its heart was only evil continually' (Gen. 6:5). After the flood, 'the imagination of humanity's heart is evil from its youth' (Gen. 8:21). Putting these clauses together shows that before and after the flood, the evil inclination of human nature remains unchanged.[29] The biblical narratives quote the same reason of corrupted human nature for God's destruction of the world, and for the covenant never to destroy the world again. Therefore the divine promise is entirely based on God's grace without any regard for change of the evil inclination within human nature. The specific way by which God chooses to assert this grace is through the promise of the covenant. Although the covenant can be bilateral, it also contains the unilateral capacity for exerting grace and mercy on the counterparties. It supports the participants' willingness of self-giving love and compassion. God confirms that He will not bring a flood to destroy living creatures on earth again (Gen. 9:8–11). The Noachic covenant presents the divine prescription for a relational order that embraces the capacity of free participation in a promise of grace.[30]

29 Rolf Rendtorff, '"Covenant" as a Structuring Concept in Genesis and Exodus,' *Journal of Biblical Literature* 108 (1989): 386–7.

30 Goldingay points out that God's covenant with Noah is extended to creation as a whole without any requirement for human response. Although there are later covenants of a more mutual kind, the Noachic covenant sets the model for human covenants. Divine fatherhood and covenanting are prior to human covenanting. See

It is a universal covenant with the whole cosmos, based on a universally applicable form of relational order.

God's promise to Abraham is first recorded in His call for Abraham to leave his father's land to go to the promised land, where Abraham will be blessed a great nation (Gen. 12:1–3). This promise is repeated as Abraham proceeds through his journey (Gen. 18:17–19), taking the literal form of a solemn oath (Gen. 22:15–18), and named as a covenant (Gen. 15:18). Similar to the promise to Noah, God's promise to Abraham contains no particular conditions, except that it assumes Abraham's faithfulness and obedience to God.[31] In contrast to the Noachic covenant, the Abrahamic covenant appears at first glance to be an exclusive one between God and the nation of Israel. Its particularity resides in the fact of Abraham being the elected one, whose name will be great and whose sons will become a great nation (Gen. 12:2). Nevertheless, the scope of this covenant, commencing with a nation of the elected people of Israel, extends to an inclusive nation of the people as all people on earth will also be blessed through Abraham (Gen. 12:3). Accordingly, the Abrahamic covenant is a covenant based on a faith that lies within the paradox of inclusiveness and exclusiveness. Indeed God calls upon a single person and his descendants to come under His special providence. From Abraham comes a new nation of Israel that is the chosen people of God. The fundamental notion of the elect and covenant carries an exclusiveness that limits its membership and benefits to a single nation. This covenant is then extended as Israel serves as a light of all nations, a nation from which the Messiah shall come to redeem the entire humankind. The Abrahamic covenant is inclusive of all the elected people of God. With the redemptive work of Christ, this election is made available to all those who believe. The universality of the covenant applies not only to salvation, but to the capability of the covenant concept to be applied to the whole cosmos because of its essential place in the creation and providential narratives. It is universal as it is the original and authentic

---

John Goldingay, *Old Testament Theology Vol. I: Israel's Gospel* (Illinois: InterVasity Press, 2003), 173–4.

31 John Bright, *Covenant and Promise* (London: SCM Press, 1977), 25–6.

way of relationships freely entered into by all humankind. This universality is revealed in Scripture as the mega-narrative continues to the climax of the coming of the Messiah and into His second coming at the end of time.

The Jewish scholar Jacob Agus asserts that an exclusive view of the covenant is contrary to the liberal and open-ended understanding of revelation that characterizes the modern Jew. Israel, the chosen people, is 'called upon to act as an example to other individuals and nations, not as an exception'.[32] The universality of the covenant is similarly affirmed by Brueggemann who sees the covenantal paradigm as a subversive one that relates to the world beyond the believing community. As such, it is also the basis for mission in a world that is yet to be liberated.[33] A rediscovery of covenant language in the human hearts is at the same time a rediscovery of the authentic way of building fundamental human relationships.[34] The characteristics of the Abrahamic covenant point towards universality within its own particularity. It is a coherent development from the Noachic covenant, serving as a continuation of the progressive covenantal relationship of God with humankind and the cosmos.

Hueglin points out that in Calvin's Geneva, those who departed from the rigid path of prescribed morality were excommunicated. The covenant between God and His people was therefore rather exclusive to the believing community. It was Althusius who proposed that faith be persuaded rather than commanded, and taught rather than ordered. As an orthodox

32 Jacob B. Agus, 'The Covenant Concept – Particularistic, Pluralistic, or Futuristic,' *Journal of Ecumenical Studies* 18 (1981): 230. The covenant concept has deep roots in Judaism, and is often reiterated by Jewish Rabbis in their teachings about God and society. However, the covenant concept has not been applied to modern economics and fundamental economic order in a comprehensive way.

33 Walter Brueggemann, 'Covenant as a Subversive Paradigm,' *Christian Century* 97 (1980): 1097.

34 Mount points out that 'if human relations and community structures are characterized by promises, commitments, and obligations rooted in shared history, it could well be that using covenant language would not be received as speaking a foreign tongue even though the persons in dialogue came from different thick identifications'. See Mount, *Covenant, Community and the Common Good: An Interpretation of Christian Ethics*, 18.

city politician and church elder, he held that those who err in religion are to be ruled by the sword of the Spirit. The magistrate in his administration is not to impose a penalty on them. This means that the covenant does not require the exclusion of non-believers from the political community. By not putting God's grace into human hands, Althusius was able to promote the idea of symbiosis as the fundamental of 'living together'.[35] Accordingly, the universality of the covenant as a relational concept is advocated in society for both believers and non-believers.

The covenant is universal because its concept and characteristics are offered to all humanity, with a capacity of unity in diversity. It allows for multilevel of associations, across different purposes and religions. The covenantal structure supports commitment according to individual quests for purpose and truth by both believers and non-believers. Stackhouse points out that 'the first element of an authentic covenant defines the parties who are in the relevant community of social interaction, now under global conditions offered not to one people or one faith, but to the world'.[36] In the light of differences in historical development, political system, societal culture, economic growth, market functions, etc., humankind shares a wide range of commonalities including intellect, reason, conscience, sense of guilt, as well as the longing for freedom, justice, love and many other virtues. The unity of humankind is claimed through faith and morality. As Bavinck asserts, 'the solidarity of the human race, original sin, the atonement in Christ, the universality of the kingdom of God, the catholicity of the church, and the love of neighbour – these all are grounded in the unity of humankind'.[37] Within this unity and diversity, the covenant concept remains universally applicable owing to its fundamental roots within creation as the divine way of relationship and societal order.

35 Thomas O. Hueglin, 'Covenant and Federalism in the Politics of Althusius,' in *The Covenant Connection: From Federal Theolgoy to Modern Federalism*, ed. Daniel J. Elazar and John Kincard (New York: Lexington, 2000), 38.

36 Stackhouse, *Globalization and Grace*, 166.

37 Herman Bavinck, *Reformed Dogmatics, vol. 2: God and Creation* (Grand Rapids: Baker Academic, 2004), 526.

The covenant concept is both paradoxical and rich in content in terms of inclusiveness and exclusiveness.[38] The inclusive covenant acts as the overall basis of moral choices. Specific covenants of various natures are entered into under this basis. Contracts are negotiated and derived from this overriding understanding. Covenants are continuously entered into and renewed as we construct a set of relationships which bind us with one another within the covenantal community. Special covenants, such as marriage vows, involve intimate relationships that are long-lasting and loving. These involve more than respect for rights and duties. Daily contracts, such as purchases from a local store, involve just and fair dealings within the structure of an ethical covenant of economic order. Inclusiveness is the very first characteristic of covenantal love. Allen points out that 'one of the most serious failings of any government occurs when it rules on behalf of some but not all its citizens: when it excludes from its concern or neglects the poor, the powerless, dissenters, the unpopular, the different'.[39] While the legal contract is an essential tool for governing and safeguarding the society, it must be complemented by a covenantal basis for human relationships. The understanding and use of the covenant are not limited to an understanding of biblical concepts or a relationship with the Divine. It embraces all humanity. The very foundation of human society and the economic order depends on the enactment of covenantal ethics. Because of its forgiving and continuing nature, the covenant transcends material considerations in satisfying human desires. With covenantal love, believers are able to relate to all humanity despite the sinful nature of humankind.

38 Cronin recognizes the multiplicity and richness of the covenant as well as its paradoxical characteristic in terms of inclusiveness and exclusiveness. He asserts that 'to refer to the human race as one family under God is to use a metaphor or model which is not literally true and yet not totally untrue either. There are points of correspondence between the more intimate form of the institution and the wider and more extended image, which are important in ethics, especially in religious ethics.' See Kieran Cronin, *Rights and Christian Ethics* (Cambridge: Cambridge University Press, 1992), 218.

39 Allen, *Love and Conflict: A Covenantal Model of Christian Ethics*, 264.

In modern society, these covenantal virtues of love, trust and sharing are in turn safeguarded by the legal contract.

The modern day individual is involved in multiple daily activities with different roles and identities, each involves potentially covenantal relationships. One needs to be 'an integrating center of identity', with a sense of divine call and empowerment.[40] Otherwise the activities become meaningless drudgeries. Each covenant is a means of grace from the point of view of divine creation. Marriage is a sacred moment, political oaths are solemn promises. Hospitals and schools represent the covenant commitment to serving the community, while cultural events mark the celebration of life. Corporations are covenantal communities dedicated towards economic means. When the contract is used in business transactions, the covenant underlies corporate and societal relationships to ensure that covenantal characteristics of trust, commitment, cooperation, honesty, etc., lay a proper foundation for mutual benefit. When covenantal love and commitment may be distorted because of human sinfulness, the contract protects the covenantal parties from exploitation. Both covenant and contract are therefore universal, relevant and essential to economic life. A lack of awareness of the necessary covenantal nature of human relationships means that the economic market can gradually be reduced to mere contractual arrangements and lead to deconstruction of societal relations.

3.4 The Mosaic Covenant: Human Freedom in the Market

As the intended way of relating between God and His people, the various covenants in the Bible reveal different forms and elements of the covenant concept. Another covenantal element that is significant to the economic order is on the issue of human freedom. Freedom in the economic market is often taken to be freedom of individual choices to satisfy needs and

40 Stackhouse, *Covenant and Commitments: Faith, Family, and Economic Life*, 156–7.

desires. This brings about the wider issue of just distribution and potential exploitation of resources. Accordingly, there is a need for theological interpretation to provide insights into the genuine meaning of human freedom in the market. I shall draw upon another important covenant narrative – the Mosaic covenant, to explore this matter.

The Mosaic covenant made at Mount Sinai contains a different pattern than the preceding covenants with Noah and the patriarchs. Rather than a promissory covenant, it contains a binding obligation for the Israelites to obey the divine commandments under threat of penalties. The Israelites are delivered from the bondage of slavery in Egypt, and are on their journey to the promised land. This celebrative narrative of freedom and deliverance at the same time contains strong demands for obedience to the divine laws. Covenant ceremonies and renewals continue to remind the people of Israel of the promises and obligations contained in the Mosaic covenant (Deut. 6:20–25, 26:5–10; Josh. 24:1–28). At this point in history, Israel was a covenant society with no king, no army and no administrative government. God's people depended entirely on divine provision and protection, under the call for allegiance to their God Yahweh and obedience to the Torah.[41]

The Mosaic covenant contains a paradox between obedience to the Torah and the freedom to do as willed. It reveals the importance of human freedom to enable voluntary participation and commitment to the covenant. The necessity and significance of human freedom are seldom disputed across intellectual disciplines. Yet the understanding of what is meant by freedom often varies. What is freedom and how does it relate to the economic or market order? What does it mean to say that freedom is one of the most important aspects of the covenant? Elazar points out that the Torah uncovered in the Mosaic Book of Covenant begins with a primary

41 For further discussion on the Mosaic covenant in the scriptural narratives, see Bright, *Covenant and Promise*, 28–31. The presence of the Torah or divine law within the covenant is a critical part of the covenantal way of life. As Meeks asserts, 'Torah is the essence of the covenant that invites and commands a human ordering of life … The law as God's gift is God's power to protect life. The law builds common expectations within the plural context of the community.' See Meeks, *God the Economist: The Doctrine of God and Political Economy*, 83.

concern for freedom. Israel is reaffirmed a free people, with slaves freed after a seven-year bondage. Other laws follow on from this first pronouncement.[42] In the Exodus narrative, Israel is freed from the bondage of slavery in Egypt, and called into a journey to the promised land of Canaan. During this journey, God's people enter into freedom within the limits of the Torah that teaches obedience. The Mosaic covenant reveals the nature of the true human freedom that resides not in the freedom of choice but the freedom in obedience. Human freedom is essentially a freedom in limitation. Authentic freedom resides within the boundaries of obedience and morality. The paradoxical nature of freedom is captured within the ability of decision and choice versus the limitation of such choices. Such theological understanding provides insights into the economic market that offers choices to satisfy needs and wants in the name of human freedom.

The almighty God capable of over-ruling human freedom summons humankind into free decision and responsibility. This human freedom is the most important basis of the covenant since it enables the capacities of decision, commitment, responsibility, justice, love, compassion, stewardship, etc., everything essential to the enactment of the covenant. It also includes the freedom to participate in the eternal covenant and to return to the eternal love of the Creator. Freedom is granted by God to humankind as a gift. Whether one belongs to the believing community or not, the significance of freedom as the essential basis for economic acts can easily be recognized.

The notion of freedom has been allotted various meanings throughout the intellectual history of many disciplines including philosophy, politics, sociology, economics, etc. It is seldom disputed that freedom is fundamental to the functioning of the modern market. Bader-Saye points out that the moral discourse of modernity takes freedom as an unquestioned good that holds together differences by affirming personal choices. However, such freedom is a freedom of choice that has led to the breakdown of relationships and misuse of resources. The Christian faith challenges the

42 Daniel J. Elazar, *Covenant & Polity in Biblical Israel: Biblical Foundations & Jewish Expressions* (New Brunswick: Transaction, 1998), 175–6.

construction of freedom as abstract personal choice by proposing the alternative of freedom as the capacity to live faithfully. God's election of Israel comprises a faithful participation in the communal covenant. In such covenant community, freedom is both a gift and a calling, both a given and a goal. It is 'freedom from sin and self-determination and freedom for risky engagement with the reign of God'.[43] The Mosaic covenant is a covenant of the priestly tradition. In the New Testament, the priestly tradition extends to all people of God in Christ, who are called to sanctification and service of the eternal God. Accordingly, the people of God are called to act in obedience within the exercise of the human freedom originally granted by the Creator. Such acts on earth represent priestly service to one another and therefore to God.

Freedom as defined by the freedom of choice holds 'choice' to be the ultimate good. In a free market sustained purely by the priority of liberal personal choice, goods are produced and distributed according to customer preferences without concern for societal goods or minorities' well-being. Ironically, consumer preferences and commodification of the means and ends of life create boundaries and limits to the freedom of choice. These boundaries are represented by allocation of monetary values to any possibility of commodification in terms of wealth and profit creation. A choice-based freedom is therefore reduced to a contractible or measure-able freedom in terms of monetary utilities.[44] In the biblical narratives of Israel, the covenant embraces God's electing grace and human freedom of voluntary participation in obedience. Freedom is embedded in the identity acknowledged and discovered as God's faithful and obedient covenant partner – a people elected by divine grace. In turning away from God by breaking the covenant through disobedience, the Israelites fall into a destructive autonomy where they lose their identity and turn from freedom

43 Scott Bader-Saye, 'The Freedom of Faithfulness,' *Pro Ecclesia* 8 (1999): 437.

44 Bader-Saye finds that Catholics, Lutherans, Calvinists and Wesleyans share a common critique of the abstract individual autonomy that results from taking freedom as choice. The freedom of modern liberalism causes slavery to the self and to desires of the moment. For a survey of the views of the different traditions on this subject and their convergence, see Ibid., 438–45.

to slavery. The Mosaic covenant presents God's faithful work in liberating His people, freeing them from the bondage of slavery and granting the Torah to renew the eternal covenant with His people. As Brueggemann points out, participants in the covenant have 'dangerous freedom in the presence of the other one'.[45] They grant freedom to each other based on faithful trust, affirming the identity and personhood of the others.

In contrast to covenantal freedom, the modern free enterprise system is developed based on the freedom of contract. As Kessler points out, a highly elastic legal institution is necessary to reasonably safeguard the exchange mechanism of the market. This need prompted common law lawyers to expand the use of the contract so that it becomes an indispensable, rational instrument of the entrepreneur. The contract protects the reasonable expectations created by the participants through a set of laws that deal with the formation, performance, impossibility and damages of contracts.[46] To some extent, this mechanism allows the participants to enter freely into transactions, and thus promotes economic freedom. Nevertheless, the freedom of contract remains a partial freedom that can only be partially governed by law. A fundamental covenantal freedom is essential to complement it. This is because it is impossible for the law of contract to anticipate the form and content of all contractual transactions, or to ascertain the specific contracting intentions of all participants. Since a contract is made primarily through the bargaining process, the freedom of contract necessarily carries the possibility of exploitation. Its proper enactment depends on underlying covenantal characteristics such as mutual responsibility, equality, commitment, trust, cooperation, etc. For example, big enterprises often have strong bargaining power because they hold the goods or services that the weaker party needs. They often offer to the weaker party, standard contracts with clauses that aim to protect their own

45 Walter Brueggemann, 'Covenanting as Human Vocation: A Discussion of the Relation of Bible and Pastoral Care,' *Interpretation* 33 (1979): 127.

46 Kessler asserts that the freedom of contract is the inevitable counterpart of a free enterprise system, promoting a spirit of individualism and *laissez faire*. See Friedrich Kessler, 'Contracts of Adhesion – Some Thoughts about Freedom of Contract,' *Columbia Law Review* 43 (1943): 629–42.

interests. It therefore becomes necessary for the law of contract to safeguard against such inequality of power. Legislations that protect the consumers can be established to tackle these issues. However, such legislations cannot anticipate an exhaustive set of infinite possibilities. The establishment and implementation of each additional law involve social costs and may in turn limit the freedom of contract.[47] There will always be a fundamental need for covenantal norms to balance the freedom of contract.

The modern economic market embraces a set of faulty anthropological assumptions and erroneous definition of freedom that requires redirection. Human freedom embraces much broader and richer contents then the economic freedom of choice. Preston points out that economists move too quickly from efficiency to freedom, with freedom interpreted in a very individualistic sense. Individuals in a contract-based market develop in isolation, competition and distrust, away from the social relations and interdependence that are in fact fundamental to the core of human living. 'A narrow view of freedom takes individuality (or personhood) as given, and ignores the social institutions and traditions within which persons relate to one another and arrive at what their social relationships enable them to be.'[48] Human persons are born into communities and interdependent relationships. To nurture and develop these bonds requires the covenant concept. The covenant is required to work simultaneously with

47 Congdon gives two example of how market freedom can be limited by imposing laws to safeguard interest of the weaker party in a contract. One is the example of upward-only rental control on commercial leases. In the 1960s to 1980s, these upward-only rental clauses in Britain were a market practice that made rents more predictable to property investors. Another example is the legislation that aims to foster prompt payment of bills to small companies by imposing statutory interest on late payments. This is in fact a form of price control. Both of these initiatives start with an intention to protect the weaker party in a contract, but tend to interfere with contractual freedom and market efficiency. They impose unnecessary restrictions on the market, and may become detrimental to the weaker contractual party when the economic trend reverses. See Tim Congdon, 'The Law: Freedom or Merit?,' *Ecoonomic Affairs* 14, no. 2 (1994): 41.

48 Ronald H. Preston, *Religion and the Ambiguities of Capitalism* (London: SCM Press, 1991), 25.

contractual arrangements to ensure that the moral and relational aspects of human nature are upheld under the pursuit of efficiency and growth. The ecclesiastic community necessarily values human freedom as the gift granted by God, to be exercised in obedience to the Word of God. The human person voluntarily confesses the commandment of God and internalizes it as the prescribed action. Accordingly, the freedom to act is not only to choose or to realize, but to realize oneself in the act. This freedom is a freedom for God, a freedom to obey Him.[49] This freedom is at the same time a freedom in relation to God and to fellow human persons.[50] Since we have established that theologically, human freedom is freedom in obedience, we need to further establish the basis for such authority within the economic order. In particular, this authority that summons freedom in obedience needs to accommodate both believers and non-believers in a pluralistic society in the modern era. Accordingly, the next theological task is to seek an authoritative measure of economic order that enhances morality and governs against exploitation through both personal agency and law enforcement. I shall examine the Davidic covenant for this purpose.

3.5 The Davidic Covenant: Authority, Morality and Personal Agency

The Davidic covenant gives a broader perspective of the covenant society as it marks a promissory gift of the kingdom (2 Sam. 7). After two hundred years of tribal confederacy, the Israelites lost their battle to the

49 Barth, *Church Dogmatics*, III/4: 13.

50 As Barth asserts, the action of human persons is a deliberate positing of themselves. Time as granted by the Creator to human life on earth is not the mere duration of animal or plant. 'Human life participates in the freedom of all God's creatures to the extent that it does not have its aim in itself and cannot therefore be lived in self-concentration and self-centredness, but only in a relationship which moves outwards and upwards to another.' See Ibid., III/4: 477–8.

Philistines, their Ark captured, their priests slain. Their land is filled with idols and shrines of foreign gods. At this time of emergency, a young hero David united Israel within a few years, broke the Phillistines, and took Jebusite in Jerusalem to be his capital. Under David's reign, the land of Canaan is recaptured, extending the Israelites' domain as far as the Gulf of Aqabah, the Sinai desert and Syria. A new dynasty is formed, with the replacement of Judges by Kings and the passing on of power under kinship. The Davidic covenant follows the pattern of the patriarchal covenant with added elements of obligations on the recipients. The king is commanded to do justice and follow Yahweh's covenant law, but the divine promise remains everlasting even in the event of disobedience (2 Sam. 7:15; Ps. 18:21, 89:30–37).[51]

The Davidic covenant is a covenant of kinship and kingship because it is relational in mutuality within a familial and communal bond, yet also hierarchical in the form of a constitutional monarchy. It involves both bilateral and tripartite covenanting. A covenant relationship is established by God with David, whereby David is anointed king of Israel. This relationship extends to covenants between David and the people of Israel.[52] Elazar identifies this new regime as one combining monarchic and federal institutions. Chronicles further affirms this kingship by asserting that David's son will be the indirect means of God's sovereign rule in Israel (1 Chron. 17:14, 29:23; 2 Chron. 9:8, 13:8). The king establishes a government to defend the needy (Ps. 72), and exercises sovereignty over other nations (1 Chron. 29:11).[53] Both kinship and kingship are essential for the authentic relationship that starts between God and the person, and extends to that among human persons. The relationship between God and His people involves both the sovereign kingdom of God and kinship of His people. God is both the King and the Father. At the same time, human persons relate to each other in various spheres comprising kinship and

51 For further details about the Davidic covenant, see Bright, *Covenant and Promise*, 50–70.

52 Elazar, *Covenant & Polity in Biblical Israel: Biblical Foundations & Jewish Expressions*, 313–14.

53 Goldingay, *Old Testament Theology Vol. I: Israel's Gospel*, 559–60.

hierarchical structures. The market is a sphere of communal exchange upon the foundation of community and kinship. A regime of law and order acts as the written authority to ensure justice within this sphere. At the same time, individuals act as personal agents in a call to exercise stewardship and uphold morality. In the economic market human persons can thus relate freely to cooperate and interact responsibly.

Moltmann points out that besides being *imago Dei*, human persons are also *imago mundi*. They stand before God as 'image of the world', representative of all creatures.[54] As a result, 'the human ownership of God's creation can only be recognized as just by the use of it in solidarity'.[55] This means that there is a duty attached to ownership, whether under divine authority for the believer or in the conscience of the non-believer. Within the covenant, all human persons are at the same time personal agents for stewardship of the world and its resources. As such, Christians are directed towards the world with a comprehensive mission in history for the kingdom of God. Moltmann identifies the economic process as one of the three major world processes of economics, politics and culture where the church must enact its mission. In economics, the church should liberate humans and nature from exploitation. It is where faith means the courage to affirm life and be loyal to the earth. The hope for the coming kingdom is vital because the contemporary world crises – economic, political and cultural, are shaking humankind to the depths of the will to live. Christians do not merely offer ethical commitment to society, but the liberation and redemption that come from the presence of its faith.[56]

The covenant assertion of divine authority over personal agency faces some difficulties in a pluralistic world. While the scriptural covenants presuppose one divine Creator, the covenantal way of life does not. Those

54 In Moltmann's theology, human persons are priestly creatures and eucharistic beings understood as *imago mundi*. They intercede before God for the community of creation. See Moltmann, *God in Creation: An Ecological Doctrine of Creation*, 190.

55 Jürgen Moltmann, *Creating a Just Future: The Politics of Peace and the Ethics of Creation in a Threatened World* (London: SCM Press, 1989), 70.

56 Jürgen Moltmann, *The Church in the Power of the Spirit* (London: SCM Press, 1977), 164–5.

things that remain common to believers and non-believers alike are the capacity for personal agency, morality embedded in human conscience, and the freedom to search for the truth. In a multilevel and multi-faith society, covenantal associations are offered time and space to search for their own truth. Accordingly, there will always be a tension among different interest groups in a pluralistic society. Continuous dialogue among these associations is an essential part of a covenantal polity. This difficulty is coupled by the problem of human sinfulness that remains a reality even among believers. The church on earth in this temporality does not reflect the kingdom of God.[57] In an economic market driven by legal laws and contractual obligations, Christians strive to live with the identity and characteristics of covenantal relationships. However, they do not always succeed. At the same time, contractual laws are necessary to govern their voluntary participation in the economy and to regulate the interaction among all the market participants. Divine authority, personal agency and morality all play their respective parts in a pluralistic society that attempts to unite diversified beliefs and interests in one harmonious societal and economic order.

Althusius uses the covenant concept to coordinate political participants so that each party is attributed original political rights. He emphasizes that justice is embedded in the divine plan for human existence, therefore adding a moral dimension to the polity. His message is that the rational logic of justice is identical with divine law, and that it must attach itself to the higher principle of mutuality, the categorical imperative of the covenantal society. Such a covenant is by no means a contractual one among

57 As Moltmann suggests, it consists of its own historically developed hierarchical constitution that arouses suspicion when it attempts to claim any direct power in secular matters. Consequently, the relational model of the church and the secular order is one of partnership and mutual complement. Christians in their secular professions and responsibilities are motivated by the will to live, the power to hope and the capacity for suffering as part of their faith. They direct themselves to the future kingdom of God, while empowered by the Spirit to strive for enactment of their faith on earth. Therefore the church seeks neither an ecclesiasticizing of the world, nor a helpless respect for the inherent laws of the secular spheres. See Ibid., 167–8.

autonomous egocentric individuals.[58] Legal rules and order provide a framework for human functions that needs to reside upon the covenantal way of relating. Both the contractual economic order and covenantal interdependence of human persons in the economy are essential to uphold market functions. These universal concepts must coexist and interact to promote healthy market norms.[59] Law is necessary because of sin and is not needed in the state of perfection. In the ideal economy of perfection, the household of God rests upon covenantal relationships in perfect bonding and cooperation. In the interim reality on earth, contracts and contractual law are necessary to govern and enact household rules because of fallen human nature.

There will always be a conflict of interests whenever economics denies the universal household of God, and remains unaware of the ways by which deformed theological concepts dominate the economy.[60] At the same time, Christians are often unaware of the distortion of religious notions brought about by dehumanized economic relationships. The Old Testament prophets' repeated call for repentance and justice presents a continuing demand for commitment, as well as the capacity for renewal of the covenant. It is the nature and will of God to remain perpetually steadfast as a party to the eternal covenant that He has initiated. After Israel anoints earthly kings to govern them, the kings are equally subject to the divine law as participants in the divine covenant. Accordingly, God's covenantal love towards His people continues, interacts with and works through the earthly kingdoms as they are established.[61] Laws and contractual order do not negate the

58 Hueglin, 'Covenant and Federalism in the Politics of Althusius,' in 37.

59 Bavinck describes the relationship between law and gospel by taking the gospel as casted and derived from the law. God who speaks in the gospel is the One who has made Himself known in the law. See Herman Bavinck, *Reformed Dogmatics, vol. 4: Holy Spirit, Church, and New Creation* (Grand Rapids: Baker Academic, 2008), 454.

60 Meeks, *God the Economist: The Doctrine of God and Political Economy*, 19.

61 'The covenant is not a contract in which God's grace is conditional on the goodness or faithfulness of his people, for he is constantly faithful to it. Even God's wrath is understood as an attempt to bring Israel back to loyalty to the covenant, loyalty

covenantal essence of divine authority, but extends it to a providential care that allows plurality and the continuing quest of each individual for the truth. Morality and personal agency work in every human heart as originally intended in creation. Under the primary and unconditional covenant with Israel, God acts to bring His people out of Egypt. The Decalogue articulates Israel's response to God's faithfulness towards this covenant. Upon the basis of the covenant, the obligations and law of the Torah are thus also sustained by God's unconditional faithfulness.[62] The ultimate goal is a covenantal renewal that unites all consociations under the divine authority of the Creator.

3.6 The New Covenant: From Scarcity to Satisfaction and Thanksgiving

The New Testament offers a renewed, covenantal ecclesiology with the coming of Christ. This new covenant builds on the worldview of creation in the Old Testament, and extends it to present an ideological order with the redemption of Christ and the kingdom of God to come. In this temporal life on earth, a fully covenantal society will always remain an ideology because of human sinfulness and finitude. The kingdom of God, and therefore the perfect form of the covenantal ideology, is only realizable at the end of time. I shall examine the new covenant not to promote it as an ideology for life on earth, but to examine what it offers in terms of our

---

expressed by both divine and human justice.' See Duncan B. Forrester, *Christian Justice and Public Policy* (Cambridge: Cambridge University Press, 1997), 208.

62 Torrance points out that the relationship between God and humanity is covenantal rather than contractual because 'the indicatives of grace precede and sustain the imperatives of law'. See Alan J. Torrance, 'On Deriving "Ought" from "Is": Christology, Covenant and *Koinonia*,' in *The Doctrine of God and Theological Ethics*, ed. Alan J. Torrance and Michael Banner (London: T & T Clark, 2006), 172.

understanding of the content of the covenant and what the covenantal way encompasses.

Most philosophers hold a teleological worldview proceeding from the order and beauty of observable things in the world.[63] As a moral philosopher, Adam Smith's concept of the 'invisible hand' asserts the teleological argument that there is an order and harmony with observable purpose underlying the free economy. It assumes at most a designer behind all things, rather than a creator. It presupposes an unconscious motive working behind the free market that contains more wisdom and certainty than conscious reflection.[64] Contradictory to this teleology, materialism in fact presents no purpose in things and objects. As natural evolution takes humankind towards an increasing focus upon materialism, the teleological view of invisible harmony is quickly taken over by the mechanical structure that resides upon unconscious functionality. The doctrine of natural law and natural religions that arises from the human quest for self-realization finds the human person autonomous and independent from God. The individual person develops the tendency to see oneself as the central focal point of perfection in his own end.[65] The familiar covenant concept and its intended relational order can easily be distorted to serve the interest of the individual through legalization and quantitative analysis of personal gains. In contrast, the covenant permits a new ecclesiology that show God's intention for a society that values all its participants, brings them together to form a common community of work and joy, and distributes its produce equally.[66]

63 Bavinck asserts that natural science takes on the impressive view of teleology, substituting cause for purpose, and then explaining the functionality of things through the theory of natural selection. For a detailed discussion of the teleological argument and its general acceptance by most philosopher, see Bavinck, *Reformed Dogmatics, vol. 2: God and Creation*, 82–4.

64 Adam Smith's system of human nature and economic mechanism is further discussed in chapter 6.1.

65 Bavinck, *Reformed Dogmatics, vol. 2: God and Creation*, 432.

66 Brueggemann asserts that solidarity on earth is possible under a new ecclesiology because the covenant construct presents God's move to solidarity. The world is

Perceiving the world as creation implies a particular worldview towards the existence of human persons and an embodiment of individuals into a wider fellowship under the Creator. Barth offers a critique of the covenant concept as it places an ontological and epistemic priority on creation, making the grace of salvation in Christ secondary to the gift of creation. This is not the case because the entire covenant tradition puts a soteriological priority on Christ. The gift of creation does not diminish the significance of grace as creation is a historical necessity prior to redemption, being restored into the original goodness through the covenants that embody the order, purposes and grace of God.[67] The understanding of an order of creation draws an attitude of thanksgiving in light of the charity of gift and self-giving love. It is the recognition of what has been received as gifts and blessings to be shared and cherished. Without such awareness, possessions and rights can be taken for granted. Stewardship and thanksgiving notions can be ignored. Human persons should not dominate and use the world as they wish, but discern the world as God's creation.[68] God creates human persons to be rational and moral beings, and thus maintains them in such ways. Accordingly, He grants freedom without coercion, relating to His people through counsel, admonition, warning, invitation and petition in the covenant. It is the way of gifting that induces gratitude without duress, and embraces universality without exclusion.[69] It is the way that provides true human freedom in the midst of decisions and choices in economic life. Through enacting covenantal initiatives within contractual bounda-

---

intended by God to be a community that covenants. See Brueggemann, 'Covenant as a Subversive Paradigm,' 1096–7.

67 Stackhouse, 'The Moral Meanings of Covenant,' 263.

68 As Moltmann points out, creation is to be understood as a sacrament of God's hidden presences, and apprehended as a communication of God's fellowship. These abilities allow humankind to consciously receive creation in thanksgiving, and to bring creation before God in praise. All God's creatures are thus fundamentally eucharistic beings. See Moltmann, *God in Creation: An Ecological Doctrine of Creation*, 71.

69 Bavinck, *Reformed Dogmatics, vol. 2: God and Creation*, 570–1.

ries, humankind receives the divine gift of creation with responsibility and thanksgiving.[70]

Creation, providence and redemption appear to be assets of the ecclesiastical community, yet they are theological articulations that affect the whole cosmos. The covenant of salvation embraces the whole human race as Abraham and Israel are elected out of the bond with humanity that remains intact.[71] The covenant between God and humanity extends from the universal Noachic covenant with nature and the covenant of grace with the elect to the eternal covenant of salvation for all humanity. This reflects a covenant among the three persons in the beings of the divine trinity itself, known as the *pactum salutis* (counsel of peace, covenant of redemption, or intratrinitarian pact of salvation).[72] The *pactum salutis* reveals the covenantal relationships and life of the trinity in consummate self-consciousness and freedom. Within this Trinitarian covenant, the covenant flourishes to its fullness. This covenantal way of relating is reflected with the character of a sovereign grant between God and humanity. The redemptive work of Christ resides at the climax of salvation history in the eternal covenant of grace granted by God as a gift to all humanity.[73]

70 Bavinck sees the covenant at work as a voluntary binding mechanism in all aspects of human life. He asserts that 'among rational and moral creatures all higher life takes the form of a covenant ... Such an agreement, whether it is made tacitly or defined in explicit detail, is the usual form in terms of which humans live and work together. Love, friendship, marriage, as well all social cooperation in business, industry, science, art, and so forth, is ultimately grounded in a covenant, that is, in reciprocal fidelity and an assortment of generally recognized moral obligations.' See Ibid., 568–9.

71 Bavinck asserts that 'humanity as a whole gathers around the cross; and the church, chosen from that humanity, is closely united with it'. See Herman Bavinck, *Reformed Dogmatics, vol. 3: Sin and Salvation in Christ* (Grand Rapids: Baker Academic, 2006), 216.

72 The *pactum salutis* idea originates from Olevianus, Junius, Gomarus and others. Bavinck finds scriptural roots for this doctrine in Christ as mediator, Son and servant, who receives a reward from the Father for the salvation task accomplished in obedience. See Ibid., 212–16.

73 This same covenant of grace is revealed in both unity and diversity in the Old and New Testament as promise and fulfilment (Acts 13:32; Rom. 1:2); shadow and substance (Col. 2:17); servitude and freedom (Rom. 8:15; Gal. 4:1, 22; Col. 2:20; Heb.

The ultimate concern of the *pactum salutis* is all humanity, through a renewed covenant of grace in Christ. However, living out the covenant concept alone is by no means the way into the covenant of God, because the covenant way of life can take on any object or ultimate concern. It is the believers' response to the covenant of grace in Christ that makes the participants children of God. Nevertheless, the covenant way is available to believers and non-believers alike because it is part of the fundamental truth embedded in authentic human nature. It is an apologetic assertion and duty of the church to proclaim the authentic way of human living in societal and economic life. In Christian worship, the Eucharist stands at its core ritual of covenantal realization that anticipates the eschatological community in the kingdom of God. It points towards the hope for an authentic household and economic order that represents the ultimate manifestation of the covenantal relationships in its perfect form.

There is a remarkable parallel to be drawn between the use of the Old Testament Law, the Torah, as a call for obedience and societal order for maintaining the covenant with God, and the use of the New Testament salvation, through grace, as redemption of all humanity in Christ. The covenant of grace presupposes that the Old Testament Law is inadequate because of humankind's fallen nature, and moves it to its fulfilment through the work of Christ. Use of the contract to govern societal and economic order provides a set of fundamental rules with covenantal intentions. Unfortunately, these intentions are often lost in the midst of exploitation of law and order through coercion, individualism and the like. Humankind has thus forgone the essence of the covenant that underlies contractual guidance. Nevertheless, God continues to uphold His eternal covenant with divine grace and providence. It remains the key to fulfilling the emptiness in human hearts through reconciliation with the Creator. The covenant of salvation is actualized through the redemptive work of Christ.

12:18); particular and universal (Jn. 4:21; Acts 10:35, 14:16; Gal. 4:4–5; Eph. 2:14, 3:6). In the new covenant, Christ fulfils all things through His role as true prophet, priest and king. His church is the true seed of Abraham, Israel and the people of God. See Ibid., 223–4.

In the economic household of creation, the covenant fulfils the work of the contract by preceding it as the underlying reality of all economic and societal relationships.

In the New Testament, the Trinitarian narrative of the Son marks an open invitation to the communal relationships of God. This divine community, the unity of the Triune God, is open for humankind, for the whole cosmos, and for the future. It reveals the nature of the eternal, covenantal bond. The entire creation shall find space and time in God under the unity of love in the Father, through the Son, and in the fellowship of the Holy Spirit.[74] Redemptive power within the relational nature of the Trinity has significant implications to economic order. It places the economic distribution process in community and relationships as opposed to individualistic satisfaction and selfishness. It means that human freedom is neither a licence of autonomy to do as one wills, nor the protection of an individual's independence from interference. Positive freedom is properly developed and exercised in fellowship through the proper distribution of resources and the empowerment of human persons to flourish within the fabric of a community.[75]

The New Testament presents us with a very different social context from the Old Testament. The gospel of the kingdom of God is for 'the poor'. These include justice to the exploited and good news to the hungry.[76]

74 Elisabeth Moltmann-Wendel and Jürgen Moltmann, *Humanity in God* (London: SCM Press, 1983), 84–9.

75 Duncan B. Forrester and Danus Skene, *Just Sharing: A Christian Approach to the Distribution of Wealth, Income and Benefits* (London: Epworth Press, 1988), 107–8.

76 The New Testament narratives contain rich resources for exploring the ethics of economic order and morality in a covenantal community. Moltmann asserts that the gospel assures a life-giving reality to those in poverty, unemployment, homelessness, sickness and sufferings (Luke 12:58, 14:21–23; Matt. 11:2–5, 18:23–25). These are the non-persons in slavery and prostitution. Christ who comes to the present brings a new dignity to the poor, liberating them from oppression and humiliation, granting them a future and identity. This gospel that pronounces the coming of the kingdom of God is part of the eternal covenant that assures equity and fair distribution. It takes the real needs of the needy seriously as Jesus heals the sick and addresses the

With the emerging churches in numerous localities and across cultures, covenantal communities are in diversity as well as unity. The ecclesiastical community is expecting an imminent end of the present order that takes them closer to the realization of the covenantal economy. Such an apocalyptic worldview testifies to the finality of the existing order of things, and nourishes a confident hope of eschatology.[77] The ecclesiastic community is the economy of God's household. Therefore the church's *oikonomia* necessarily includes Christians' relationship with society and economy. In the modern context, the church works in the presence and power of the Holy Spirit in solidarity with the world. It seeks to live for the transformation of the world into a household of God in constant strive and hope.[78]

The *imago Dei* places the human person in community. It is a gift that embraces the whole of humanity through time and space in all dimensions and characteristics. As such, the cosmos is a unity with humanity to be conceived as an organism that comprises of one household and family. This notion takes humanity in its historical meta-narrative that serves to unfold God's revelation towards fulfilment of the whole cosmos as both a gift and a mandate. The church is thus the bride of Christ, the temple of the Holy Spirit, God's dwelling and the new Jerusalem in all its glory. Its fulfilment is the kingdom of God where the human destiny is found in community and perfect unity.[79] Restoration of humankind to the *imago Dei* is achieved through the messianic redemption by which believers become *imago Christi*. In the new creation believers become 'conformed to the image of the Son' (Rom. 8:29). This salvation is completed through the work of Christ, who redeems all His followers through calling, justification and sanctification. God reveals His faithfulness to the covenant through His eternal salvation plan. The covenant is therefore both an indicative gift and an imperative

exploitative power of the rich (Luke 1:46–54, 6:24, 19:1–10). See Jürgen Moltmann, *The Way of Jesus Christ: Christology in Messianic Dimensions* (London: SCM Press, 1990), 99–102.

77 Duncan B. Forrester, *On Human Worth: A Christian Vindication of Equality* (London: SCM Press, 2001), 91–3.

78 Meeks, *God the Economist: The Doctrine of God and Political Economy*, 23–4.

79 Bavinck, *Reformed Dogmatics, vol. 2: God and Creation*, 576–7.

charge. It is promise, hope and glory in the echaton. At the same time, it resides in a continuing mode in history whereby being human means becoming human in community with God and with one another.[80]

The ideal divine covenant community is one in which participants are in perfect communion with God and others. Within such community there is no scarcity or competition. Fear and coercion are replaced by complete trust, commitment and respect for each other. Interests and benefits are shared with common allegiance to the divine law and grace. Complete obedience to the divine governing allows the full realization of the covenant society. Unfortunately, this perfect covenant society cannot be realized within life on earth. It can only be realized eschatologically, when the heavens and earth are renewed by the Creator God in the redemption of Christ. In this already-but-not-yet temporality, covenant living is a target to work towards. It complements the earthly governance of contractual regulations to set the boundaries for humanizing market relationships. This prototype requires a balance between individual responsibility for the self and collective responsibility in relation to each other in the wider community.

> If private interest and individual economic calculation – even if guided by the most enlightened personal motivations – are accented rather than social harmony, economic chaos results. If the accent falls entirely on collective action and class solidarity, even given a profound struggle for a just community, the inevitable result is economic czarism.[81]

Accordingly, the covenant as a fundamental reality in the original intent of creation must be balanced with individual freedom and protective justice to ensure harmonious social and economic order. This balance requires appropriate interaction between covenant and contract in a complementary manner. Chapter 4 presents a conceptual analysis of the two concepts, and derive the Two Pillars paradigm that provides the framework

80 Moltmann, *God in Creation: An Ecological Doctrine of Creation*, 226–7.

81 Stackhouse, *Public Theology and Political Economy: Christian Stewardship in Modern Society*, 65.

for maintaining a well-balanced economic market. Before I proceed to present this paradigm, our final step is to critically evaluate the ideology that may result from a pure theological understanding of economic order, so that a realistic theological response can be formulated without falling into idealism.

3.7 Economy of Grace, Gift or Covenant?

We have seen that early Christians in the New Testament hold a distinctive eschatology that shapes their daily living. The central focus is for Christ to come again during their age, and therefore the new age is considered to be taking shape. They live together in a kind of eschatological community that is largely covenantal. Jewish Christians and Gentiles are bounded together to form a people of Christ. In this early Christian community, wealth and family are secondary to the eschatological community. Their covenantal community is united by a common faith and eschatological hope, inclusive of any race and social class.[82] To the believers, the practices of almsgiving and communal property are responses to the call of the kingdom of God.[83] Through individual and communal commitments, they redistribute their resources by participating in shared values for the well-being of the community. The divine law reigns with the greatest commandment of loving God and neighbour as oneself (Matt. 22:34–40). The patterns and boundaries of properties ownership are demolished, giving participants the security and freedom with respect to possessions and their distribution.[84] This is not to say that the eschatological ideology of an ultimate covenantal

82 Thomas W. Ogletree, *Hospitality to the Stranger: Dimensions of Moral Understanding* (Louisville: Westminster John Knox Press, 2003), 130–3.

83 The practices and narratives of almsgiving and communal property in the early Christian community are described in Acts 2:43–47; 4:32–37; 5:1–11; 6:1–6.

84 Ogletree, *Hospitality to the Stranger: Dimensions of Moral Understanding*, 143.

community of mutual sharing is the blueprint of life on earth. In reality, the early Christian community is a unique covenantal association that continues to relate to non-believers in mission. This no doubt involves ordinary economic dealings to purchase daily necessities in the form of contractual exchange. An economic order relying entirely upon covenantal grace and sharing is the ultimate hope that is realizable only in the end of time. In the temporality of life on earth, the believing community strive to enact the covenantal order within the limitations imposed by human sinfulness. Accordingly, a balance between covenant and contract is necessary for a harmonious society that enables cooperation among all the participants, regardless of their ideological or religious beliefs.

The covenant community of the early Christians is built based on the teachings of Jesus Christ. Ogletree identifies two important characteristic of Jesus' teaching based on the Gospel of Matthew. First, obedience of the divine law involves devotion of the self rather than mere acts. This means that intentions, attitudes and feelings are significant, contrary to the assumptions of abstract relationships in contract law. Second, obedience also involves radical vulnerability to adversaries. Jesus and His disciples are often at odds with the social order. Under the new covenant, they submit to the authority of earthly governance, while at the same time refusing to compromise to its violence in a community of love.[85] This covenant community presupposes a strong common allegiance of all participants to the divine law in submission and obedience. Even then, perfection cannot be attained in this already-but-not-yet temporality on earth because of the corrupted nature of humankind. The narratives of this early Christian community contain incidences that point towards the need for reprimand and enforcement of the covenantal order. Some examples include the narrative of Ananias and Sapphira who lied about their property (Acts 5:1–11), and the need for appointing seven men to handle the conflict about daily distribution of food between Grecian Jews and Hebraic Jews (Acts 6:1–7). Such situations suggest that there are times when rules and regulations need to be clarified and upheld. The contract provides a valuable complement

85 Ibid., 134.

to the covenant in these circumstances by safeguarding economic functions. It helps to clarify and enforce laws and economic order within the covenantal community.

The covenant way of economic life in its eschatological stage contains certain similarities with the economy of grace advocated by theologian Kathryn Tanner. The economy of grace is based on unconditional giving in a structural sense. It is built upon social relationships with the motive of giving. Tanner attempts to define unconditional giving as a social and economic matter without consideration of feelings or returns. Hence an economy of grace is depicted to reflect the characteristic of God's unconditional giving in creation and redemption. This unconditional giving is universal because God gives to everyone. The resulting economy operates in a community of noncompetition for the benefit of all.[86] The unconditional aspect of this economy is in line with the covenant concept of shared possession and redistribution. Tanner goes further to point out that the values of materially different things are in fact too abstract to compare for exchange in the market. Setting a price value is an attempt to set a common norm for incomparable things. In a simple example of barter whereby one party prepares dinner while the other offers a haircut in return, the transaction is based on values more abstract than measurable costs. Money makes these abstract notions of value explicit and regulates them by external norms.[87]

While Tanner is correct in pointing out the abstract incomparability of values, the convenience of money as the measuring unit has its own benefits. The use of money as a measuring unit enables multiple market transactions and cross-market exchanges. Commodities are given monetary values so that contractual arrangements can become unambiguous. The use of money as exchange unit allows for wider trades and cooperation. This need not be detrimental. What Tanner should be arguing against is the lost of the transcendent and ordering of values when monetary units are involved in transactions. The ideal arrangement based on gratuity and

86 Tanner, *Economy of Grace*, 62–85.
87 Ibid., 16.

abolishment of monetary units can be attained in the eschatological covenant community, but not the already-but-not-yet temporality. In this earthly market, the solution is not to abolish monetary units, but to properly balance relational covenant concepts with the contractual exchange of material commodities. The use of money is to serve the market of exchange within its own functionalities and limits. At the same time, unquantifiable nonmarket values must be properly acknowledged and enacted. Two friends who exchange their services in terms of cooking dinner and performing haircuts can and should continue to do so without excessive concerns for the accuracy of monetary unit involved. This relational act is carried out under the concept of sharing and covenantal love. Two strangers on the streets, one requiring dinner while the other needs a haircut, can satisfy their respective needs through mutually beneficial contractual market arrangements. In such case, the covenant concept allows the strangers to give and receive services in an ethical manner. In reality, people do start to build relationships as they interact. A satisfied customer who gives a tip to a hairdresser or waiter may do so beyond mere contractual requirements. Why do people dine out or shop? The standard economic answer is for a satisfaction of needs and wants. In reality, such market exchanges and interactions are part of society and community living. These seemingly generic activities can come from a range of motivations. While shopping is considered a leisure activity by some, others shop for expensive items to show their social status. Still others shop on a need basis only. Some people buy gifts for others out of appreciation, while others find it an undesirable obligation. Similarly, money may become the mammon of human lives, but can also be used appropriately to serve as units of exchange to facilitate communal living.

Another similar alternative to the economy of grace is the economy of gift advocated by a group of radical orthodox theologians including John Milbank, Catherine Pickstock and Stephen Long. The economy of gift is marked by the nature of gifting in its market exchange. In such markets, participants are bonded together politically and socially by the obligation and indebtedness of reciprocal gifts. These obligations remain in perpetuity. Unfortunately, the mechanism of reciprocity in gifting reduces the essence of gifting to an obligation of gifting in return. 'Gifts' as defined in these markets are therefore not free but obligatory because they demand something in exchange. Participants are required to be both donors and recipients as part of mutual ties. Obligations become the essence of relationships in contrast to the independence provided by contractual arrangements upon completion of the contract.

In a gift exchange, gifts are never unconditional or disinterested because the demand for reciprocity is the necessary element that binds the participants and sets them free at the same time. Nevertheless, the notion of gifting presents some advantages over the use of monetary measurement. Long and Fox assert that 'a gift from another and the consequent return leads us more fully into the life of the other while also fulfilling my own life. For this reason, a gift economy is a virtuous economy.'[88] They challenge traditional economic views of value by asserting the theological view that value cannot be produced but can only be discovered by seeking God above all things. Therefore the reception of gifts cultivates the reception of virtues. They point out that public goods have been left out of the economic models not only because of a focus on the calculation of individual interest, but also because of the economic conception of value.[89] The market essentially focuses upon commodities and their value in exchange. As a result, the first attempt is to commodify everything in sight for assigning a relative value. These include commodification of abstract concepts such as labour hours, risks, property rights, etc. Further attempts in commodification penetrate human relationships in the form of caring or marital contracts. Once the item in question is commodified, a value in exchange can be assigned for it to be tradable in the contract-based market. However, this value in exchange often differs from the value in use.[90] For example, basic necessities such as air and water have significantly higher value in use then jewelleries and rare antiques that have high value in exchange. The market then attempts to maximize value in exchange by creating commercial norms and lifestyle

88 D. Stephen Long and Nancy R. Fox, *Calculated Futures: Theology, Ethics, and Economics* (Texas: Baylor University Press, 2007), 194–8.

89 In fact, their claim is only true of the basic models. Public goods are an integral part of many economic models and analyses.

90 Long and Fox, *Calculated Futures: Theology, Ethics, and Economics*, 47–51.

urges that speak to the human desire. As the market structure is deeply embedded in daily living, these value measurements from the market in turn drive human lives and eventually become their master.

While these criticisms of the monetary market contain some truth, non-commodity gift exchanges also have serious shortcomings. In models of non-commodity gift exchange, possessions are shared to meet needs in an imitation of Trinitarian love. Such gift exchanges are markets for exchange of alienable things motivated by reciprocal expectations. While commodity exchanges are based on reciprocal independence, gift exchanges involving non-commodities are simply those of reciprocal dependence. These gift exchanges promote trust and interdependence, focusing on relationship building rather than individual needs. In such markets, social status increases with the increase in material possession given away. Accordingly, the priority is to maximize net personal outflow in order to attain maximum prestige. With gift exchange as the community's fundamental organizing principle, social relations continue through an obligation to give. The exchange of money completes and breaks off a transaction cycle, but gift relationships are self-sustaining through a continuation of indebtedness. Gifts can circulate in similar ways as money to become capital. The arrangement involves goods or services in exchange for consideration of different kinds which is essentially contractual in nature. As a result, gift exchanges also have a competitive tendency in terms of social status and reciprocity.[91] Gifting eventually deteriorate into exchanging and contracting with calculated indebtedness. Therefore, gift exchanges are implicitly contractual by virtue of their conditions involving reciprocity and imposing obligations. At the same time, contractual terms that are implicit and vague in the non-commodity exchange lead to misunderstanding and breakdown of trust. Once the contractual terms become explicit again, one returns to a market that is contract-based.

As Tanner asserts, what gives the gift exchanges their unique form is the charitable giving aspects whereby gifts meet the needs of the recipient. A true gift has to be free from any tit-for-tat attachment. This means

91 Tanner, *Economy of Grace*, 49–54.

that the gifting is not circulating and reciprocal, but settled in the hands of the giver and the needy. The act of giving is without self-concern and solely for the others. In reality, donors seldom build a continuing relationship with the recipients. Therefore in a market of grace, the goal is not to maximize benefits or relationships, but to focus on charitable giving. Since no personal obligations or pressures are attached to the recipient, status concerns need not infiltrate the giving of gifts. This allows the giving to be purified of motives that draw the market towards commercial exchanges. Purely disinterested gift exchanges stand in contrast with purely interested market exchanges.[92] An economy of free gifts, however, does not resolve all the problems. Reliance on charitable giving does not build relationships or encourage cooperative production. It cannot form the basic structure of economic order because gifting needs to be voluntary and disinterested. Eventually, personal motives and preferences enter into the decisions of free giving, and a lack of self-interest cannot be sustained.

A covenantal market embraces the unconditional giving notion of the economy of grace, as well as a redistribution of resources described as extension of benefits in the economy of grace. The priority of extending benefits maximizes aggregate utilities to all recipients, without consideration of reciprocity or exchange. This extension of benefits is inclusive of oneself, meaning that disinterest is no long the norm. Since participants are free of the danger of losing what they have, they can be freed to give to others. When gifting freely and unconditionally, the participant also receives freely and unconditionally. The elimination of scarcity and fear are theologically attractive and feasible under the reign of the Divine. However, such an economy of grace presupposes a people of God not only comprised exclusively of believers, but also one that is sanctified and redeemed in its entirety. The finitude and sinfulness of human persons become fully cleansed and renewed through the coming of Christ. This is the believers' eschatological reality. In the meantime, while residing on earth in anticipation of the second coming of Christ, modern believers are called to live in communities that comprise pluralistic values and beliefs.

92 Ibid., 55–85.

In such reality, believers continuously encounter the paradox of striving towards a covenantal eschatology while maintaining a market order that is inclusive of both believers and non-believers. The challenge of the church in this temporality is to enact its mission of covenanting and continuous covenant renewal with this day and age. To allow for a relevant and realistic theological response to the economic market, insights from theological concepts need to be placed within a practicable paradigm universally applicable to believers and non-believers alike. This will be the focus of my study in part II of this book.

3.8 The Quest for a Theological Response to the Market

The theology of the covenant provides a view of human nature in finitude and sinfulness that explains the inadequacy of contractual arrangements based on natural evolution of legal concepts. It also reveals that the covenant is rooted in genuine human nature, creation, freedom and divine authority. Scriptural narratives offer resources for understanding the contents of the covenant to be universal, relational and redemptive. These resources offer valuable insights and reminders for the continuing quest towards a theological response for the economic market. Reformed theologians speak of the covenant as God's plan that spans the economy of salvation from creation through redemption and consummation. Covenantal thinking affirms God's sovereignty, His relationship with creation, and the freedom and responsibility of humankind. Through covenantal living, humankind cares for creation and the economy in ways intended by the Creator. The covenant concept invites us to envision a world of community and relationships through developing mutual bonds that foster human life. The self-sufficient and abundant nature of the Trinity presents liberation from insecurity and economic scarcity. In an eschatological covenantal household of God, the need of every individual is taken care of through trust, cooperation and sharing under the lordship of the divine Creator. Possession, rights and justice are not objects of power but realities that enable fulfilment of individual uniqueness as well as pursuit of the common good. In the temporality of life on earth, the believing community strives towards covenantal living while remaining loyal to the law and order that regulate society. In doing so, the church offers the vision and hermeneutics through the formulation of a covenant response to economic life. The world remains God's good creation but the divine kingdom has not been realized in this already-but-not-yet temporality. Accordingly, the church is positioned in a wider world that is the field of mission. It seeks the peace and harmony of the kingdom of God on earth through a continuous quest for covenantal living based upon the Word of the Creator.

The covenantal way faces many difficulties when applied to temporal life on earth. It is a qualitative concept that is difficult to measure in economic models. Any attempt to extract its rich content leads to an abstraction that may distort its true meaning. The concept is easily distorted into a legalistic form, resulting in confusion with notion of the contract.[93] In a multilevel and multi-faith pluralistic society, the struggle among different interest groups will always cause tension. The covenant concept does not offer easy solutions to economic issues but provide a platform for open dialogue. We are provided with a glimpse of the ideological covenantal society in the New Testament, yet even the early Christian community does not represent a perfectly covenantal community. Believers remain sinful human persons who tend to distort the innate covenantal goodness in human nature. Accordingly, a perfectly covenantal society can only be realized in the end of time. Yet the covenant way is a relational order of creation, known to humankind as part of an innate human nature. Our task therefore is to rediscover and implement the covenantal contents in a realistic manner to the economic order on earth.

Since covenant is the intended way of relational order on earth as revealed and enacted by the Creator God in reaching out to build a relationship with His people, it is therefore the foundation of any society that

93 I shall address this confusion by clarifying and distinguishing between the two concepts through a conceptual analysis in chapter 4.2.

seeks authentic communal relationships. Economic life is to be protected not only under law and justice, but within the relationships and moral principles that guard the economic order. Covenant expresses the urgency and immediacy of the relationship between God and humanity. This relationship is equally shared among members of humankind. In a covenant, the destructive powers of cruelty and injustice can be overcome through renewed common life. The covenantal parties are inspired to envision a world of interdependence not through profit maximization but through mutually supportive bonds. Such covenantal bonds foster human life and take care of the vulnerable. Human beings become God's representatives invited to participate in the stewardship and care of creation through covenantal living.[94] Christian participation in the economic household of this world is a participation in Christ. The covenantal economic agent is the ecclesiastic community. Therefore as Jesus proclaimed under the new covenant of economic order, that whatsoever the believer does unto the least among them is equivalent to serving Christ Himself (Matt. 25:40).

Our exploration so far suggests the possibility of a covenantal market that may be realized when all creation reconciles and resides within the household of God. At the same time, the realization that this is an ideology for the end times affirms the need for a realistic framework for the covenant concept to be rediscovered in temporality. In part II of this book, I shall present the Two Pillars paradigm that promotes complementary interaction between the concepts of covenant and contract in order to support a well-balanced economic market.

94 Botman, 'Covenantal Anthropology: Integrating Three Contemporary Discourses of Human Dignity,' 85.

PART II

The Two Pillars Paradigm: A Dialogical Framework

CHAPTER 4

Covenant and Contract: A Two Pillars Paradigm for the Market

This chapter presents a Two Pillars paradigm for the economic market. It traces the development of the modern market into a contract-based exchange, gradually eroding the covenant characteristics that are originally embedded in society and the economic order. Having rediscovered the significance of the covenant concept in part I of this book, part II argues that both covenant and contract are significant and essential to a well-balanced economic market that promotes the well-being of the whole person. In the Two Pillars paradigm, covenant and contract act together in complementary ways as the Two Pillars that are both essential to uphold the proper functioning of the market. The two similar but distinct concepts of covenant and contract are analysed in detail in this chapter to show their differences, implications and interactions. The Two Pillars paradigm contributes a dialogical framework for interdisciplinary discussions and for further examination of specific economic issues. The economic quest for efficiency and productivity is explored in light of the covenantal characteristics of sharing and cooperation to show the place of both productivity and cooperation in a balanced market. The notions of private possessions versus public goods are examined to show how the covenant interacts with the contract to support both individual property rights and promote common societal interests. The ultimate target is to build a well-balanced economic market that enhances human relationships, freedom and inclusive care for all members of society.

4.1 Development of the Contract-Based Market

In medieval societies, relationships are customary, with trades and crafts inherited through kinship. Economic and ethical ideas are closely connected. Land is held and not owned. There is a strong sense that freedom should be exercised under ethical constraints and under the duty to God and others. These medieval traditions place justice above the freedom of choice. During the same time when social contract and contract law developed in the eighteenth century, the church gradually withdrew from its central role in the social order. Although Christian ethics were still professed, the church increasingly focused on matters of purely spiritual concern, leaving the morality and functioning of the market to the state. When tracing the rise of capitalism, Tawney laments that 'the very concept of the Church as an independent moral authority, whose standards may be in sharp antithesis to social conventions, has been abandoned'.[1] An ideal of personal character and conduct gradually replaced the 'kingdom of Christ' commitment. Economics was separated from ethical interests. 'Individualism in religion led insensibly, if not quite logically, to an individualist morality, and an individualist morality to a disparagement of the significance of the social fabric as compared with personal character.'[2] For example, addressing poverty becomes the obligation of good conscience and therefore an individual responsibility, not a social obligation. Under the governance of the state and the development of contract law, trade and commerce flourish. At the same time, the economic market becomes increasingly contract-based.

The word 'contract' originates from the word 'pact' or the Latin *pacta*. The most significant development of the concept relates to its primary use as an instrument of private law for commercial transactions. A *contract* is

1 Ronald H. Tawney, *Religion and the Rise of Capitalism* (London: John Murray, 1948), 192.

2 Ibid., 255.

an agreement with one or more counterparties for the exchange of goods or services.[3] This form of contractual mercantilism is based on the understanding that community is rooted in self-interested arrangements governed by law.[4] Contract law is based on the principle expressed in the Latin phrase *pacta sunt servanda* (pact must be kept).[5] On the positive side, development of the contract provides a method of entering into mutual agreement for activities conducted in the market, allowing voluntary relationships that shape the modern notion of human rights and individual freedom. It nurtures the modern culture of personal worth, human dignity, entrepreneurial spirit, individual freedom and right of participation.[6] However, the sovereignty of contract has a negative side. The contract atomizes individuals, who then pursue their own advantages without the necessity of regard for other people. The contractual mechanism turns land and labour into market commodities. It then in turn imposes its own assumptions and values that affect human mindsets and community relationships. In focusing on contracting for self-interested individuals, the contracting individual is removed from the need for tradition, history and narratives. The overall result is that contract-based market encourages arms-length transactions so that commercial interests can be

3 The definition of contract in this book is that of a purposive contract that serves as the characteristic of a market oriented exchange economy based on the use of legal tenders. This definition differs from the status contract that denotes a voluntary agreement for a continuing relationship. Since the focus here is on the economic market and exchange mechanism, detailed discussions of the status contract or social contract are beyond the scope of this book.

4 Adela Cortina, *Covenant and Contract: Politics, Ethics and Religion* (Leuven: Peeters, 2003), 6.

5 Wehberg finds Christianity to have exercised a great influence on the sanctity of contracts, as the demand to keep one's word is expressed in Matt. 5:33–37. This principle also takes on a religious meaning in the Islamic Koran. The common interest for a regulated commerce is then added to the religious motive by the Romans. See Hans Wehberg, 'Pacta Sunt Servanda,' *The American Journal of International Law* 53 (1959): 775.

6 William Johnson Everett, 'Contract and Covenant in Human Community,' *Emory Law Journal* 36 (1987): 558–9.

segregated from personal relationships. Under this arrangement, political and economic society no longer comprises communities of human persons but individual human persons.[7] The need to direct resources to societal interests in turn leads to the necessity of government intervention in the market. Taxes, regulations and welfare services are then put into place to address these needs.

General principles of contract law emerged during the late seventeenth to eighteenth century in accordance with the development of the free market and political economic ideals. There was a shift from particular relationships to general contract principles, and from executed to executory contracts.[8] In the nineteenth century, the classical theory of contract developed into its modern form. Classical contract law is based on definition of terms, conditions and liabilities by the voluntary parties involved. It is characterized by an impersonal nature that extends to become a characteristic of the contract-based market. The contract does not regard who the participants are, or what the matter of exchange is. The removal of all particularities of persons and subjects in the law of agreement gives rise to what is known as abstract relationships in classical contract law.[9] Liberal

7 For a comprehensive background of the historical development of contractual ideas before the eighteenth century, see P.S. Atiyah, *The Rise and Fall of Freedom of Contract* (Oxford: Clarendon Press, 1979), 11–41. Atiyah concludes that 'the new man of the eighteenth century, who was the true descendant of post-Reformation man, was an individualist; and one of the essential differences between the social and political theory of the pre- and post-Reformation eras concerned the way in which individuals made up a community. It was only through the free choice of these free individuals that societies and political communities existed at all.'

8 An executed contract is a completed contract with no outstanding actions beyond the completion date. An executory contract is one that requires some future act. For example, an on the spot buy and sell arrangement is under an executed contract, while an agreement to buy a house to be built in six months is an executory contract. See Ibid., 398.

9 Lawrence M. Friedman, *Contract Law in America: A Social and Economic Case Study* (Wisconsin: University of Wisconsin Press, 1965), 20–4.

economics in the nineteenth century capitalizes on this development to derive theories of individual economic units with complete mobility and freedom of decision.[10] The significance of contract in modern life continues as it penetrates other aspects of societal living in the form of public regulations, labour law, insurance legislation, business order and social welfare.[11] Commerce, finance and economic markets gradually came to depend entirely upon contractual arrangements of abstract relationships. Atiyah summarizes the key presuppositions in the thoughts of Hobbes and Locke that develop as part of the market economy ideology. Under the contract, human persons are free of the control of any other. They can choose and decide freely. Their relationships with others are voluntarily entered into and motivated by self-interest. The labour of each person is placed under a contract belonging to the individual just like land or property. Society comprises a series of market relationships.[12] Not only is the market increasingly contract-based, but the contractual notions of impersonal relationships, freedom of choice and maximization of self-interest increasingly penetrate social aspects of economic and community life.

Classical contract law has undergone modifications and has branched into many different forms. It gives way to neoclassical contract law as the courts impose legal obligations on the contracts as a matter of public policy. For example, an employment arrangement that involves obvious exploitation of labour may be deemed unenforceable by the courts because it

10 Scholars in the legal profession including Lawrence M. Friedman, P.S. Atiyah, E. Allen Fransworth and Grant Gilmore generally agree that classical contract theory develops relatively recently in the eighteenth and nineteenth centuries, although the roots of contract in English law can be traced back to the Middle Ages. This development is largely coextensive with emergence of the liberal laissez-faire concept of the free market.

11 Everett uses land contractualism to demonstrate the subordination of value to market calculations. Since land use shapes community structures, communal memories are destroyed when land use is subordinated to the priority of market contracts made for private gain. See Everett, 'Contract and Covenant in Human Community,' 564–5.

12 Atiyah, *The Rise and Fall of Freedom of Contract*, 70.

is against public interest. *Neoclassical contract* extends the basic contract by tying the individual advantage of each contracting party to the success of their mutual venture. This means that some communal standards of responsibility are injected into the contracts. Values such as liberty, efficiency, trust, fairness and cooperation are weighed by the courts when deciding the scope of contractual liability. This allows contract to develop into formulation of general standards rather than mechanical rules.[13] The introduction of these general standards promotes fairness in the market. However, market relationships remain abstract and impersonal as values remain subordinate to quantifiable contractual arrangements in the name of economic freedom.[14]

4.2 Conceptual Analysis of Covenant and Contract

The Concepts

The terms 'covenant', 'pact' and 'contract' have been used interchangeably in early literature.[15] They are explored and applied in various ways in the disciplines of theology, law, economics and sociology. In religion,

13 Jay M. Feinman, 'Significance of Contract Theory,' *University of Cincinnati Law Review* 58 (1990): 1285–8.

14 Other forms and variations of contracts are discussed in the legal literature. Examples of these include meta-theory, relational contract, empirical contract and critical contract. Since neoclassical contract theory is at the center of the status quo in legal scholarship, general discussion of contracts in this book will be based on neoclassical contract theory. The only exception will be an extended exploration into relational contract in chapter 5 as part of the discussion on long-term employment contracts.

15 Lovin gives a useful account of the historical development and political application of the covenant concept and the contract theories. He also provides a comparison that shows the distinctiveness of these two concepts. See Robin W. Lovin, 'Equality and Covenant Theology,' *Journal of Law and Religion* 2 (1984): 241–62.

a contractual God is one who obligates humankind in reciprocal duties. In marriage, a contract denotes calculative means for the goal of common advantages rather than unlimited commitment. In political society, contractual participants are only committed to limited and refutable purposes. According to Torrance, covenant and contract mean the same thing in Scots law. However, theologically the two concepts must be carefully distinguished. 'Theologically speaking, a covenant is a promise binding two people or two parties to love one another unconditionally. … A contract, in common parlance, is a legal relationship in which two people or two parties bind themselves together on mutual conditions.'[16] Confusion between the two concepts means that gradual erosion of covenant characteristics can easily be neglected. The result is an increasing reliance on the legalistic contractual exchange and disregard of the covenant fundamentals that are essential for authentic human relationships.[17]

As we have defined earlier, a contract is an agreement with one or more counterparty for the exchange of goods or services. A covenant is a promise with one or more counterparty under common pursuit of shared values for long term cooperation and the well-being of the community. Table 1 provides an overall conceptual comparison of contract and covenant. The various differences between the two concepts are discussed in the following subsections.

16 Torrance, 'The Covenant Concept in Scottish Theology and Politics and Its Legacy,' 228–9.

17 Niebuhr points out that in the mist of confusions between the two concepts, 'contract always implies limited, covenant unlimited commitment; contract is entered into for the sake of mutual advantages; covenant implies the presence of a cause to which all advantages may need to be sacrificed. The tendency of the covenant idea to degenerate to the limited contract idea is evident in all the later religious and social history.' See Niebuhr, 'The Idea of Covenant and American Democracy,' 134.

Table 1: Conceptual Comparison of Contract and Covenant

	Contract	*Covenant*
Form and Duration	Specific Condition/Circumstance Relatively Short/Fixed Disengage on Penalties	Open-Ended Relationship Long Term/Continuing Failure on Breakdown of Unity
Structure and Intention	Impersonal, Individualistic Exchange, Obligatory	Personal, Communal Sharing, Willingly
Relationship	Self-Interest, Insecure, Possible Coercion/Fear	Common Good, Secure, Trust, Love, Bond
Authoritative Basis	Government, Institution Law and Regulations	Divine Order Personal Agency
Process and Result	Bargain, Competitive Price as Consideration/Measure Result in Agreement	Promise, Cooperate Aim for Common Purpose Result in Commitment
Morality	Individual Ethics Personal Decisions	Personal and Communal Ethics Culture Norms

Form and Duration

The Jewish Rabbi Jonathan Sacks is a long time advocate of the covenant concept in its application to society. He summarizes the difference between covenant and contract into three basic aspects – form, duration and nature of the relationship.

> A covenant is not a contract. It differs in three respects. It is not limited to specific conditions and circumstance. It is open-ended and long-lasting. And it is not based on the idea of two individuals, otherwise unconnected, pursuing personal advantage. It is about the 'We' that gives identity to the 'I'. There is a place for contracts,

> but covenants are prior and more fundamental. They form the matrix of mutuality within which contractual relationships can exist.[18]

Sacks sees the social covenant as one that creates society with acts of moral engagement, while the social contract creates the state and its constitutional structure. Accordingly, the contract can bring together a global political structure, but a covenant truly frames a shared vision for the future of humanity.[19] The covenant bond is an open-ended one, entered into with mutuality and loyalty. Although one may argue that contractual arrangements can also be long term and continuing, scholars who examine the fundamental differences between contract and covenant generally find that contracts tend to have shorter duration.[20] This is because the stronger covenant characteristics of personal bond, trust and promise support a longer lasting duration for covenantal arrangements.[21]

The logic behind covenant and contract forms has also been examined by sociologists. Bromley and Busching identify covenant and contract as alternate methods of organizing intentional social behaviour based on different logic and form.

> Contractual social relations are those in which individuals coordinate their behavior through pledging themselves to specific reciprocal activity. Thus, contracts are articulated through a logic of calculative involvement and individual interest; covenants are articulated through a logic of moral involvement and unity.[22]

18 Jonathan Sacks, *The Dignity of Difference: How to Avoid the Clash of Civilizations* (London: Continuum, 2003), 202.

19 Ibid., 205–6.

20 One example of a continuing contract is the situation of a long-term employment contract. This example is examined in chapter 5.

21 For example, Mount points out that 'contracts tend to be minimal, short term, and presumptive of little or no community bonding. Covenants presuppose community, lasting commitment to the other's total well-being, and the assumption of obligations to each other and to shared values that change one's life.' See Mount, *Covenant, Community and the Common Good: An Interpretation of Christian Ethics*, 21.

22 David G. Bromley and Bruce C. Busching, 'Understanding the Structure of Contractual and Covenantal Social Relations: Implications for the Sociology of Religion,' *Sociological Analysis* 49 (1988): 16.

Many social relations contain elements of both covenant and contract, whereby the two forms exist in rather complex relationships to one another. For example, employment may commence based on a contractual arrangement while friendship and commitment may develop during the course of the work relationship. Such specific behaviours are not inherently contractual or covenantal, but are results of conscious or unconscious choices within the given circumstances. In covenantal relations, participants express connection, involvement, identification and commitment. In contractual relations, participants exert prudence and individual interests, conveying a certain separation from personal involvement. While covenantal relations call for sensitive response and affective commitment, contractual relations are oriented towards rational objective and alertness. Contracts are reliable, astute and fair; covenants are loyal, sensitive and caring. The qualities within contracts or covenants are not inherent but are developed through social interactions. Persons are shaped by their own intentionality, contributing to the qualities of the other, while at the same time being shaped by the circumstances and people they encounter. Economic transactions negotiated and completed with contractual aspirations differ from those of covenantal nature in their fundamental concerns, processes and possible outcomes.[23]

Contractual relationships carry the logic of divided components in sequenced time-phase, leading to its completion. They embrace the concept of efficiency and are thus driven and evaluated by it. On the other hand, covenantal relationships tend to build continuing relationships that involve mutual commitment on promises in anticipation of mutually beneficial future outcomes. Therefore they are driven by an integrative logic based on unity. When disputes arise, the contractual burden of proof is for each party to demonstrate its mandated performance. The covenantal burden of proof is for each party to demonstrate the activity that is not relevant to the covenant. Bromley and Busching further assert that the receptor within contractual relationships is the mind or the brain, while in covenantal relationships it is the spirit or the heart. This is because contractual partners

23 Ibid., 18–19.

adhere to the laws of the market and operate under operational mechanistic forces. Covenantal partners make reference to spiritual or personal agents that are equally compelling. In contracts, violations are linked to penalties. In covenants, violations are breakdowns of unity.[24]

The covenant paradigm presupposes an on-going, long-term commitment because it is based on relationships. Consequently, it calls for continuous renewal in a loving and forgiving manner. The Protestant view of sinful human nature that 'all are sinners in need of the grace of God' allows for inevitable failures within the covenantal emphasis while striving towards the ideal.[25] The covenantal community experiences continuous renewal and respect for each other.

Personal or Impersonal Market?

Since Bromley and Busching work from a sociological stance, they take contractual relationships as social relations that are essentially commercial or impersonal in nature, while covenantal relationships are taken as those that involve human connectedness. They find that both of these relationships are necessary for societal functions. Religion and family are listed in the domains of covenantalism, while labour and trade are considered contractual.[26] On this issue, economists Hill and Lunn assert that markets have developed from the personal systems in history to the impersonal systems in modern times. They argue that the move from personal to impersonal markets is necessary for the division of labour and production efficiencies

24 Ibid., 20–3.

25 Stackhouse points out that sin is a basic condition rather than the intentional betrayal of some principle or norm. Rationalized forms of denial of sins or justifications for sins are even more distorting. Accordingly, continuous reminders and alerts to the covenantal characteristics and their enactment are necessary in light of human finitudes. See Stackhouse, *Covenant and Commitments: Faith, Family, and Economic Life*, 28–30.

26 Bromley and Busching, 'Understanding the Structure of Contractual and Covenantal Social Relations: Implications for the Sociology of Religion,' 30.

that lead to higher standards of living in the developed world. Therefore they conclude that the ethical systems which theologians apply to modern markets are outdated and inappropriate for impersonal societies.[27] Are markets necessarily impersonal in the interest of size, efficiency and growth? How do we humanize the market and retain the essence of genuine human relationships that are valuable to human life?

The nature of contractual arrangements supports impersonal bargaining of terms and voluntary participation. According to this contractual system, the only requirement is to understand the rules and conditions. Intentions and motives are irrelevant to these types of arrangements. Hill and Lunn point out that economic markets enable cooperation among the participants without the need to explicitly recognize their intentions or overall character.[28] The contract-based market is therefore indifferent to the objective good of the person. Such a dynamic system of impersonal market activities is much more complex than a direct personal exchange because of its capability to expand in terms of scope and geographical horizon. Based on this contractual infrastructure, markets are ever evolving and changing along with institutions and legal systems. By focusing on the rules rather than intentions, moral duties are left to the individual level and growth across difference spheres is enabled. Workers produce goods and services that are utilized by people they do not know. To Hill and Lunn, the contract-based market is relatively efficient because of its impersonal nature. They therefore consider this impersonal characteristic necessary and essential. This conclusion leads to their support for two systems of ethics – one for the world of impersonal exchange in order to regulate market actions, another for the world of personal relationships where the moral framework is assumed to be much richer and more demanding.[29]

Indeed the contract enables an extended order of exchange because it is based on a set of rules and regulations. Such rules and regulations

27 Peter J. Hill and John Lunn, 'Markets and Morality: Things Ethicists Should Consider When Evaluating Market Exchange,' *Journal of Religious Ethics* 35, no. 4 (2007): 627–53.

28 Ibid., 628.

29 Ibid., 648–9.

are necessary to guide the functioning of the market that involves multitudes of human needs, wants and intentions. Nevertheless, human needs cannot be satisfied through materialistic concerns alone. The market also serves a communal and relational function that is intrinsically significant to human life. The authenticity and self-integration of human intentions and actions are necessary to maintain the well-being of the self. This means that contrary to the underlying assumption of the impersonal contract market, intentions are highly relevant to economic acts. If the intention is egocentric and focuses on maximizing personal gains, then the market becomes competitive with acts of coercion and feelings of insecurity. On the other hand, where the intention is in terms of mutual interest and sharing, a culture of community and mutual care can be realized.[30] Although Hill and Lunn argue that intentions may not be related to outcomes, e.g. self-interested intentions can lead to cooperative ends, economic intentions do initiate market actions. This is shown through the fact that when the covenant culture of mutual interest and moral is gradually eroded, it becomes necessary to increase the number of rules and regulations in order to govern contractual arrangements. These rules that attempt to regulate market intentions and activities, whether effective or not, tend to replace the human initiatives of genuine care for others by prescribing the boundaries and content of the tasks involved in a commercialized way. The failure to align contractual rules with personal intentions leads to the failure of the contract-based markets to support moralized and authentic cooperation. The covenant must be restored and renewed continuously to enable authenticity and well-being, rather than leaving the task of satisfying human needs to legalistic rules.

Although markets are complex and are continuously evolving, human nature and the need for personal relationships and authenticity remain

30 O'Neill points out that the element of trust is vital to community life. We can set high standards with the law and define professional responsibilities, but these incur legislative and auditing costs. Therefore trust cannot be replaced by law or contract. The objective is not to impose blind trust but trust based on good judgement and mutual responsibility. See Onora O'Neill, *A Question of Trust* (Cambridge: Cambridge University Press, 2002), 1–19.

unchanged. The advocate of two different sets of ethical standards is absurd and hypocritical. It encourages the human person to put up different personae when dealing with different situations. This is a major dehumanizing characteristic of the contract-based exchange which is detrimental to societal relationships. A moral community consists of ethical persons within a community who pass these norms on to later generations. Relying on individual ethics at the contract level by rules and coercion cannot lead to a harmonious exchange in the long run. This is particularly important within the complexities of the economic market. In this regard, size and scope cannot justify an impersonal exchange. For the customer of the supermarket, purchase and sale appear impersonal on the surface because of the contract-based mechanism. However, a covenantal presupposition of community care and customer concern must precede the transaction and act as the underlying foundation for mutual trust. Such degree of trust and comfort relies not only on rules and regulations, but on a communal sense of caring and goodwill.[31]

The covenant cannot be fully captured in a contractual manner in legalistic terms. Any intention to quantify or legalize it reduces covenant to contract. This is because covenant involves identities and relationships. It is an organic relational order that defies any calculative exchange. Relationships in community require virtues to be exercised during a given encounter between the parties involved. These virtues in turn become the basis of covenantal trust and commitment. Therefore market exchange cannot be purely impersonal. The authentic human person needs to align intentions and acts. Without such authenticity, material needs can still be exchanged and consumed, but true satisfaction cannot be attained. The contract enables exchange of goods and services. The covenant enables satisfaction from the supply and consumption of goods and services above the extrinsic activities

31 Economists argue that long-term contracts inherently contain elements of trust and goodwill because of their continuing nature. For example, supermarkets exercise due care to build trust and goodwill so that customers return for their goods and services. This is part of the covenantal goodness that interacts with the economic contract. The interaction between covenant and contract is further explained in chapter 5 through the example of long-term employment arrangements.

involved. Workers may not know the persons consuming the goods they produce, yet in a covenantal market they can experience the consumers' gratitude for their services from the general respect for their work within their organization and community. The covenantal market culture in turn allows participants to experience a sense of security and care within the market exchange. Market transactions are arm's length and enforceable by law due to their contractual nature. At the same time, they are not entirely impersonal. They have everything to do with personal interest, integrity and social norms. Although market relationships cannot extend indirectly to the end-user level, it is important for individuals to take personal interests in market relationships with the people they encounter on a daily basis. This need is intensified as market relationships extend across geographical horizons because the covenant network relies on participants at each and every stage of the economic exchange to cultivate.

Nature of Relationships

Sacks points out that the contract is about 'interest', while the covenant is about 'identity'. Covenants turn a plurality of 'I's into a collective 'we'. Marriage and friendship often take this form. In the Bible, Jonathan covenanted with David because he loved him as himself (1 Sam. 18:3). Contracts aim at mutual gain while covenants aim at mutual give. Self-interest motivates parties to enter into contracts for mutual benefits. These are based on mutual consent to fulfil certain obligations. Covenants are open-ended. Their moral commitments are sustained by loyalty, fidelity and faithfulness. Within a covenant, people can live together despite their differences and be inspired to share values and the common good.[32] Similar to Bromley and Busching, Sacks finds both contract and covenant necessary, but for different reasons. He locates social contract within the relationship between the individual and the state, while social covenant is about relationship between people. The common good, being covenantal rather

32 Sacks, *The Home We Build Together: Recreating Society*, 109–10.

than contractual, belongs to society. Contract associations are for self-interest, while covenant is about association in a shared identity.[33] The advantage of covenant over contract is in the fact that covenant embraces a relational concern that is fundamental to the ontology of human nature. Such relationships become impersonal and unsatisfactory once they are placed under purely contractual terms.

A proper understanding of human economic behaviour needs to go beyond a system of egocentric self-interest. Human persons are social beings not only in terms of interdependence for economic ends, but also during their quest for social connections among one another.[34] The problem with a purely contractual arrangement lies deep within human nature. Hobbes identifies the reason for entering into a mutual contract as one that is not based upon cooperation or love, but is based upon fear. This presupposes an insecure and egocentric view of human nature, where one fears losing one's life to another. Therefore alliances are formed to protect themselves from being subject to the predator of another. This calculative reasoning suggests that the economic person joins the polity and economic order in fear and distrust.[35] It is negative, dehumanizing, and contradictory to the covenant concept that promotes sincerity, security and trust. The proper use of contracts requires an underlying covenant awareness and foundation in order to maintain a humanized economic order in the market.

This does not mean the market is to be eliminated. On the contrary, the market has shown itself to be a natural means of human exchange throughout history, contributing to economic growth and productivity.

33 Ibid., 157–8.

34 As Polanyi points out, the human person 'does not act so as to safeguard his individual interest in the possession of material goods; he acts so as to safeguard his social standing, his social claims, his social asserts. ... Neither the process of production nor that of distribution is linked to specific economic interests attached to the possession of goods; but every single step in that process is geared to a number of social interests which eventually ensure that the required step be taken.' See Karl Polanyi, *The Great Transformation: The Political and Economic Origins of Our Time* (Boston: Beacon Press, 1957), 46.

35 Cortina, *Covenant and Contract: Politics, Ethics and Religion*, 5.

Markets and competition have their inherent advantages. They generate wealth, lower prices, increase choices and promote advancements. Economic growth brings the possibility of decreasing poverty. The problem is when the market goes too far to govern relationships and abolish human identity. As Sacks asserts, 'the idea that human happiness can be exhaustively accounted for in terms of things we can buy, exchange, and replace is one of the great corrosive acids that eat away the foundations on which society rests; and by the time we have discovered this, it is too late'.[36] However, humankind need not proceed down the road of destruction with the market. Sacks adds that the 'market exchange is the paradigm of the win-win scenario and the non-zero-sumness of human relationship'.[37] It is a platform for human interaction that is not necessarily tragic. With the awareness and enactment of the covenant concept, human persons can operate through the market by maintaining a balance between covenantal and contractual means to achieve cooperative ends.

Life in community encompasses participation, responsibility, and respect for individual differences. Through participative acts of relating, sharing and receiving, participants affirm their identities as individuals and in community with each other.[38] The pursuit of common interest does not belong to the believing community alone, but to society as a whole because of the common fundamental goods shared by all humanity. Mount sets individuals in community within both the common good and the covenant by stating that both traditions 'affirm the centrality of community and resist the extremes and neglects of Western individualism with its suspicion of any effort to advance a common good because of plural versions of the good and its tendency to make all associations

36 Jonathan Sacks, 'Markets and Morals,' *First Things* 105 (2000): 28.

37 Sacks, *The Dignity of Difference: How to Avoid the Clash of Civilizations*, 101.

38 Sacks asserts that 'covenant-making is a highly distinctive form of politics, predicated on active interpersonal responsibility. Other forms of politics do not assume that responsibility is shared by all.' See Jonathan Sacks, *To Heal a Fractured World: The Ethics of Responsibility* (London: Continuum, 2005), 115.

voluntary and contractual'.[39] Working from this model, he finds the contractual idea, such as the social contract of bargaining, inadequate for the whole of moral life. The common good is to be understood as a community quest and not a given. It is embedded in the covenantal way of relating.[40]

The self-interest view of the market also takes on a legalistic counterpart. Trebilcock argues from a legal perspective that the convergence of public welfare and autonomous market choices are tenuous. When the market operates under the Will or Autonomy Theory of Contract Law, arrangements among individuals arise from voluntarily assumed, self-imposed obligations reflecting convergent intentions of the contracting parties.[41] In such a community, there is no collective consensus for common economic goals or values. A number of elements work to destroy the integrity of the voluntary nature of such contracts. Examples of these include commodification of contractual elements, external influences, coercion, information imperfections, paternalism, discrimination, etc.[42] These limits to the contractual arrangement can only be alleviated through a collective or covenantal awareness of community. As Allen points out, consent and coercion are always intermingled in social life.[43] Similarly, numerous other social factors influence the written contract to impose limitations in its use. The contract should remain as a tool to serve the market rather than to direct how human persons relate to each other.

39 Mount, *Covenant, Community and the Common Good: An Interpretation of Christian Ethics*, 1.

40 The relationship of the common good concept with welfare economics and the covenant is further discussed in chapter 6.4.

41 Michael J. Trebilcock, *The Limits of Freedom of Contract* (London: Harvard University Press, 1993), 241.

42 For a detailed discussion of these limitations, see Ibid., 23–240.

43 Allen, *Love and Conflict: A Covenantal Model of Christian Ethics*, 259.

Authoritative Basis

To protect individuals and society from the negative aspects of corrupted human nature, an authoritative basis is needed to mediate human relationships. This is particularly important in an age of plurality, when a variety of ideologies and associations resides together in search of the truth under different or contradicting means and ends. The authoritative basis of the covenant is the divine order and communal norms, while the contract relies on individual morality and is safeguarded by law. Tucker analyses the covenant and contract forms in the Bible and Ancient Near East, and concludes that covenants are centred upon the oath formulae while contracts may or may not be.[44] The contract requires an operative description of the underlying transaction, thereby giving it a focus on what has happened or is happening. On the other hand, the content of an oath is a promise for the future. Therefore, covenant and contract are governed by two distinct authorities. As a purely covenant society is only attainable under universal commitment to a common faith, the authority of laws and regulations is required to mediate the market in coherence with the covenant order.

From a legal point of view, the core nature of a contract lies in the fact that it is a promise that is enforceable by law. Its elements include mutual assent and some detriments on the part of the promise. Newman points out that a covenantal relationship fails to be a contract because there is no bargaining involved. The offer and acceptance assent is missing as the divine covenant is granted as a gift without a bargained-for-exchange. In the covenant of God with Israel, its scope is contained in the text of the Torah. Here, sovereignty belongs to the Divine. The covenant serves as a means of gift and guidance for establishing a relationship of promise. On the other hand, a contract is under sovereignty of the law. It binds the parties to service a bargained relationship of exchange. Living under

44 Tucker asserts that 'the contract is an economic, legal agreement, a witnessed transaction which would either be committed to writing or solemnized before the assembled court. Covenants, being sworn agreements, did not require the apparatus of the court for their solemnization.' See Gene M. Tucker, 'Covenant Forms and Contract Forms,' *Vetus Testamentum* 15 (1965): 501–3.

the sovereignty of God versus that of contractual law has basic implications for the functioning of the relationship. The laws set out in the Torah for ancient Israel represent only part of what God demands. Those who strictly adhere to the Torah may still be lacking in true piety or love. The covenant cannot be reduced to a legal formula since it is indispensable but not exhaustive.[45] In the contract-based economic market, a payment in exchange for goods or services carries autonomous duties of delivery and responsibility bounded by legal requirements and penalties. In a covenantal relationship, the pre-existing moral duty is derived from a genuine and free response to the offer of cooperation and mutuality.[46] Accordingly, individual choices and cooperation are respected and honoured through continuous voluntary mutual commitment.[47]

Building Trust and Keeping Promises

During the development of contract law, the contract originally based on moral theory turned into a bargaining concept. Consideration shifts from the purpose for a promise to a price paid for the promise. Liability involved in the contract changes from fault to absolute obligation, relying on the terms of the contract.[48] These are shifts in fundamental presuppositions that contain relational and moral implications. During the development

45 Louis E. Newman, 'Covenant and Contract: A Framework for the Analysis of Jewish Ethics,' *Journal of Law and Religion* 9 (1991): 93–7.

46 Newman points out that Israel's response to the covenantal offer is genuinely free and therefore arising out of Israel's gratitude for God's prior acts of salvation and protection. This covenant is then grounded in pre-existing moral duties that are not autonomous in nature but out of benefaction. See Ibid., 103.

47 As Sacks points out, 'in an act of covenant, both parties agree to respect one another's integrity as free agents: this is so even when one of the parties is God himself. The key element in covenant is neither power, nor the past, but a verbal declaration and a mutually binding promise.' See Sacks, *The Home We Build Together: Recreating Society*, 109.

48 Harold J. Berman, 'The Religious Sources of General Contract Law: An Historical Perspective,' *Journal of Law and Religion* 4 (1986): 116–17.

process, certain basic assumptions of the original contract idea become eroded, causing the nature of contract to deviate more and more from that of the covenant.

A contract is generally perceived to be promise-based in the same way as a covenant, especially in legal literature. However, this notion is questioned by legal scholar P.S. Atiyah. The traditional view is that contracts can be benefit-based subject to payment or consideration, reliance-based subject to guaranteeing or expectation, or promise-based subject to future execution. Promise-based contracts are expected to turn into benefit-based or reliance-based at their future time of execution. Atiyah points out three misconceptions of the promise-based contract. First, the protection of expectation is not the same as restitution or reliance. A disappointed party has a relatively weak claim since full performance of the promise or redress based on such entitlement may not be possible. Second, a promise-based contract involves a method of risk allocation or transfer. One typical example is an insurance arrangement. Such arrangements can be cancellable and may indeed be beneficial to do so upon changing circumstances, as long as alternatives are available. A contract based on continuing evaluation of future risks can therefore be perpetually refuted and reconstituted. Third, promise-based liability is usually seen as a subsidiary way of ensuring compliance with benefit-based and reliance-based obligations. This argument is relatively weak because of the two preceding misconceptions.[49] Atiyah's analysis has profound impact on the structure of moral and legal obligations of contracts. It implies that a contract holds a relatively weak promissory characteristic, especially in terms of future expectations.[50] For the same

49 Atiyah, *The Rise and Fall of Freedom of Contract*, 1–6.

50 Other legal scholars have commented on the deficiency of contracts as binding promises. Craswell argues that philosophical theories of the binding nature of promises are irrelevant to the background rules of contract law. Rather than theories of human freedom, economic efficiency or ethics, background rules such as remedies for breach, duty to perform, implied warranties, etc., govern the binding nature of a contract. Feinman asserts that contracts are based on the doctrine of 'commercial convenience', with its contradictory nature concealed in service of the illegitimate status quo. Since rules and languages cannot be precise, and doctrines do not fully

reasons, a contract works best when it focuses on the immediate executable duration. Its relatively short term characteristic is therefore inherent to the nature of the contract. At the same time, the contractual mechanism encourages continuing evaluation of risks and benefits, therefore a perpetual uneasiness of the need for calculative measures.

Allen reminds us that covenant theory differs from contract theories over why we are obligated.[51] Contract theorists are concerned with the duty of fair play. Fairness obligates one to fulfil the duties and rules as defined by the contract. However, fair play is deficient because it deals only with one part of human obligation. Covenant offers a broader interpretation of obligations to fellow participants, as we accept others' trust in us. Through mutual entrustment, the participants risk what they have to each other. A contract breaks down with the breakdown of a system. A covenant binds the participants and continues to do so under unforeseen circumstances. Trust and commitment are therefore critical covenant characteristics that ensure individuals are mutually respected and provided with authentic identity and freedom in the economic order.[52] The encounter with another elicits compassion, trust and bonding, making the covenant a necessary basis of authentic market relationships. This mutual bonding breaks through egocentric self-interest into a freedom of mutuality, empathy and dialogue. It enables the openness of human hearts to one another.[53]

---

represent social behaviour, contracts always remain ambiguous, their contents subject to exploitation and contradictions. See Richard Craswell, 'Contract Law, Default Rules, and the Philosophy of Promising,' *Michigan Law Review* 88 (1989–1990): 489–529; and Jay M. Feinman, 'Critical Approaches to Contract Law,' *UCLA Law Review* 30 (1982): 829–60.

51 Allen, *Love and Conflict: A Covenantal Model of Christian Ethics*, 259–61.

52 As Niebuhr asserts, 'in the covenant conception the essence of freedom does not lie in the liberty of choice among goods, but in the ability to commit oneself for the future to a cause and in the terrible liberty of being able to become a breaker of the promise, a traitor to the cause'. See Niebuhr, 'The Idea of Covenant and American Democracy,' 133.

53 Mount, *Covenant, Community and the Common Good: An Interpretation of Christian Ethics*, 26.

Upholding Market Morality

To the free market advocates, self-interest is the answer. This notion of self-interest presented by Adam Smith differs from egoism. Smith argues that self-interest regulates the contracting interests so that individuals will honour their promises. 'When a person makes perhaps twenty contracts in a day, he cannot gain so much by endeavouring to impose on his neighbours, as the very appearance of a cheat would make him lose.'[54] This view presupposes that morality depends upon the integrity of human nature and natural evolution. Unfortunately, human nature and natural evolution do not always lead to desirable outcomes. Values within the market are derived through the way participants interact within it.[55] Therefore freedom of the market demands high personal moral standards. The paradoxical truth pointed out by theological anthropology is that corrupted human nature prevents the realization of freedom in a purely contractual free market. The covenant is needed to bring out the relational nature of humanity and the morality embedded within.

The covenant community is a moral community in which each person participates freely in his or her own right. In the covenant community the human person is not merely something useful to society. Rather, human persons are participants in the moral community. They entrust themselves to others, accept the entrusting of others, and uphold continuing responsibility to one another.[56] Covenant does not carry the necessary condition that the others are actually trustworthy. It presupposes a gifting concept that starts from the willingness of oneself to voluntarily trust and give to

54 Adam Smith, *Lectures on Jurisprudence* (Indianapolis: Liberty Press, 1982), 538.

55 Sen points out that 'defenses of the market are instrumental in terms of the goodness of the results achieved. It works "efficiently"; it serves our "interests"; it is "mutually beneficial"; it delivers "the goods"; it contributes to "utility"; it serves as the "invisible hand" by which man is led to promote an end which was no part of his intention.' See Amartya Sen, 'The Moral Standing of the Market,' in *Ethics and Economics*, ed. Ellen Frankel Paul, Fred D. Jr. Miller and Jeffrey Paul (Oxford: Basil Blackwell, 1985), 2.

56 Allen, *Love and Conflict: A Covenantal Model of Christian Ethics*, 17.

others.[57] Participants in a covenantal community work together for justice and compassion, starting not from receiving but giving. The practice of morality and the common good ensures social cohesion. The covenantal community is then created and continuously renewed through festivity and celebration of life together.[58] For example, parents do not calculate the future monetary return from their children when they provide for their needs. They do so out of natural covenantal love and human instincts. The covenantal community cannot be promoted through legislation alone. It must be conjured through culture, education and social cohesion. Is the shift from the modern contract-based market a more covenant-based community feasible? I shall now explore the potential for a paradigm shift to the Two Pillars market.

4.3 The Paradigm Shift

As we have seen, the human nature of the economic person in a competitive, contract-based market is assumed to be egocentric and self-interested. The self-interest idea has been derived and developed over the years ever since Adam Smith has written his most widely quoted and misinterpreted description of the butcher, brewer or baker, who does not serve dinner from benevolence but out of self-interest. Over the years, the philosophical intentions of self-interest, sympathy and moral sentiments in the original Smithian system are gradually reduced to a narrow notion of selfishness and

57 Cronin points out that we entrust ourselves in the hands of others daily in our basic activities such as seeing the doctor, going to the car mechanics, riding a bus, etc. This means that covenant is not only an obligation but a respect for others as respectable human persons. 'Covenant appears to be a more profound moral reality then, say, a business contract which prescinds from such ontological judgements and concentrates instead on pragmatic considerations.' See Cronin, *Rights and Christian Ethics*, 211–12.

58 Sacks, *The Home We Build Together: Recreating Society*, 126–7.

egocentrism as the market increasingly relies on the contractual mechanism. The self-interest assumption understood as self-focused utility maximization in turn encourages market participants to become more individualistic. Numerous economic models and theories have been developed to explore, analyse, and enhance this assumption. Economists excel in identifying the *Pareto optimum* for competitive market situations.[59] However, is egocentric individualism a proper representation of human nature or human behaviour in the market?

Amartya Sen, winner of the 1998 Nobel Prize in Economic Science, has been offering constructive critiques of traditional economic assumptions and practical contributions to welfare economics. His work shows that a paradigm shift in economic models is not only feasible but also necessary. Sen finds that a simple reason why human nature is presupposed to be egoistic in economic models is that no matter what a person chooses in an isolated act, it can be defined as being based on self-interest. This definitional egoism is considered to be rational choice as long as it is consistent.[60] According to this observation, self-interested human nature is at least partly a self-fulfilling paradigm. If this is the case, market participants fall into a kind of helpless coercion that stands against the assumed characteristics of freedom and cooperation within a free market. I assert that this helpless and coercive scenario is not definitive because humankind is equipped with the ability for making intentional choices. To derive and enact responsible choices that contribute to the well-being of humankind, we need to continuously reflect upon our economic assumptions, become aware of market limits, and be willing to enact market alternatives. The market choices we make concern not only the commodities we purchase and consume, but more fundamentally, the means and structures of market exchanges and how individuals participate in market activities.

59 Named after the Italian economist Vilfredo Pareto, the Pareto optimal is the point of optimal efficiency when no one can be better off without someone else being worse off.

60 Amartya Sen, *Choice, Welfare and Measurement* (Oxford: Basil Blackwell, 1982), 84–9.

Sen finds it a traditional misconception to consider that moral behaviour is generally detrimental to economic benefits. Similarly, upholding covenantal characteristics may be misunderstood to have a negative impact on profits. In fact, the use of egocentric self-interest in pursuing preferences and fulfilment does not necessarily maximize utilities to the individual. This is because unforeseen consequences and external influences may occur at any time. Also, the individual may not be able to accurately measure his or her own utility, or to define a measure of utility that leads to actual well-being. For example, smoking or gambling may seem to yield high short-term utility to an individual, but leads to detrimental results and lower aggregate utility over time. For similar reasons, focusing on quantifiable measurements alone does not guarantee maximization of profits. Covenantal characteristics add to the intrinsic considerations or the underlying concerns of economic activities. For example, employees who act morally may build more trusting relationships, contributing to increases in team spirit and efficiency in the long term. Companies that promote covenantal norms may have higher levels of employee morale that in turn increases productivity. Sen asserts that markets are about trust and relationships as much as self-interest. Relying merely on legalistic and contractual means to prevent destructive self-interested behaviour will make economic activities in the market expensive and slow because of the costs and time involved in additional legal processes and safeguards. Similarly, the need to engage legalistic means to regulate workers' productivity, e.g. hiring additional supervisors, involves additional costs for the company.

Sen presents 'public goods' as an illustration of the limitations of a self-interest market. The mechanism of such a market breaks down when it comes to non-competitive goods that are not exclusively provided to the buyer who is willing to pay the highest price. In such cases, the combined benefits of the general public must be compared with the production costs. Besides the problem of resource allocation, there is also a need for embedding social concerns in the market processes. These factors are not necessarily detrimental to maximizing economic benefits. Behavioural codes such as anti-corruption, maintaining goodwill and business norms, etc., generate the trust and assurance that are necessary for the market to function properly.[61]

Sen's work shows that economic modelling and measurements based entirely on egoistic self-interest are deficient in their ability to enhance life values. It also means that important qualitative human values such as justice and freedom have not been adequately captured or considered in existing efficiency models. More importantly, Sen questions the self-interest maximizing assumption of efficient markets. In the pursuit of opportunities and freedom, the self-interest assumption in the welfarist assessment turns out to be irrelevant. This means that when human persons are empowered with the priority of freedom in preferences, self-interest maximization becomes irrelevant. Sen asserts that a focus on freedom shifts economic analysis towards more ethically and politically sound approaches. He demonstrates that once the economic scientist is willing to shift the paradigm from egocentric self-interest to higher common human values, the horizon becomes largely broadened.

At first sight, the market equilibrium based on efficient market transactions appears to yield good results. When a given model assumes no externalities, the competitive equilibrium is Pareto optimal. Under even more stringent conditions, especially with the absence of economies of large scale, the 'converse theorem' shows that every Pareto optimal is a competitive equilibrium that corresponds to certain initial distribution of resources. If this is true, it means that given the appropriate set of initial conditions, the market mechanism will reach an optimum social state. The problem is that the converse theorem only applies under stringent circumstances demanding a 'right' initial distribution of resources, right prices, incentives and decisions. These are practically impossible in a complex and imperfect world. Hence one returns to the first theorem that generates Pareto optimality. The problem becomes one of distribution and inequality, when there can be large disparities in terms of wealth distribution at a Pareto optimum. When conflicting versus congruent interests of individuals are added to

61 Amartya Sen, *Moral Codes and Economic Success* (London: London School of Economics, 1993), 1–21.

the analysis, the Pareto optimum contains no alleviation for exploitations. When public goods and common interests are put into the picture, the situation becomes more complex. As Sen points out, the market mechanism is good at specific types of congruent issues, but cannot handle conflicts or congruent public interests.[62]

Sen offers basic capability equality as an alternative to the utilitarian approach. This model is based on an interpretation of needs in the form of basic capabilities of each human person. It shifts focus from goods to the effect of goods on different human persons. The capabilities of a given good vary substantially from person to person due to the ability to take advantage of the good, personal taste, preference, pre-existing conditions, etc. The indexing of capabilities is not simple, but the shift in focus allows for more humanized and morally relevant analysis of the market.[63] Sen's capabilities approach can be traced to the perspective of 'functionings' in the work of Lagrange, a mathematician from Smith's time who pioneered the pursuit of the variability of physical functionings from food intakes, with reference to activities, location and other factors. While Lagrange pioneers the physical functionings concept, Smith shows the relationship between achievements of social functionings and opulence. These concepts of functionings and capabilities become largely neglected in later economic discussions. As economic models become increasingly inclined towards utilitarianism, the human aspects of societal living also become largely neglected.

The capabilities approach contains some resemblance to the biblical concepts of vocation and stewardship. First of all, each human person is uniquely created and equipped with different capabilities, preferences and needs. Each is to contribute and serve the community while receiving and being cared for within it. This is a fundamental part of the covenant community. Second, a shared notion of ownership and contribution within the covenant community starts from the concept of stewardship for God. The

62 Amartya Sen, *Resources, Values and Development* (Oxford: Basil Blackwell, 1984), 93–8.

63 Sen, *Choice, Welfare and Measurement*, 367–9.

concept of capabilities supports realization of one's limitation, broadening an individual worldview to include not only self needs but the needs for others. Sharing and contribution are put in perspective. These form essential parts of the covenant community and economic order. However, the capabilities approach faces some challenges in terms of its application in economics. It is understandable that some capabilities are naturally inborn, but most remain at least partially nurtured. The investment of time and resources in education and the access to opportunities affect the continuing development and therefore the capabilities of individuals. By the same token, capabilities cannot be objectively measured and can change significantly due to contextual or other circumstances.[64] Nevertheless, the capabilities approach contributes to redirecting the focus of economic models to a concern for the individual human person. It marks the awareness for the need of a paradigm shift in economic approaches, and offers an alternative that takes into account concerns for the human person.

The market has developed naturally over time because it assists economic growth and efficient economic development through trades and exchange. Such activities form part of human life in which community and cooperation are necessary. Although these activities are primarily material exchanges that can be made at arm's length, the underlying relational aspects cannot be neglected. As Sen asserts, 'it is not so much a matter of having exact rules about how precisely we ought to behave, as of recognizing the relevance of our shared humanity in making the choices we face'.[65] In this regard, the covenant concept reminds us of the important human qualities

64 Pressman criticizes the capabilities approach for being ambiguous and incomprehensive. For a list of the critics' views on Sen's work, see Steven Pressman and Gale Summerfield, 'Sen and Capabilities,' *Review of Political Economy* 14 (2002): 429–34. In particular, Gasper finds that freedom in the capabilities approach focuses too much on available choices to an individual, and too little on the needs of others. The approach rejects the neoclassical view of people as utility maximizers but does not offer and alternative theory of the person. See Des Gasper, 'Is Sen's Capability Approach an Adequate Basis for Considering Human Development?,' *Review of Political Economy* 14 (2002): 435–61.

65 Amartya Sen, *Development as Freedom* (Oxford: Oxford University Press, 1999), 283.

such as responsibilities, commitment, justice and compassion within our shared humanity that support freedom and the proper exercise of freedom. Freedom is a necessary but not sufficient condition for morality and humanized living. As Sen asserts, 'the value of the living standard lies in the living, and not in the possessing of commodities, which has derivative and varying relevance'.[66] He shows that self-interest need not be the only way, and more importantly, it is unlikely to be the 'best' way.

4.4 The Two Pillars Market

Re-introducing covenant into the contract-based market is non-subversive in the sense that I do not seek to over-ride modern economic structures or to abolish market exchanges. Nevertheless, the covenant concept appears subversive when re-introduced to the contract-based market because of its fundamental relevance and significance to basic economic activities. A realist's view of the market quickly points towards the fact that contract-based market exchanges have become indispensible in every aspect of economic life. On the other hand, Christian eschatological hope for a shared economy of grace presents a possibility inert within creation that the church must work towards. The question is not how one eliminates the market for another alternative. Sharing and grace can function efficiently through the market exchange where participants cooperate for mutual benefits. The critical issue for the Christian community is to act in humility and embrace all creation with an awareness of the natural tendencies within human nature to reduce covenantal grace to legalistic contract.

Law and contract play critical roles in society. It is unrealistic and unnecessary to advocate an eschatological truth as a here and now reality during the already-but-not-yet life on earth. The high moral demands

66 Amartya Sen, *The Standard of Living* (Cambridge: Cambridge University Press, 1985), 22–9.

and relational basis of the covenant must be safeguarded through legal boundaries to support its universal application in the secular world. At the same time, the contract is not self-sufficient.[67] It must work together with the covenant that lays the foundation of human relationships. The covenant is the authentic human pathway to ensure the market functions according to its original intention of human cooperation and interdependence. The economic market provides a platform for exchange that aims at mutual benefits. Whether it is a loan, service or sale, the parties involved are to derive a higher combined value of benefits based on such exchange. The Two Pillars market does not advocate a total reliance on gift or grace but maintains the qualities of fairness and cooperative exchange as the characteristics of economic markets. This fairness of exchange is necessary to uphold freedom within the market based on responsible entitlement, individual capabilities and mutual respect.

The human tendency towards contractual arrangements over the covenant is not without cause.[68] Rational, legal, logical and calculated means are much easier to work out and defend. Such arrangements provide a natural order that is essential to society, especially in terms of justice. Law and order must be maintained in any society to protect the rights and freedom of individuals. In these manners, the contract is an important mechanism to facilitate law and order. In terms of economic order, it is important that the market not only provide a platform for exchange, but a lawful and orderly one for individuals to deal efficiently and freely with one another. Contract law helps to initiate transactions between complete strangers, thereby expanding the scope of cooperation and exchange across

67 Cortina points out that the contract cannot stand alone without a number of presuppositions before it. These presuppositions include a moral duty to observe an agreement, relationships of trust among the participants, authoritative standards, fairness, justice, rights, recognition, etc. See Cortina, *Covenant and Contract: Politics, Ethics and Religion*, 26–8.

68 Cortina appropriately points out that the capacity to contract and to enter into the covenant are two non-eliminable forms in human coexistence, and that 'the discourse of the contract has gone far beyond the sphere in which it has any legitimacy and has colonised that of the covenant, sending this into exile'. See Ibid., 13.

communities and geographical locations. It provides a set of default rules that enforces reasonable prices, fair terms, good faith and quality warranties. Through constructive conditions of contracts, the participants can deal with potential performance disputes and establish channels for mediation of non-performance. Mediation and court enforcement are made possible with formalization of the written contract. At the same time, continuing contracts help to build trust and on-going relationships, which can develop into covenantal bonds.[69] Nevertheless, the market must not be purely contract-based. In order for the market to retain the communal qualities and protect individual freedom in association, the market platform must be embraced by an underlying covenantal concept by the participants. Without the covenant, the market loses its life as a gathering place for human persons to relate and cooperate with one another. Rather, it becomes a mechanical place where individuals calculate their own interests and protect themselves against each other in fear and trembling.

The legal contract that is essential to guard against abuses must not be allowed to override human relationships and compassion. Extreme forms of legalism lead to political tyranny and economic destruction. Kraus asserts that in the covenant way of life, the dominant elements are peace, justice and right. Peace marks the unbroken good condition of all relationships, justice denotes faithful behaviour, and right is the basis of law established by the commands of God. Solemn commandments and the divine Torah reside in the core of Israel's worship and obedience to God with the covenant relationship. This covenant is exclusive to the household of God, final and irrevocable in terms of its political power and solidarity. Accordingly, covenant and right are intimately connected in the Deuteronomic theology.[70] In Deuteronmic history, Israel as God's chosen people answers to the Creator's authority and His commandments as granted in the Torah.

69 Erin Ann O'Hara, 'Trustworthiness and Contract,' in *Moral Markets: The Critical Role of Values in the Economy*, ed. Paul J. Zak (New Jersey: Princeton University Press, 2008), 179–89.

70 Hans J. Kraus, 'God's Covenant: Old and New Testaments,' in *A Covenant Challenge to Our Broken World*, ed. Allen O. Miller (Atlanta: Darby Printing, 1982), 79–80.

The Bible does not offer a comprehensive theology of contract because the intended relational order commanded by God is covenantal. However, both covenant and contract are essential to the formation of Israel in the Old Testament. Although against His will, God allowed the Israelites to establish a social contract by choosing their king (1 Sam. 8). Sacks points out that the formation of the state of Israel under this social contract differs from the formation of the society of Israel under the social covenant at Mount Sinai, when Israel accepted the sovereignty of God and the authority of His commandments. By the same token, America is founded upon the Declaration of Independence of 1776 as its covenant base, and formulated its social contract, the Constitution, in 1787.[71] The social contract is applied to create a state through a constitution, but a covenant is needed to form a society of common duties and belonging. The economic contract represents a structured way derived by humankind to facilitate cooperation and exchange, but it has to be complemented by covenantal elements of sharing and love. As such, the contract is an important and practical tool for maintaining social and economic order, especially in a society with non-believers. Full realization of the covenantal way of life in the end times means that contractual safeguards will be replaced entirely by obedience and submission to divine authority. Egocentric self-interest and coercion will be replaced entirely by sharing and love. However, the eschatological stage is not realizable until the end of time. In the pluralistic modern society where believers and non-believers reside together, both covenant and contract are necessary to enable a well-balanced societal and economic order.[72]

Covenant and contract work together through a range of types and forms. Two distinct types of covenant, the unconditional promissory covenant and the conditional obligatory suzerain-vassal covenant, have been

71 Sacks, *To Heal a Fractured World: The Ethics of Responsibility*, 125.

72 Niebuhr points out that 'political society was neither purely natural nor merely contractual, based on common interest. Covenant was the binding together in one body politic of persons who assumed through unlimited promise responsibility to and for each other and for the common laws, under God.' See Niebuhr, 'The Idea of Covenant and American Democracy,' 133.

identified in the Old Testament.[73] These covenants are similar in form but serve different functions. From these distinct types of covenant numerous forms and meanings of covenant emerge.[74] In the Old Testament, the act of 'cutting' a covenant is derived from a ritual meal in the context of invoking the presence of God to establish a system of justice within duties and rights. In its practical application as a relational order, a covenant may take place among equals or between superiors and subordinates.[75] Within the covenanting processes, deals are made and participants share duties and rights that nourish each other.

Covenant and contract interact to serve the earthly economic order as a balancing mechanism. They address different aspects of our lives. The covenant and contract pillars of the Two Pillars paradigm work together in the form of a continuum of relationships. The balancing point and interaction between the pillars differ according to the nature and complexity of the transaction involved. Towards the end of the contract pillar, we have the example of a buy and sell transaction of daily supplies. This transaction is based on a simple contractual act of purchase and sale. The buyer and seller may not have a personal relationship. For obvious reasons, the buyer may have developed a relationship with the corner store owner when the purchases are made on a regular basis. Similarly, the urban consumer who buys daily supplies at the supermarket may develop brand loyalty to some products or get to know some of the employees in the supermarket. These

73 Kraus, 'God's Covenant: Old and New Testaments,' 89.

74 In the history of the people of Israel, covenants take the form of commandments (Ex. 34:28), peace (Gen. 31:43–54) friendship (1 Sam. 18:1–4), marriage (Mal. 2:14), etc. It occurs between God and His people, as well as among individuals. The covenant between God and Israel passes though continuous stages of renewal, whereby the outward law becomes written inwardly in the people's hearts (Jer. 31:31–33). This continues to the new covenant in Jesus' times, extending the parties involved to all believers of Christ. See Klempa, 'The Concept of the Covenant in 16th and 17th Century Continental and British Reformed Theology,' in 132. For more details on covenant characteristics in the scriptural narratives, see chapter 3 of this book.

75 Covenants can have many variations including 'binary, mutual form; a pluralistic, federated form; or a hierarchical-subsidiary form. All established a "constituted association".' See Stackhouse, 'The Moral Meanings of Covenant,' 250.

relationships are fundamental to communal life. However, they are not intimate. In these simple purchase and sale transactions, contractual elements play a strong part while covenantal elements remain present in the background. Farmers or manufacturers who supply the products take on a moral responsibility within the covenant with society to ensure that their products are safe, and to transact business in good faith. All parties within this supply chain remain participants in a wider societal covenant that ensure covenantal elements are embedded in the economic activities.

Towards the other end of the spectrum lies the family unit, a covenantal arrangement in which participants voluntarily love and contribute to the well-being of one another. It is a consociation where oaths are solemnly taken and love becomes self-giving. The transactions within such units are based on sharing and non-calculative means. Children are raised not through calculation of their potential return. Human associations are based on bonding and care. Within the family unit, the contract plays a relatively small part, but remains in place to set the ground rules and to protect the consociation from injustice and abuse. For example, it comes into play when educating the children or displaying proper respect for the rights of family members. From the family unit the covenant concept spans a spectrum of relationships to the extended family, associations of friends, colleagues and co-workers, superiors and subordinates, community, and finally to the stranger on the street. All manners of economic relationships between human persons take on certain elements of both covenant and contract.

Sacks asserts that a covenanted nation is a story-telling one. Its history is memory in narrative form, being celebrated continuously and passed on to future generations. The covenant community is future oriented with a continuous vision and purpose. 'Stories create memory, and memory creates identity. That is why covenant and narrative are at the heart of nations consciously created out of diversity.'[76] He points out that covenant complements the state and the market by putting forth human persons as altruistic

76 Sacks, *The Home We Build Together: Recreating Society*, 118–20.

individuals seeking the common good.[77] While the state and the market compete for power and wealth respectively, covenantal institutions do not compete. Instead, they cooperate to serve society. Similar to contract and covenant, competition and cooperation need to coexist in society. On the one hand, total competition leads to egoism and inequalities. On the other hand, total cooperation leads to sectarianism and totalitarianism. Such dreams for utopias have led to the worst bloodsheds in history.[78] The market is not only a platform of exchange, but contains certain persuasive priorities within itself merely due to its underlying mechanism interacting with an egocentric human nature. In the modern market, the economic agent is encouraged to chase after trendy fashions, leisure and lifestyle in the place of personal uniqueness and identity. In the market of mass production, the human person becomes reduced to the product of mass production itself. Sacks identifies this as the anti-traditional nature of markets.[79] Personal identity is given to us through the historical horizon in which we are born. By presenting us with an alternate set of norms based on the promotion of transaction volume, the market abolishes personal identities and binds the economic person to a blind chase towards vanity.

The covenantal and relational aspects of the Two Pillars paradigm ensure a long-term, continuing commitment to human living within any transaction that takes place in the market. Covenant carries a chance for continuous renewal, with faith that the divine truth surpasses all human disruptions and distortions. It contains an eschatological hope for a new

77 Critics find that Sacks' concept of the covenant contains a tendency to take diversity as the will of God, and to downplay the universality of God's revelation. While Sacks finds affirmation of human diversity in the Babel narrative, Gorsky points out that diversity on humankind was imposed as a punishment for overstepping the limits of creaturely existence. See Jonathan Gorsky, 'Beyond inclusivism: Richard Harries, Jonathan Sacks and The Dignity of Difference,' *Scottish Journal of Theology* 57 (2004): 366–76. I take the view that the covenant concept offers a way of life supporting both universality and diversity. This is demonstrated through the respective characteristics of universality and particularity in the Noachic and Abrahamic covenants. See chapter 3.3 of this book for a detailed discussion of these covenants.

78 Sacks, *The Home We Build Together: Recreating Society*, 234–5.

79 Sacks, 'Markets and Morals,' 24.

economy of grace, sharing and love. The call for humanization of the market challenges the fundamental economic paradigm, adding excessive externalities to economists' neat and tidy analytical models.[80] Bromley and Busching point out that relational soundness appears problematic when a given contractual relationship is seen as affective. For example, 'in financial circles market stability is viewed as problematic when buying selling patterns are significantly out of alignment with what are perceived as rational predictors of market performance.'[81] This mathematical and calculative approach stands in contrast with the personal and affective engagement with covenantal partners in a relation that targets mutual well-being. The solution is not to exclude the externalities, but to build models and methods that reflect authentic human nature with embedded covenant concepts, and to clearly articulate the qualitative limitations that simple models cannot portray. In doing so, a continuous discernment of a balance between eschatological truth and reality is essential. To rediscover the covenant characteristics in the market, one needs to start from the human person and persons in community. Morality is made possible when human persons encounter each other in community.[82] Through covenant awareness and

80 As Meeks asserts, 'a community that through shared understanding could designate a good or service as a gift rather than a commodity requires face-to-face communicative life and sustained association, communal qualities that are themselves increasingly threatened by the spreading commodification of life. The humanization of economy thus demands that we once again recognize that economy is embedded in community and exists for the sake of the enhancement of community. The viability of human community is a greater value than free trade and the increase of wealth through financial markets.' See M. Douglas Meeks, 'The Economy of Grace: Human Dignity in the Market System,' in *God and Human Dignity*, ed. R. Kendall Soulen and Linda Woodhead (Grand Rapids: Eerdmans, 2006), 209.

81 Bromley and Busching, 'Understanding the Structure of Contractual and Covenantal Social Relations: Implications for the Sociology of Religion,' 19.

82 As Everett asserts, the first task of recovering a covenantal approach to contractual relationships is cultural. The image of covenant needs to be restored within the different spheres of societal living – kinship, association, schools, government, etc. The failure to build a covenant culture means that state coercion is necessary. This in turn falls back to the need for contractual bonds. See Everett, 'Contract and Covenant in Human Community,' 563–4.

relationship building, the market can rediscover true moral norms through development of a covenantal culture that embraces authentic intentions, personal responsibilities and concern for others.

To the believer, economic life forms part of the celebration of created life on earth. The emphasis on integrity and ethics has been part of the covenantal life since the Old Testament times. Early rabbinic teaching states that integrity in economic affairs is part of the fulfilment of religious life. The Talmud considers study and practice of the ethical laws in commerce and finance as part of the way to sainthood.[83] There is a natural tendency for human persons to reduce such teachings to legalistic norms, therefore transforming relational covenants into commercial contracts. The Christian's mission is to exert a renewal of the covenant paradigm into the economic order that is increasingly tilted towards purely contractual and legalistic terms. Both covenant and contract are concepts essential to the proper functioning of the economic order. Accordingly, the Two Pillars must be allocated their proper places within different types of market functions and aspects of human life. There remains an undeniable reality that while Christians continue to reside as resident aliens on earth, legal requirements continue to be necessary to act as authoritative governance for a secular age that otherwise contains no higher standards. A fully covenantal economic order is only realizable eschatologically. Yet during the already-but-not-yet temporality, humanity must work towards covenant living. The Two Pillars paradigm outlined in this chapter takes into account practical applicability to actual market situations, and the rediscovery of authentic human nature embedded in the goodness of creation. It recognizes fundamental human needs for sharing and cooperation during the quest for efficiency and productivity, thus ensuring a balance between humanization of the market and satisfaction of material needs.

83 Sacks, *The Dignity of Difference: How to Avoid the Clash of Civilizations*, 88.

4.5 Sharing and Cooperation in the Quest for Productivity

The market is concerned with how the economics of the order of creation is actualized. Its rules and boundaries should be set with good intentions of governance and safeguarding. Legal order and contractual limits serve to protect and govern economic order, and to promote productivity. These positive aspects of the contract-based market need to work together with covenant characteristics to ensure fundamental humanizing values are encouraged and upheld in the market during the quest for productivity. Economic notions of efficiency and competition in the modern market must be balanced with covenant assertions of sharing and cooperation. At the same time, the covenant characteristics of sharing, love and compassion must underlie the contractual exchange to derive authentic communal cooperation. The responsibility of serving the market and the community is deeply rooted in the election and calling of humankind from within the order of creation. The creatures of God find ultimate life and nourishment only when standing in creaturely relationship to God. Such goodness is poised for eschatological realization through the redemptive work of Christ. Until then, in the already-but-not-yet transition of time and space, humankind continues to long for authentic covenant relationships within the community – the true essence within human nature that has given way to our sinfulness.

Economic activities start from the ontological needs and wants of humankind. Efficiency and competition serve to increase productivity and satisfy as many needs and wants as possible. Modern economics focuses on the material aspects of these needs and wants as its sole concern. In reality, human needs and wants encompass many different scopes and interacting categories including material, social, spiritual, etc. These ontological requirements become the foundation of human interaction and relationships within society. Material need and wants, though essential, are not sufficient for the well-being of the whole person. Efficiency and positive competition can facilitate productivity in the contract-based market, but the notions of sharing and cooperation must be simultaneously considered when making economic decisions. This is because the economy not only serves a material exchange purpose, but represents the platform for providential care of all human persons in community with each other. It is a 'household' of participants exchanging goods and services in a spirit of sharing and cooperation.

The word 'economy' is derived from the Greek word *oikonomia*, which means the 'law of the household'. Accordingly, Meeks identify the living relationships essential to survival of human beings in society as *oikos* – the household. In the *oikos* of God, people serve each other through mutual self-giving, thereby forming the basic economy of relationships among those within the household. The economy is an agent of God's work in which all of God's creatures find access to life.[84] Out of nothingness God created the heavens and the earth, with the human person as part of the creaturely creation within the cosmos. This means that from the very beginning, the economy of God is within the household of creation itself, representing the commencement of the household order called into being by the Creator.[85] Within the creation and continuing providence of God, we identify a covenantal history with a narrative that points towards the original design of the relational order that must be rediscovered to derive an economic order that originates from creation and points towards eschatological perfection.

Creation is a sphere willed and established by God before its existence. Consequently, the worldly order involving human relationships and economic activities is called into being within the time and space of divine will and design. Within the goodness and intention of creation and creaturely existence, there is an economic order posited and willed by God

84 Meeks, *God the Economist: The Doctrine of God and Political Economy*, 33–45.

85 Creation is the ordering of the cosmos in which the economic order that sustains human life and relationships is granted cosmological, ontological and ecological significance. Therefore creation is the origin of economic order, an order of which the original meaning and purpose must be identified through the intention of its Creator as He reveals to us. As Meeks suggests, 'God's economic work is not completed with the original creation, but is only begun'. See Ibid., 89.

under covenantal and providential care.[86] The nature of this eternal, perfect covenant reveals to humankind the nature of authentic love and perfect freedom. The bonding and pledge of love in freedom within the covenant forms the economy or relational order intrinsic to the triune God. It is also the nature of perfect economic order in the free love of God's economy. This economy is revealed in the history of creation, whereby humankind is invited to participate in work and the Sabbath, as well as the joy and rest it carries. The human being is 'set in the service of the ground from which he was taken', and that it will 'bear and produce in the power and goodness of God'.[87] The ground becomes a hope for the fulfilling of man's needs with his existence and ability to work.

This notion of sharing and cooperation as part of the order of creation must be reiterated in the modern market. It is the original purpose for humankind to work and plant the earth, integrating into the totality of the created world.[88] In a sharing community, production and growth originate from the purpose of cooperation, rather than self-satisfaction. Economic activities such as work and production that deploy resource and later develop into trading and market exchanges, all start from the ordination of humankind by God to work and serve the earth. This ordination is not meant for individuals alone, but for human persons to work together, to cooperate for mutual benefits, and to share the results in celebration and thanksgiving. The duty to cultivate and keep the earth means that humankind as gardener is blessed through a giving relationship with all creation, revealing the beauty, glory and fullness of creaturely life. The original inten-

86 In the narrative between God and humankind, God gives to creation what He undertakes to give when He first gave it its being and nature. This gift is compelled by God Himself in perfect freedom. It is not in terms of discharging a debt but out of free love. Barth describes covenant as the goal of creation and creation as the way to the covenant. Accordingly, the inner basis of the covenant is the free love of God, and the external basis is creation. See Barth, *Church Dogmatics*, III/1: 96–7.

87 For a discussion about human stewardship and service of the ground, see Willis Jenkins, *Ecologies of Grace: Environmental Ethics and Christian Theology* (New York: Oxford University Press, 2008), 163–5.

88 Barth, *Church Dogmatics*, III/1: 250–3.

tion of covenant partnership is shown here through the relational order amongst creatures and the cosmos.[89] Economic necessities and desires are thus placed within the much wider context of the whole cosmos in serving, sharing and cooperating during the process of work and production.

Modern economic persons have no idea of a covenant of grace freely established and maintained by God. When grace is unknown, we dwell under insecurity and strive for material abundance to fulfil both external needs and internal desires. The attempt to become self-sufficient economic persons places us in isolation, destructive competition and coercion. When human persons focus entirely on organizing economic life around our own needs and desires, the market becomes a place for exploitation of resources and other people. Such individualism reduces all relationships to rivalry or manipulation. In such a market, human persons lose their identity through commodification into headcounts, labour hours or purchasing power. The providence of God is essential to redeem and reconcile the market. Gifting and self-giving love are the ontological characteristics of God from whom all wellsprings of life originated. The isolated economic person is perpetually haunted by insecurity because self-satisfaction continuously fails to deliver. Through covenantal participation, individuals enter into a common economy of providential care. In contrast, a focus on maximizing material ends narrows economic relationships to self-satisfying means. Materialism presents a mechanism based on the investigation of atomic science, without consideration for the richness and diversity of the created world and its meaning.[90] It brings about an unconscious fate that is elevated to replace

89 'Heaven corresponds to the being and action of God. Earth corresponds to the being and action of man. The conjunction of heaven and earth corresponds to the covenant in which the divine and human being and action meet.' See Ibid., III/2: 12.

90 God's covenant with His people embraces them within the continuing care and promises of the Divine while calling for the voluntary obedience of human persons in the freedom granted. On the satisfaction of external needs, it is the Creator who provides the world with abundance (Gen. 1:22–25) and a viable life according to each person's needs within the community (Exod. 16:17–18). See Bavinck, *Reformed Dogmatics, vol. 2: God and Creation*, 435.

the transcendental. What appears to be quantifiable and controllable inevitably turns out to betray its intended purpose.[91]

If humankind continues to focus entirely on productivity and efficiency, our natural desires drive economic development to the exhaustive deployment of the environment and calculative means of market exchange. Well-defined legal concepts are then developed to facilitate efficiency and effectiveness. While these rules and judgements may achieve productive ends, the intrinsic goodness of the covenantal order easily give way to contractual finality. In contrast, the essence of the Two Pillars market is a covenant relationship of giving and receiving, governed by the boundaries and clarified by the contractual arrangement but transcends calculative legal limits. The relationship is active and positive, enabling the participants to work together towards a common objective with mutual benefit. No earthly creature can escape the necessity of cooperation and coordination with one another. The relational, self-giving nature of the covenant cannot be perfected in the earthly duration because of corrupted human nature during this already-but-not-yet temporality. Nevertheless, God's original intention of the covenant order is not concealed. It is revealed in Scripture through the history of the covenant of grace, and in world events where divine providence continues to uphold the temporality necessary for participation in the covenant in communities that uphold both productivity in the form of stewardship, and sharing in the form of care and cooperation.

91 Biblical covenants contain a providential commitment from the more powerful party that invites a gratuitous response from its counterpart. The more powerful and resourceful accept some responsibility for love and care towards the more vulnerable and powerless. The relationship therefore transcends self-interest and coercion to that of care and justice. This care and justice originating from the divine call for human communities to reflect a quality of relationship that is based on service and charity towards our neighbours. See Forrester, *Christian Justice and Public Policy*, 208–9.

4.6 Private Possessions and Public Goods

When human persons share and cooperate in production activities, questions about private possessions versus public goods arise. A proper understanding of the covenant concept helps to place these concerns in their proper context, lifting our focus from material possessions to notions of gifting and receiving within the relational covenant.[92] In a covenantal market, responsibility and stewardship receive their meaning by taking creation and therefore material matters as gifts from God. Without the immanence and transcendence of divine authority, covenantal intentions quickly deteriorate into mere contractual pursuits. Without the doctrine of creation and the gratuity of receiving from the Divine, irresponsible deployment of resources can lead to exploitation and adverse ecological consequences.[93]

92 Moltmann points to the relationship of God with the world through both His immanence and transcendence by asserting that 'God does not manifest himself in the forces and rhythms of nature; he reveals himself in human history, which is determined by his covenant and his promise'. Indeed, divine blessings that may be expressed in the form of earthly resources and possessions are not the primary drivers or manifestations of human life. God sets Himself over and against the world in revelation of His transcendence and immanence through the covenant that draws upon the faith and obedience of His people. See Moltmann, *God in Creation: An Ecological Doctrine of Creation*, 13.

93 There are increasing concerns over scarcity and exploitation of natural resources in modern times. Creation and covenant remind humanity to act as good stewards in protecting and preserving the environment. Proper stewardship over both private and public possessions extends to a concern for the common good and the welfare of future generations. Daly and Cobb distinguish between the *chrematistics* nature of modern economics versus the *oikonomia* (household) concept that the word – 'economics' is originally derived from. *Chrematistics* concerns the manipulation of possession and property to maximize short-term monetary value. The lack of covenant awareness shifts modern economics away from *oikonomia* towards *chrematistics*. For discussions on the use of land and other resources for the common good, and the related policy issues, see Herman E. Daly and John B. Cobb, Jr., *For*

While acknowledging the right to private possession in the form of contractual entitlement, the covenant opens up the participant to simultaneously embrace the notions of social capital and the common good. The Calvinistic concept of common grace provides insights for opening up private grace and advantages to the public arena. Reformed theologian Abraham Kuyper explores and applies this concept to divide grace into the dimensions of a saving grace that abolishes sin, and a temporal restraint that holds back the effect of sin. The common grace concept prevents a division of the spiritual versus secular, reminding Christians that they remain Christians whether inside or outside of church premises. The same grace of spiritual and material abundance is offered to the believer and non-believer alike. No sphere of life for the Christian falls outside Christ. Similarly, no sphere of creation falls outside the sovereignty and covenantal plan of the Creator.[94] Through this common grace, Kuyper places all spheres of existence and divergence of worldviews under the sovereignty of the Creator. At the same time, Kuyper acknowledges the sphere sovereignty concept to enable different levels and purposes of human association, reflecting the essence of the covenant concept in society. To Kuyper, sphere sovereignty reflects a similar sentiment deriving from the covenant concept to that of the consociation in the federal society depicted in Johannes Althusius' polity.[95] Kuyper argues that spheres of life such as family, business, art, etc., develop spontaneously in an organic way. The different organic spheres share common concerns in the form of morality and the common good.

Creation in the *imago Dei* provides the basis for an inclusive family that values diversity as much as unity. The Two Pillars paradigm embraces private right and property, as well as public goods and common interest. Individual difference is an asset that enables and contributes to covenant

---

the Common Good: Redirecting the Economy Toward Community, the Environment, and a Sustainable Future (Boston: Beacon Press, 1989), 121–455.

94 James D. Bratt, ed., *Abraham Kuyper: A Centennial Reader* (Grand Rapids: Eerdmans, 1998), 167–87.

95 The philosopher and theologian Johannes Althusius applies the covenant concept to present a polity of consociations for political society. Details of his work are discussed in chapter 2.

relationships. Such differences are not results of sinful human nature, but represent the intention of the Creator to grant uniqueness to each individual person. Human sins turn differences into divisions while covenant enables differences to converge and cooperate. Covenant encourages uniqueness and multicultural coalitions by identifying common grounds for identity, participation and responsibility.[96] These common objectives converge to the public good within the common grace of God.[97] Ultimately, the common good serves the interests of all its participants.

Vatican II defines the common good as 'the sum of those conditions of social life which allow social groups and their members relatively thorough and ready access to their own fulfilment'.[98] The three features that support this idea of the common good are human dignity, interdependence and participation. Human dignity is rooted in creation of the human person in the *imago Dei*. Interdependence means that human persons are bound together in communities. Participation refers to entitlements such as food, shelter and education, as well duties to contribute to social political and economic institutions. Hollenbach identifies the approach of Vatican II as 'dialogic universalism'.[99] It assumes common outlines of well-being for all human persons while dialogical engagement with pluralistic cultures remains part of the human good. Social capital is an obvious common sphere for all societal participants. At the same time, individuals reside in a diversity of private spheres that interact within a dynamic network of relationships. I claim that the covenant is a more comprehensive concept

96 Mount, *Covenant, Community and the Common Good: An Interpretation of Christian Ethics*, 45–6.

97 Allen summarises common good to include justice, goodness and shared objectives. The pursuit of the common good need not conflict with the good of each member, because 'from the standpoint of covenant love the common good includes as part of its meaning respect for the worth and therefore for the rights of each member of the community'. See Allen, *Love and Conflict: A Covenantal Model of Christian Ethics*, 267–9.

98 Mount, *Covenant, Community and the Common Good: An Interpretation of Christian Ethics*, 42.

99 David Hollenbach, *The Common Good and Christian Ethics* (Cambridge: Cambridge University Press, 2002), 152–9.

that serves to enable authentic relationships within such diversities.[100] It supports smaller communities of common goals and interests at the social spheres, while at the same time enables participation in a wider society for unity and the common good.

In contrast to shared objectives and the common good, modern society tends to reduce commonalities into quantifiable measurements for contractual purposes. For example, Moltmann points out that money is the only universality in the contemporary world. It has become the only medium of economic communication that enables communities of exchange and trade. Human persons enter into communication as *homo oeconomicus*, in the form of labour hours and as units of purchasing power or consumption. In light of these economic relationships all other designations appear insignificant because they cannot be translated into monetary terms. The economy thus offers a social ethics and ruling power of its own. The highly complex systems of relationships among humans, nature and the Divine have transformed into continuous hunger for growth, expansion and conquest. As human persons seek security from satisfying their needs and wants, mere material existence constantly fails. The goal of human lordship over the world and its resources fails to offer the paradise that fills the emptiness in humankind. Lordship captures for itself more and more possessions. Possessions and possessing power lead to exploitation of both human persons and ecological resources.[101] The protection of private right and property is a concern for individual economic freedom, security and respect. In order to enable this private sphere of contractual functionality, concerns for social capital and the common good must coexist. Otherwise, possessions easily turn into egocentric exploitation or materialism. The covenant allows private possession to open up towards charity and community concerns. It lifts the participant from a quest for material security to a higher level of freedom and security in mutual care and sharing.

100 See chapter 6.4 for further discussions about the relationship between the covenant and the common good.

101 Moltmann, *The Church in the Power of the Spirit*, 169–71.

Moltmann asserts that economics cannot be excluded from the lordship of Christ because the *oikoumene* of God is to be kept under His will and order. Under the universal lordship and salvation of Christ, Christian theology is also economic theology or 'materialistic theology'. The living testimony of Christians penetrate every sphere of life to enact God's will and order as they strive towards the kingdom of God and the hope of perfecting His household order. Christians choose to turn away from the ruthless satisfaction of demands to community, living in solidarity with others and with nature. They do not see others as competitors in the struggle for existence, but live towards the vision of symbiosis with others. Under covenantal living, they are able to see the persons behind the monetary terms, and the essential social bonds behind the contractual exchange. They enjoy freedom within the rules and boundaries of the market mechanism, but turn away from the domination and suppression that result from exploitation of market freedom. The covenantal fellowship and participation in equal responsibility and just distribution of goods enable survival of human persons individually and collectively.[102]

Private possession and property rights are often placed in the context of individual freedom in the modern market. Moltmann points out that freedom as lordship differs from freedom as community. In the former, persons find themselves in their possessions and as proprietors. They maintain a lordship over themselves, taking freedom as the ability to be their own ruler. The limit of individual freedom is the freedom and property of the other. Therefore freedom of others is respected in order to claim freedom of the self. In contrast to freedom as lordship, freedom as community is based on the love that brings human freedom to its truth. Through love in relations to others, human persons are recognized and accepted in community, becoming free as they open and shares their lives with one another. This freedom is communal, mutual and participative.[103] It is covenantal in nature.

102 Ibid., 173–6.

103 Moltmann-Wendel and Moltmann, *Humanity in God*, 62–5.

The law that intends to govern common life does not take into account individual persons and their characteristics. It relates to a hypothetical legal citizen of a particular society in general, calling for conformity through a presupposed social agreement. The legal system provides an image of the human person who resides in a given time and place. It grants status and rights within the given society, and sets out the penal code relating violations. In doing so, it presupposes moral self-determination, calling for responsible decisions at all times. The person's social situation is not taken into account under an abstract view of the legally framed individual.[104] In terms of economics and distribution, this means that legal and contractual systems alone become inadequate to articulate social good. Choices and material satisfaction must be used properly for life's preservation and not for its destruction. Its goal is not the increase of power, but the freedom from compulsion and necessity, and the striving for the realization of the good.[105] Moral purposes must be considered in order to attain quality and community in property rights and the common good.

4.7 The Two Pillars Paradigm as a Dialogical Framework

The covenant concept is subversive because its self-giving, sharing and forgiving aspects are high standards difficult to maintain unless trust and commitment are always present in a community. Balancing the covenant concept with contractual arrangements makes the Two Pillars approach realistic to the secular community. The Two Pillars paradigm maintains that both covenant and contract are essential to economic activities, and should interact in complementary ways to uphold the economic market.

104 Jürgen Moltmann, *Man: Christian Anthropology in the Conflicts of the Present* (Philadelphia: Fortress Press, 1971), 68–73.

105 Jürgen Moltmann, *The Trinity and the Kingdom of God: The Doctrine of God* (London: SCM Press, 1981), 213–14.

It results from a public theology that thinks on behalf of humanity as a whole, rather than starting from the interest of the church. The paradigm starts from an accent of fundamental human nature and the order of creation that is universal, while offering a structure that allows for communal particularity. As such, the paradigm forms an important framework both for interdisciplinary dialogue and for discussion of economic issues. The covenant and contract pillars together offer a spectrum of possibilities for regulating economic activities. A balance is required between covenant and contract to support healthy economic order. Detrimental consequences result when society relies solely upon, or overly inclines towards, the contractual approach. The believing community must strive to demonstrate the relevance of covenantal living, and to bring the covenantal aspect of relating to the contractual world in witness and in pursuit of a balanced and humanized market. To further clarify the Two Pillars paradigm and to illustrate its practicability and dialogical nature, I shall demonstrate its application through the example of long-term employment arrangements in the next chapter.

CHAPTER 5

Illustration of the Two Pillars Paradigm in Long-Term Employment Arrangements

This chapter focuses on the specific aspect of work as a continuous, long-term arrangement between an employer and employee. Through this example, I demonstrate the relevance and application of the Two Pillars paradigm in terms of a given economic activity. Work and work arrangements are integral parts of human life and economic cooperation. I shall explore the underlying presuppositions of work, development of the employment contract, and the economic relational contract models that attempt to capture the relational aspects of long-term employment. The covenant approach to employment is then compared and contrasted with the relational contract arrangement. Finally, the Two Pillars paradigm is presented by analyzing its effects and implications with respect to different components of the long-term employment arrangement. This illustration shows the relevance and practicability of the Two Pillars paradigm, and how the covenant and the contract are mutually dependent and shade into one another. Both the covenant and the contract are needed to promote humanized relationships and the overall well-being of the market participants.

5.1 Human Nature and Economic Presuppositions About Work

According to a simplistic view of the market, the purpose of work is to produce goods and services in return for money to spend in exchange for other goods and services. This process assumes that the market mechanism is the best way to distribute work and resources. Human persons enter the labour market to earn their living through market exchange. The market system in turn demands a degree of commitment and performance from its participants. Whether intentional or not, norms that focus upon productivity and efficiency easily cause human work to degrade to labour commodities. Modern economics embraces the two dominant philosophical ideologies of naturalism and materialism.[1] In the employment arrangement, a presupposition of materialism presents a monistic view about the material or physical existence of all things that tends to minimize the relational aspects of employment relationships. A presupposition of naturalism tends to minimize the need for active interference or structural enhancement to the workplace. The modern person falls naturally into negative notions of work, placing work in contrast to leisure. Consequently, the tendency is to avoid labour and to impose it on others.

Markets are originally formed to serve human persons and communities. When such roles and functions are reversed, the quality and value of human life deteriorate. In the Smithian system of self-interest and division of labour, work is an instrumental means to obtain material ends. This self-interested motive in turn benefits the aggregate common interest. According to Smith, division of labour brings about separation of trades and employments, creating a network of consumption interdependencies. Therefore the division of labour gives rise to market relationships. With the creation of private property and segregation of work responsibilities, individuals can earn a living according to their capabilities, and own the assets necessary to provide for their daily needs. Accordingly, it is possible to attain a kind of economic independence through work. This Smithian view of economic exchange finds work and economic relationships to be essential and dynamic. Division of labour creates a functional structure of cooperation and interdependence that significantly increases productivity and efficiency. While these are appealing, commercial exchange

1 For a discussion of the definitions and limitations of materialism and naturalism, see Paul K. Moser, 'Human Persons: Their Nature, Faith, and Function,' *Ex Auditu* 13 (1997): 17–36.

relationships can also become calculative and coercive when left to evolve entirely through self-interest. Although wealth brings material satisfaction, power and status, it can also turn into a driving force for measurement of value and identity.

The division of labour shapes a mechanism of cooperation and interdependency based on functionality. When this mechanism is further enhanced through the development of employment contract law, contractual arrangements flourish and permeate our daily lives. Such a mechanism promotes economic growth and productivity, leading to higher standards of living. Together with these advantages, over-reliance on contractual arrangements brings adverse effects on human relationships. In neoclassical economics, the contract promotes discrete and impersonal exchange. In a purely contractual model, it will always be beneficial for a given party to minimize performance if that non-performance does not affect the counterparty's probability of performance.[2] Through these models, we can see that contractual arrangements carry both advantages and disadvantages. They show that the tendencies to prioritize performance and self-interest can be detrimental to basic human relationships when these mechanisms are left without scrutiny. Human persons naturally motivated by self-interest tend to find increasingly egocentric and calculative means to meet quantifiable ends in the form of material gains. Work is reduced in the labour market economic models to a commodity measured by labour hours and wages as part of a market exchange.

What are the meaning and essence of work? The significance of work as an essential human activity is strongly asserted in the Catholic *Encyclicals*. In *Rerum Novarum*, the human person is to engage in gainful occupation for 'a true and full right not only to demand his wage but to dispose of it as he sees fit'.[3] Economic rights and freedom are seen as essential parts of personhood. The right to private possessions is affirmed although

2 Victor P. Goldberg, 'A Relational Exchange Perspective on the Employment Relationship,' in *Firms, Organization and Labour: Approaches to the Economics of Work Organization*, ed. Frank H. Stephen (London: Macmillian, 1984), 129.

3 Pope Leo XIII, 'Rerum Novarum,' *Encyclical Letter* (1891): par. 9.

common interest is considered at the same time. Products of the earth serve as compensation for human labour. This is the natural scheme that allows the human person to secure a livelihood. Since the ability to work for a living is a natural right, it is the duty of employers to respect the dignity of workers by ensuring just demands and proper compensation.[4] In *Laborem Exercens*, work is taken to bear the mark of humankind and of humanity as a sign signifying that a person is operating within a community of persons. It is a perennial and fundamental aspect of human life that yields dignity to human existence, supports science and progress, and cultivates civilizations. Accordingly, considerations over work and work arrangements are of decisive importance in the human quest to 'make life more human'.[5]

What then happens, when the nature of human work falls under the anthropology of the modern market? Meeks points out that in the anthropology of the modern market, human persons are tailored to fit the market mechanism and technological advancement. The notion of *homo economicus* simplifies human persons to fit as actors in the market by an implied adherence to the market solution for the distribution of goods. Human persons necessarily become economic persons and market participants who are drawn into the commodification of all goods and services into marketable units. This in turn leads to a commodification of the self, and a self-making identity based on market sentiments of production and sale.[6] The labour market is a typical example of commodification of the self in respect of the contribution of human effort to society.[7] Meeks asserts that ideologies that attempt to exalt work present work as justifi-

4 Ibid., par. 14–32.

5 Pope John Paul II, 'Laborem Exercens,' *Encyclical Letter* (1981): par. 1–3.

6 M. Douglas Meeks, 'Being Human in the Market Society,' *Quarterly Review* 21 (2001): 254–8.

7 As a result, Meeks concludes that 'work is a central theological issue because nowhere are the relationships of authority and subordination more apparent than in the relationships of work. Work is the most immediate way in which human beings dominate and exploit each other.' See Meeks, *God the Economist: The Doctrine of God and Political Economy*, 127.

cation for one's existence. Coupled with the commodification of work, such ideologies place the human person under slavish manipulation by work arrangements. As human persons seek for meaning and justification of their own existence through work, they fall into the traps of commodification and dehumanization in the labour market. With the concerns for human identity and purpose in life, work is viewed as the functional and organizational basis of life, contributing to the self-image and social recognition of the individual. The possibility and quality of work determine the meaning of life. In such situations, the domination of efficiency over work reduces work to its functionality and labour to a means to an end. When the value of the human person is measured in terms of productive work, the unemployed may find themselves secondary citizens who cannot access the basic necessities of life.[8]

The complex nature and multiple implications of human work render any simple definition or single anthropological viewpoint inadequate. Perhaps one of the more comprehensive explorations of the theology of work is the threefold nature of work proposed by Darrell Cosden. Cosden asserts that work is constituted by its instrumental, ontological and relational aspects existing together in a mutual and interdependent relationship. Work as an instrumental activity means that it serves certain outcomes, such as self-satisfaction and contribution to society, which are beyond direct consequences of the activity itself. This instrumental aspect is essential but cannot stand on its own because work is quickly dehumanized if the human person is taken merely as an instrument or tool to achieve certain

8 Instead of placing value on the functionality of work, Meeks presents a Trinitarian perspective by identifying work as distinctively personal, cooperative, egalitarian and self-giving. The Trinitarian view describes each person of the Trinity as working and acting on a specific contribution to the divine work. They cooperate or co-work to attain the eternal goal, taking equally crucial roles within the hierarchically arranged work of God. The Triune community's work is integrated through self-giving love towards each other. In a system that reflects the nature of the Triune community, the unemployed are freely taken care of through inclusive, self-giving love. The fullness of life in the other motivates the Triune community's work in faithfulness and steadfastness. Such characteristics are embedded in human nature as humankind is created in the *imago Dei*. See Ibid., 132–43.

results. Consequently, the ontological nature of work as part of life itself cannot be overlooked. Human work is in itself an activity of human life, and represents a gift from God. The working process builds discipline and character that play a part in spiritual development. One meets the needs of each other and acquires the means for charity through performance of work, leading to co-creation and interdependence in the communal sense. The relational aspect of work addresses ethics, social relationships and existential realization in work. It concerns how work is organized, and the promotion of appropriate social order such as equality and justice within the social structure.[9]

Theological anthropology proposes an evangelical humanism that emphasizes the ontology of the human person. Human nature and destiny reside in their identity and action in the reciprocities of relationships with God and others.[10] The workplace is one of the most important arenas for the development of unity, identity and presence of the human person. Through work and acts, the participant is placed within the spectrum of historical narratives and economic transactions. Work being ontological is therefore essential to human worth. This theological view finds adverse circumstances, such as structural unemployment, immoral because the exclusion of individuals from work rejects the value of human persons.[11] Mutual trust and cooperation are important foundations for human identity and overall well-being. These tend to breakdown when the zeal for profits dominates the market culture. At the same time, the sinfulness of human nature implies that egocentric market participants are characterized by continuous desires to satisfy pleasure and avoid pain through material ends. This sense of insecurity and perpetual desire is a distortion that leads to an insatiable desire, drawing the human person away from God.[12] To examine this distortion under the natural development of the employment

9 Darrell Cosden, *A Theology of Work: Work and the New Creation* (Cumbria: Paternoster, 2004), 10–12.

10 Meeks, 'Being Human in the Market Society,' 219–29.

11 Timothy L. Smith, 'Work and Human Worth,' *Christian Century* 84 (1967): 1094–6.

12 Meeks, 'Being Human in the Market Society,' 258–9.

contract, we turn to the development of employment contract theory in legal scholarship.

5.2 The Development of the Employment Contract and its Relational Aspects

In modern society, contracts are often thought of in legal terms. From the negotiation process to the drafting and enforcement of a transaction, participants are drawn into a set of formal presuppositions that characterize the contract mechanism. Even a single, discrete transaction at a retail shop occurs within relationships that involve a wide network of producers, suppliers and retailers. Development of the employment contract provides the basis for further developing the division of labour in terms of individual interests and social status, as well as the commodification of labour hours by laying out predetermined terms and conditions. As contract theories are studied and developed, the limitations of contracts in capturing relational aspects of employment arrangements become apparent when put into practice. Consequently, the legal profession starts to develop extensions and variations to the simple contract in an attempt to alleviate these limitations. Major examples of extended contractual forms include the psychological contract, implicit contract and relational contract.

Rousseau defines the *psychological contract* as 'an individual's beliefs regarding the terms and conditions of a reciprocal exchange agreement between that focal person and another party'.[13] She asserts that subjectivity is inherent in all contracts. Such subjectivity can occur in written or oral agreements, intrinsically residing as part of any agreement from a

13 Denise M. Rousseau, 'Psychological and Implied Contracts in Organizations,' *Employee Responsibilities and Rights Journal* 2 (1989): 123.

relationship or interaction over time.[14] Employment contracts are essentially relationship-based agreements that go beyond economic exchange to relational concerns. They involve not only promise and contribution, but extend into cognitive limits, divergent frames of reference, and the formative nature of relationships. The main concerns here are the beliefs and expectations within the contract, binding the participants into some reciprocal obligations. While other contractual structures reside among the participants to the contract, the psychological contract is perceived by the individual person when reciprocity is expected of the counterparty. It reflects the individual's commitment to an organization, involving the acceptance of organization values, the willingness to exert effort, and the desire to remain an employee.[15] Since psychological contracts are implicit in nature, they can be considered a form of implicit contracts.

An *implicit contract* is 'a non-contractual employment arrangement that corresponds to a Nash equilibrium of the repeated, post-hiring, bilateral trading game other than the degenerate agreement consisting of a sequence of Nash equilibria to the one-shot trading game'.[16] Bull examines the rea-

14 The psychological contract has been studied as part of organization behaviour since the 1960s. See Robert C. Bird, 'Employment as a Relational Contract,' *University of Pennsylvania Journal of Labor and Employment Law* 8 (2005):154–8 and 165–70, for a description of the four stages of employment relationship within a psychological contract, the historical development of the concept of psychological contract, and discussion of its characteristics.

15 Although the idea of psychological or implicit factors affecting the contractual arrangements has developed over many years in organizational research, they remain unstudied in economic models until presented in the form of new contract structures and analysed through alternative mathematical approaches. These approaches attempt to capture the patterns of relational interactions not previously captured in transactional models. See Rousseau, 'Psychological and Implied Contracts in Organizations,' 121–39. Besides being analysed in economic models, these notions are studied and further developed by scholars in the fields of law, business and psychology.

16 Nash equilibrium is a way of formalizing the idea of a self-enforcing agreement, so that each party has incentives to carry out the contract even when it is not legally enforceable. In other words, it is an understanding of how each party behaves reciprocally for mutual benefits over and above what happens if there is a breakdown of trust. It does not provide for the capacity of sacrificial acts because reciprocal acts

sons for and values of implicit contracts. His model shows that in the labour market hiring process, informational asymmetries among the company, potential employees and third parties cause a contract to be incomplete and provide incentives to form an implicit contract. This is largely due to the complexities in monitoring employee effort that tend to be implicit rather than explicit during the employment process. Implicit contracts mediate a large proportion of the employment relationship. However, they appear worthless from an enforcement point of view because implicit qualities in the contract may be observable but are not verifiable in a court of law.[17] Implicit contracts extend beyond psychological contracts because they contain implied expectations that are based on past experience or circumstantial reality beyond subjective beliefs. Examples of these implicit elements may include employee performance or job security, for which expectations can be implied from continuing performance measurements or company policies. Psychological contracts concern individual beliefs in the reciprocity of a relationship, while implicit contracts represent mutual obligations characterizing the nature of the employment relationships. Implicit contracts share similar attributes with the relational contract, described below, since these theories are developed simultaneously under different terminologies.

A *relational contract* recognizes the relational nature of contractual arrangements. Legal scholar Ian Macneil is widely known as the original advocate of relational contract theory. He points out that contracts can never reside outside social relationships. The fundamental roots of a contract are society, specialization of labour and exchange, choice, and awareness of the future. It involves reciprocal exchange based on extensive specialization where individuals contribute their own specialization while relying on others to do the same. It necessitates a sense of choice whereby individuals are equipped with perceived freedom to elect their own

---

by the other party must be anticipated before one would carry out the agreement. See Clive Bull, 'The Existence of Self-Enforcing Implicit Contracts,' *The Quarterly Journal of Economics* 102 (1987): 149.

17 Ibid., 147–59.

behaviours. His work points towards the need for contractual participants to have a conscious awareness of a future for the contract. This awareness and expectation for continuing relationships provide the relational basis for a given contract to fully develop and realize.[18] Relational contract theory attempts to capture the relational aspects of contracts that may be over and above the formal contractual agreement. From a legal point of view, the relational approach to contract is informed by four core propositions. First, each transaction is embedded in a complex network of relationships. Second, all formal and informal elements significant to a transaction must be considered in order to understand a transaction. Third, all relationships and sequences relevant to a transaction must be recognized in order to analyse the transaction effectively. Fourth, such contextual analysis is more sensitive to the contractual relationship than an approach that privileges the formal agreement.[19]

Having identified the relational nature of contracts, the next step is to examine the behaviour and implications involved within the relational exchange. These may include a multitude of variables such as trust, cooperation, communication, justice, equality, solidarity, reciprocity, etc. Different context and group dynamics give rise to different norms and culture. Relational contract theory makes the self-maximizing notion of the neoclassical contract appears too simplistic even for the most individualistic discrete transaction.[20] A multitude of other factors such as coercion and dependence may occur among the participants. The neoclassical contract assumption of equal bargaining power in a transactional relationship is often

18 Macneil asserts that 'contract between totally isolated, utility-maximizing individuals is not contract, but war'. See Ian R. Macneil, *The New Social Contract: An Inquiry into Modern Contractual Relations* (New Haven: Yale University Press, 1980), 1–4.

19 Linda Mulcahy and John Tillotson, *Contract Law in Perspective* (London: Cavendish Publishing, 2004), 49–50.

20 As Feinman points out, 'values other than wealth maximization figure importantly in exchanges, even discrete contracts and market exchanges because the non-economic, non-market aspects of relations pervade market transactions.' See Feinman, 'Significance of Contract Theory,' 1302.

not the case.[21] When applied to employment arrangements, the neoclassical model disregards the participants' identities and fails to account for the complexities of employment relationships. The contract may be useful for protecting the interests of the relevant parties and for providing a means of formal and fair negotiation. However, a pure contractual model overlooks the underlying dynamics outside of the contractual structure, as well as the continuing nature of personal relationships and unwritten norms involved when people work together in an employment environment. Future events and unforeseeable circumstances can never be adequately represented in a written contract.[22]

Relational contract theory is formulated to capture economic relationships among contracting parties that involve planning, trust, cooperation and other personal norms. Relational contracts attempt to embrace unwritten terms among the contracting parties. It is a tool developed to understand commercial contracts in better ways. The relational contract recognizes the long-term nature of some contractual arrangements, e.g., in a long-term employment relationship, within which the extended duration and relational aspects prevent participants from calculating full value of the exchange on the outset. It recognizes that future cooperative behaviour and governance mechanisms are necessary, that unforeseen contingencies are expected, and that continuing accommodation to contractual terms is required. During the process, bonds of friendship, interdependence and altruism may develop. At the same time, there may be conflicts and dissatisfactions. The relational aspects of the contract lie outside of the written arrangement, and may result in gains or losses implicit to the contract. The commitment and cooperation involved in a relational contract is far more complex than the bargain for a single transactional exchange.[23] The

21 For example, Blau points out that the wage contract is fundamentally unequal in its nature. Workers have no alternatives other than selling their labour, putting them in a weak position susceptible to exploitation. Therefore the social contract and wage contract are often in conflict with each other. See Judith R. Blau, *Social Contracts and Economic Markets* (New York: Plenum Press, 1993), 81–3.

22 Bird, 'Employment as a Relational Contract,' 163–4.

23 Ibid., 152–4.

long-term employment relationship is typical of relational contracts that involve both explicit and implicit characteristics. It is a type of relationship involving both quantitative economic exchange and qualitative human living.

All employment contracts involve the very basic unquantifiable relational aspects between the employer and employee.[24] Fox points out that in order to adapt the contract to business organizations, contractualism has to be combined with the traditional master-servant model. While contract theory allows equity and discretion to the participants in defining the nature and terms of the contract, when the law is applied to the employment relationship such discretion reverts authority and control to the employer. This is because employers generally retain greater coercive power within the relationship from their status and resources. The master-servant model thus enters the employment contract, legitimizing the employer's prerogative. This status differentiation reduces the employment contract to a legal device for the employer to make rules and exercise discretion. In addition, the long-term and continuous nature of the employment contract prevents definition of specific obligations of the employee over time. It is hardly practical to exhaustively fix the obligations of participants in the employment relationship at any given point in time. The employment contract is therefore necessarily a continuously renewing and open-ended one.[25] Legal scholars identify the open-ended nature of the employment contract as an essential incompleteness. This means that employment arrangements necessarily contain self-enforcing notions. Scholars therefore proceed to

24 Hviid finds it impossible to locate a definition for relational contracts that adequately distinguishes relational and non-relational contracts. This is because the relational aspects and unforeseen contingencies cannot be fully captured within a specific set of defined rules. This means that relational contracts cannot be made legally operational in a distinct form from general contracts. Accordingly, Hviid suggests that contracts should be taken as a combination of legally enforceable and self-enforceable obligations. See Morten Hviid, 'Long-Term Contracts and Relational Contracts,' in *Encyclopedia of Law and Economics*, ed. Boudewijn Bouckaert and Gerrit de Geest (Cheltenham: 2000), III: 58–9.

25 Alan Fox, *Beyond Contract: Work, Power and Trust Relations* (London: Faber, 1974), 186–90.

model these long-term relationships in repeated games by studying the participants' ability to cooperate in trust and good faith.[26] Undoubtedly, the contract mechanism cannot be expected to capture all the essential elements within employment relationships. In particular, human factors such as trust and commitment cannot be explicitly formulated. Informal or implicit agreements necessarily coexist with the formal written contract.

Informal agreements are identified and studied by scholars in economics, law and business alike.[27] MacLeod and Malcomson analyse a series of wages and performance outcomes that are implicit in employment contracts. They focus on contractual terms such as piece-rate or informal bonuses that cannot be legally enforced because of their unverifiable nature. These self-enforcing, implicit contracts resemble actual employment contracts more than those in the standard principal-agent models.[28] When

26 Hviid finds that in order to allow optimal renegotiation, it may be preferable to leave the long-term contract more incomplete than it needs to be. Bernheim and Winston argue that incompleteness is an essential feature of a well-designed contract. Their models show that when observable but unverifiable behaviours are involved, the contract should be written in a way to leave open some potentially contractible aspects. The optimal degree of contractual incompleteness may be related to the economic environment or other externalities. See Morten Hviid, 'Relational Contracts, Repeated Interaction and Contract Modification,' *European Journal of Law and Economics* 5 (1998): 179–94; and B. Douglas Bernheim and Michael D. Whinston, 'Incomplete Contracts and Stategic Ambiguity,' *American Economic Review* 88 (1998): 902–32.

27 Informal agreements in organizations have been widely explored by organization behaviour scholars such as Chester Barnard, Peter Blau, Alvin Gouldner, Philip Selznick and Herbert Simon. See George Baker, Robert Gibbons and Kevin J. Murphy, 'Relational Contracts and the Theory of the Firm,' *The Quarterly Journal of Economics* 117 (2002): 39–40, for the importance of informal agreements with respect to relational contracts and the organization.

28 In principal-agent models, the principal is a person or group of persons hiring another or others to achieve an objective of the principal. The agent is the person or group of persons hired to achieve the principal's objective. An economic inefficiency occurs in the principal-agent problem because taking each player's strategy as given, the agent's personal goal reduces the principal's welfare. Standard principal-agent models are built around the variables of agent effort, output, bargaining power, wages,

modelled in a repeated game, MacLeod and Malcomson find that many potentially perfect equilibria may result for these contracts.[29] Vacancies and unemployment may coexist. When the renegotiation process is applied as a criterion for selecting equilibria, this potential mismatch in employment is eliminated, but division of potential benefits from the employment outcome remains ambiguous. Various other assumptions and externalities are further explored in the models, leading to the conclusion that equilibria selection depends largely on the participants' beliefs about employment expectations, benefits and outcomes. These determinants reside beyond the technology and utility functions of the participants involved.[30]

5.3 Employment Contracts as Repeated Games

The relational contract approach to employment portrays the employment relationship as one of functional interdependence. Pearce and Stacchetti build a repeated agency model to capture the interplay of explicit and implicit contracts, in which the agent's actions are observable to the principal but not verifiable in court. They find that optimal cooperation between the players requires the use of both explicit and implicit contracts. The constrained efficient equilibria of supergames based on a standard agency

---

and risk taking levels of the principal and agent involved. See Don E. Waldman, *Microeconomics* (Boston: Pearson Addison Wesley, 2004), 568–72. Accordingly, self-enforcing, implicit contracts assume a higher level of trust, cooperation and unwritten understanding between the contracting parties.

29 In game theory, an equilibrium is a strategy combination that consists of the best strategy for each player in the game. Perfect equilibria must satisfy an additional 'credibility' restriction about how players react to deviations from the equilibrium, taking everyone else's strategy as given (formally, each subgame must also be in equilibrium). Ibid., 352–8.

30 W. Bentley MacLeod and James M. Malcomson, 'Implicit Contracts, Incentive Compatibility, and Involuntary Unemployment,' *Econometrica* 57 (1989): 447–80.

model show that the presence of bonuses discourages cheating and smooths the agent's consumption pattern with reference to salaries and utilities.[31] In such situations, the long-term employment contracts are in effect continuously renegotiated, although they are perceived to be a single, anticipated arrangement by the participants involved. Explicit contacts that are short-term in nature should therefore be designed to enhance the effectiveness of long-term implicit contracts.[32] Levin studies the trade-off for organizations to have a multilateral relational contract with their workforce as a whole, versus bilateral relational contract with individual employees. He finds that while bilateral contracts are more flexible in terms of workforce changes, multilateral contracts that bind the organization more strongly to implicit commitments improve workforce motivation.[33] The findings of these studies add to our understanding of the functional relationships in the employment situation, yet they are necessarily economic abstractions that present observations limited to the instrumental aspects of the relationships under the assumptions of rational self-interest.

The use of repeated games to model relational contracts in employment situations involves a number of parameters. In an explicit contract, verifiable conditions of employment such as wages and working hours can be specified. At the same time, the employment contract may also involve implicit terms such as a discretionary bonus and quality measurements. In repeated game models, threats to the relationship may include decrease in trust, expectation of lower bonus levels, job security concerns, morale problems, etc. Termination of employment involves severance pay and breakdown in relational bonds that parallel 'punishment' in the prisoner's dilemma model. To further explore the use of repeated games in modelling relational aspects of economic behaviour, I shall discuss the example of the Prisoner's Dilemma.

31 The constrained efficient equilibria of supergames are the best that can be achieved given the constraints of informational imperfections or other factors.

32 David G. Pearce and Ennio Stacchetti, 'The Interaction of Implicit and Explicit Contracts in Repeated Agency,' *Games and Economic Behavior* 23 (1998): 75–96.

33 Jonathan Levin, 'Multilateral Contracting and the Employment Relationship,' *The Quarterly Journal of Economics* 117 (2002): 1073–1103.

The Prisoner's Dilemma is a familiar illustration in the social sciences, and widely used to model strategic behaviour in economic theory. It is an interesting scenario where rational individual self-interest appears to leave the participants worst off. This model is presented here to illustrate the covenant response to economics behaviour, and the limitations of economic modelling with reference to the covenant concept. In this model, two prisoners who have committed a crime together are asked to confess their crime for a reduced sentence. If neither confesses, the evidence for conviction is mild so both receive a light sentence, say one year each. If both confess, they receive five years each. If one confesses but not the other, the confessor will go free while the other receives a heavy penalty of ten years. The prisoners are held in different cells without knowing the decision of the other. This means that without knowing the decision of the other prisoner, a prisoner who confesses either gets five years if the other confesses or goes free if the other does not. A prisoner who does not confess either gets ten years if the other confesses, or one year if the other does not. This is a simple 'game' scenario where it is better to confess no matter what the prisoner thinks the other is going to do. This means that prediction of the other's action or strategic intentions is not necessary. Under such a simple self-interest maximizing scenario, both prisoners will confess and end up with five years of imprisonment. As a result, their individually rational actions work against their social interest because if they cooperate on not confessing, they only get penalties of one year each.

When Prisoner's Dilemma situations occur in real-life situations, cooperation does occur in some cases. This starts the social scientists' quest in modelling different situations around the phenomenon and placing the model in parallel to real life conditions such as business decisions or employment negotiations. Cooperation based on reciprocity has been observed in numerous situations including breach of contract, political negotiations and international trade. The answer lies in considering the repeated play of the Prisoner's Dilemma game, when a strategy such as Tit for Tat quickly emerges in experiments with real players as the participants respond to the decision of each other.[34] In a sense, this is not cooperation but a rational calculation taking into account future circumstances in the pursuit of egocentric self-interest. Nevertheless, it affirms the complexity of human behaviour and the fact that cooperative behaviour can be taught intentionally.[35]

The Prisoner's Dilemma is an interesting and useful illustration because it captures the reality of possible inefficiencies in the market exchange in a simple way. Maximization of individual interests does not always add up to optimal common advantage. When the market is left on its own to operate through fate of natural law, the results can be against the social interest. As a government policy administrator, Adam Smith realizes this fact.[36] Law and order are necessary to administer contracts in the market. At the same time, a covenantal polity is necessary to ensure proper human relationships and cooperation for the common good. In the context of the workplace, employment relationships portrayed as repeated games assume rational calculative intention from all participants. The relational

34 For a detailed discussion of the Prisoner's Dilemma and the Tit for Tat solution, see Robert Axelrod, *The Evolution of Cooperation* (London: Penguin, 1990), 21–86.

35 David Warsh, 'How Selfish Are People – Really?,' *Harvard Business Review* May–Jun (1989): 26–34.

36 Tullock considers the Prisoner's Dilemma with insights from Smith's system of economic theory. He points out that in a competitive market, reputation matters because the participants are allowed to choose the player they play with. Under the scenario of a multiple participants Prisoner's Dilemma game played repeatedly with information about the reputation of previous players, ethics or commitment influence future gains. A one-time gain is possible by cheating, but participants do not regard this as being profitable in the competitive market where the participants are to remain for the long term. The cooperative solution is an optimum because the cost of cheating when discovered by the other participants is too high. This is very similar to the prisoner's dilemma situation discussed above. When a person changes partners, one's history of play continues to be observable by all parties. Tullock ties this back to Smith's comment that 'the discipline of continuous dealings' leads people to cooperate and that sympathy influences social behaviour in the market. See Gordon Tullock, 'Adam Smith and the Prisoners' Dilemma,' *The Quarterly Journal of Economics* 100 (1985): 1073–81.

aspects captured in the economic models therefore remain contractual rather than covenantal.

Economists have applied the Prisoner's Dilemma to model numerous different situations. Leibenstein finds that it is useful to view productivity as a Prisoner's Dilemma problem. He argues that productivity can be viewed as an interactive game involving numerous interdependent variables under the decision of multiple decision-makers. Workers who are part of this 'productivity game' are employed under incomplete contracts that can specify remuneration but cannot fully monitor the effort exerted. Therefore productivity partly depends on the effort made by individual workers. Under these scenarios, effort conventions are usually non-optimum. Accordingly, Leibenstein concludes that the invisible hand does not produce a Pareto optimal result.[37] Arce, Daniel and Sandler find that in their experiments, when a variation of public versus private incentives are given to the participants, public benefits facilitate cooperation in repeated plays of the Prisoner's Dilemma.[38] Dayton-Johnson shows that a critical level of social cohesion must precede cooperative behaviour, while social cohesion can be facilitated by information and cooperative norms.[39] Cooperative norms mitigate the inefficiencies that arise in the Prisoner's Dilemma. These norms must be embedded in an ethical market climate and a culture for moral economic relationships.

Frank places the self-interest model in contrast to a commitment model in which workers assume a considerable level of commitment to the employment contract. He recognizes that beliefs about human nature in turn shape human nature itself, especially in terms of its consequences for material welfare.

37 Harvey Leibenstein, 'The Prisoners' Dilemma in the Invisible Hand: An Analysis of Intrafirm Productivity,' *American Economic Review* 72, no. 2 (1982): 92–7.

38 M. Arce, G. Daniel and Todd Sandler, 'The Dilemma of the Prisoners' Dilemmas,' *Kyklos* 58 (2005): 3–24.

39 Jeff Dayton-Johnson, 'Knitted Warmth: The Simple Analytics of Social Cohesion,' *The Journal of Socio-Economics* 32 (2003): 623–45.

> [T]he traditional self-interest model says that people who love, who feel guilty when they cheat, vengeful when they are wronged, or envious when they get less than their fair share will often behave in ways that reduce their material payoffs. But the commitment model tells us that precisely because of this, they may also enjoy opportunities that would not be available to a purely opportunistic person. In many cases, a person or society armed with this knowledge will make better choices than one exposed only to the self-interest tradition.[40]

Frank's model identifies emotional predispositions as the driving forces behind moral behaviour. Workers feel guilty when they cheat, vengeful when they err, and envious when things are unfair. Instead of attempting to free ride on other workers, committed employees are responsible and cooperative. The finding shows that the commitment model needs to be supported by an appropriate working environment that promotes proper norms. An increase in personal ties among the workers leads to a decrease in motivation to shirk on the job. Being moral and doing the right things impose economic costs on the workers but most people have the capacity to be educated and to behave in a committed manner.[41] While cooperative norms and commitment can be present in either the covenant or contract situation, the essence of non-egocentric cooperation and commitment in true human bonding must be based on covenantal relationships. Such covenanting capabilities can be educated and nurtured.

The wide application of the Prisoner's Dilemma to economic theories such as optimum savings, taxation, allocation involving externalities, etc., demonstrates that cooperation and commitment are beneficial under many real-life circumstances. Sen points out that the problem here is actually what the person presupposes under the Prisoner's Dilemma. In a rational economic model where people act on self-interest, one assumes participants to be self-interested. The choice of cooperating in view of self-interest is based on rational calculation. On the other hand, a choice of not cooperating follows a moral code of behaviour or a set of personal values beyond calculative rationality.[42] Numerous possibilities begin to emerge when externalities

40 Robert H. Frank, 'Beyond Self-Interest,' *Challenge* Mar–Apr (1989): 8.

41 Ibid., 4–13.

42 Sen, *Choice, Welfare and Measurement*, 65.

such as on-going relationship, coercion, conflicting interest, etc. are added to the interactions. If one continues to focus on the self-interested assumption of economic human nature, this can mean that cooperation simply starts from a calculated risk or expectation of reciprocity. This story can continue. On the other hand, if the horizon is opened up to include the possibility of irrational acts, social interests or even sacrificial intentions, the story becomes a human narrative of non-calculative bonding.[43] This may not fit the classical view of the self-interested economic person, yet it carries some truth to the relational aspects of human life.[44]

The Prisoner's Dilemma has a number of limitations when modelling human relationships. The observable behaviour in economic modelling may not reflect the true essence of the underlying human relationships and motives. Gilbert questions the validity of the Prisoner's Dilemma by pointing out that 'the central assumptions of the Prisoner's Dilemma are devoid of any vision of enduring, mutually beneficial connections between the human beings who create and sustain such institutions as business and the modern corporation'.[45] Accordingly, we imprison ourselves by using the Prisoner's Dilemma to model human interactions. Gilbert challenges the Prisoner's Dilemma in terms of five assertions: commitment, cooperation, trust, mutual benefit and defection. The commitment concept in the Prisoner's Dilemma game has nothing to do with human relationships. It only represents the prudence of an egoist. The cooperative person builds a reputation in the game over time that does

43 As Axelrod discovers, cooperation among the participants can start from the few individuals who have a chance for brief interaction with others. See Axelrod, *The Evolution of Cooperation*, 21.

44 As Cortina asserts, the Prisoner's Dilemma and related game theories are often used in the study of public goods. Nevertheless, 'it proves difficult for these designs to be successful in practice if this is done without relying on the human capacity to appreciate what is in itself valuable, going beyond the game of self-interests and utility and recognising that there are actions and beings – people – that are worthy in their own right'. See Cortina, *Covenant and Contract: Politics, Ethics and Religion*, 17.

45 Daniel R. Jr. Gilbert, 'The Prisoner's Dilemma and the Prisoners of the Prisoner's Dilemma,' *Business Ethics Quarterly* 6 (1996): 165.

not necessarily contribute to relationships. The game itself does not allow for evolving relationships in which trust can be anchored. It also does not capture any mutuality or the common good. Since a history of relationship is not provided for in the game, defection as a departing strategy has little ground.[46] Gilbert's observations point towards a deeper meaning of ethics that goes beyond the modelling approach. The five questions converge to the lack of recognition of human identity in the Prisoner's Dilemma. The fact that human persons act in relationship with each other must first be presupposed before the model takes on any meaning. This is the underlying covenant concept that embraces society, even before any analysis can actually commence.

In the eschatological sharing economy of grace, the participants in the Prisoner's Dilemma will act in self-giving, covenantal love to uphold the oath and bonding with each other. Within the covenant, perfect trust and total commitment in the form of authentic relationships will ensure reciprocity. Such a paradigm is ideological in the already-but-not-yet realm. During this temporality, a balance between covenant characteristics and contract legalities is needed. The Two Pillars paradigm offers a balance between unconditional compassion and economic justice. A participant acts in self-giving, covenantal love and trusts the others to do the same. When faced with a breach of trust, the participant reassesses the situation under the view of a covenant renewal, rather than taking the exit route in the first instance. Covenant renewal is balanced with justice to derive a decision based upon loving-kindness and personal judgement. This decision cannot be calculated empirically. To the social scientist, this is irrational behaviour that cannot be modelled. The social scientists' objectives of modelling through the Prisoner's Dilemma are to simulate human behaviour. Accordingly, alternatives to the self-interested, contractual model such as the altruistic model or commitment model are measured by their results. Under the covenant concept, the intrinsic value of human

46 Ibid., 169–70.

relationships, trust and compassion need to be taken into account in measuring results. These highly valued human qualities are often destroyed when one focuses entirely on the means to achieve immediate economic results, with the negative impact on society long-lasting and unaccounted for. In a repeated Prisoner's Dilemma scenario where trust is eventually breached and relationships broken, community shatters. Contractual arrangements and laws to guard against the breach of contracts are necessary because of the natural sinful tendencies of fallen human nature. Yet at the same time, humankind must strive against such tendencies in pursuit of the covenantal relationships that bond human persons together and truly uphold the market in its proper function, i.e. to serve humankind rather than be served by it. Relational norms are much needed to complement the contractual arrangement in employment relationships.[47] These can best be served by enacting covenant characteristics to balance the contract.

47 Further to the discussions on psychological, implicit and relational contracts in section 5.2 above, Bird applied these concepts to identify three sources of relational contract norms for employment relationships – the psychological contract, company credo and organizational culture. First, psychological contracts are employees' perception of mutual obligations within the employment relationship. It is perceived between the individual employee and the organization as a whole, but not necessarily representing organizational expectations. It can remain within the mind of the particular employee, changing over time as the employment relationship progresses. Violation of the psychological contract occurs when the employee perceives a failure of fulfilment. Second, the company credo is the document of ethical rules for employees. It lays out the explicit standard of employment behaviour within the company, usually including requirements for commitment to integrity and appropriate business conduct. Company credos affirm the law, demand honesty, call for loyalty and promote fairness. Third, organizational culture is the consistent set of goals and norms within an organization that influences the values and behaviour of its employees. It represents the beliefs, values, assumptions and norms that define the organization and how its employees behave. See Bird, 'Employment as a Relational Contract,' 170–80.

5.4 A Covenant Approach to the Employment Arrangement

The predominant Protestant understanding of work starts from the doctrine of vocation, which involves work to meet physical needs, as well as personal obedience to God in the context of a 'calling'. Forrester finds Abraham to be the first person who received an explicit sense of calling and vocation from God. God commands Abraham directly to embark on a pilgrimage within a personal relationship with God Himself. This marks the beginning of the election of Israel as the chosen people within the covenant with God. It is this sense of vocation that makes and keeps Israel a people under God's covenant. Within this national vocation, God keeps Israel prosperous and safe, while charging them with obligations and duties towards God and other people. The meaning of vocation and calling in the context of the Old Testament is much richer than work alone.[48] Yet the essence of being charged with the covenant entails a communal essence of work that embraces both privileges and responsibilities of the acts of working together. This covenantal essence enriches the meaning of work as understood in the secular context.[49]

In transactional contracts, employees' involvement and contribution is limited to the offering of skills and abilities that are instrumental to the outcomes sought within the contract. Accordingly, the participants are steered to focus on maximizing self-interest and managing expectations. In comparison, a relational contract is more open-ended, subjective and evolves over time. It is based on long-term fairness, obligations

48 W.R. Forrester, *Christian Vocation: Studies in Faith and Work* (London: Lutterworth, 1951), 23–7.

49 As Stackhouse asserts, 'a calling is more properly understood as a spiritual matter in the context of covenanted social arrangements, and one theological reason for treating work in terms of calling is to deny the notion of a fixed, naturally determined status in life for which there is no moral responsibility and no exit. We are responsible first of all to God and to those given to us to love, and not merely to "nature," for how we live our lives.' See Stackhouse, *Covenant and Commitments: Faith, Family, and Economic Life*, 69.

and reciprocity. Such social exchanges support psychosocial ties between the employee and employer. The participants involved tend to focus on equity and exchange of contributions to the relationship. It safeguards the employment relationship by providing a minimal fallback position upon its breakdown. In comparison, a covenantal relationship takes a further step into promoting healthy employment relationships. It is yet another form of relational concern based on mutual commitment and shared values of the participants. It focuses on normative and moral commitments, allegiance to shared values, and willingness to sacrifice self-interest for the common good. Therefore covenantal relationships necessitate loyalty and long-lasting personal relationship within the work environment.[50]

The covenant approach to work places work in the context of co-creation, stewardship and vocation. Herman defines covenant as enduring commitments that withstand durable contingencies. When applied to employment situations, covenanting is 'a process for creating a community of mutual accountability by engaging the wills of management and employees in the marking and fulfilling of commitments oriented to shared goals and self-restraint in the use of power'.[51] It involves promises, respect, the common good of the firm and concern for wider social goods. This covenantal view puts the notion of work in its proper place as a constructive and positive element of human life.

As shown through the concept of incomplete contracts discussed earlier, employers and employees may bring into the workplace many contingencies such as changes in the working environment or absenteeism due to unexpected illness. These contingencies are often uncontrollable and unpredictable intentions and actions generated by external complexities. They contribute to changes in expectations and outcomes. Herman points out that employers and employees are continuously present to each other with their own capacities to define and pursue purposes during the

50 Tim Barnett and Elizabeth Schubert, 'Perceptions of the Ethical Work Climate and Covenantal Relationships,' *Journal of Business Ethics* 36 (2002):280–1.

51 Stewart W. Herman, *Durable Goods: A Covenantal Ethic for Management and Employees* (Notre Dame: University of Notre Dame Press, 1997), 4.

employment process. Employees may place higher priority on job security and wage increases, while employers seek to promote productivity and control costs. Accordingly, the participants derive their own strategies and tactics ranging from the more negative means of coercion to the positive ways of empowerment. Struggles within the employment relationship may be non-vocal or invisible, and are continuous in nature. They can either lead to negative conflicts or positive cooperation. Contractual arrangements help to alleviate employment contingencies. They are behavioural devices for social actors to reduce their vulnerability to each other.[52] Terms and conditions within the contract are designed to neutralize contingencies. However, the continuous nature of the employment relationship cannot be adequately captured in a contract. The contract as a mediating tool is not self-sustainable when faced with the complexities and contingencies of employment relationships. A covenantal interpretation of the employment relationship means that the participants are united to pursue the common interest of the organization, and bind themselves not to exploit their advantage over the other during the employment process. As Herman points out, 'a covenant ethic enjoins management and employees to express lovingkindness and justice in the tactics they apply to each other ... the idea that both sides respect the moral principle central to each other's actions'.[53]

In a 2002 study, Barnett and Schubert studied 194 employees of a large retail department store to find out the relationship between work climates and covenantal relationships. They define covenantal relationships to be those based on mutual commitment and shared values, as compared to relational contracts of social exchange which rely primarily on equity and fairness. Employees who build covenantal relationships with their employers feel valued by, and value, their organization. Their findings affirm the importance of ethical climates for development of a covenantal relationship between the employee and employer. Climates that promote benevolence and moral principle foster covenantal relationships. On the other hand, those that incline towards egoism promote self-interest. A one-sided focus

52 Ibid., 34–9.
53 Ibid., 99–100.

on company profit and efficiency tend to be detrimental to development of covenantal relationships.[54] The contract relies on covenantal elements to humanize the economic arrangement, so that profits and efficiencies can be complemented by humanizing characteristics to support overall well-being. At the same time, covenant characteristics rely on the contract to safeguard the relationship against exploitation.

Within a covenantal employment relationship, employers may not be able to promise lifetime employment, but can promise best efforts to sustain conditions of employment. Employees may not be able to promise total satisfaction and compliance to employers' expectations, but can promise integrity in pursuing the best interests of the organization. Covenantal bonds develop through mutual respect, and trust is built through refraining from taking advantage of the counterpart. Covenanting is real and desirable in employment relationships because whether this awareness surfaces or not, the participants are already making and breaking promises during the continuous struggle with contingencies in the employment process.[55] Qualities such as trust, respect, integrity, love, justice, honesty and other virtues are imperatives in the well-being of employment relationships as part of fundamental human goodness.

Another advocate of the covenant approach, Mount, points out that 'covenant constitutes the community of identity and provides a vocation to work, worship, and rest in a commitment to the reign of God and its justice that encompasses all of life'.[56] However, he also identifies the dangers of corrupted covenantal relationships in the workplace. Where there is an imbalance of power and influence, the covenant can become paternalistic. Where over-reliance on trust transcends the need for record keeping and fairness, employee interests can be compromised. Misuse of the language of loyalty, teamwork and employees development can create conflicts and

54 Barnett and Schubert, 'Perceptions of the Ethical Work Climate and Covenantal Relationships,' 279–90.

55 Herman, *Durable Goods: A Covenantal Ethic for Management and Employees*, 39–40.

56 Mount, *Covenant, Community and the Common Good: An Interpretation of Christian Ethics*, 82.

abuses. Adverse workplace cultures such as excess competition or workaholic addiction can be elevated in the name of the covenant. These situations can lead to rationalization and exploitation of employees. Healthy covenantal communities encourage dissent and communication. The essence of the covenant is to promote genuine participation. Instead of suppressing contrary opinions, such communities seek to empower rather than take advantage of vulnerabilities. A covenantal workplace needs to go beyond the minimum through mutual respect and loyalty by taking into account the welfare of all its members.[57] The contract acts as a complementary means to balance the potential misuse of the covenantal relationship. It serves to maintain economic order and protect against inequality and coercion by subjecting the participants to a commonly accepted legal authority.

Just as humankind remains in the fallen state until the end of time, the workplace on earth will continue to remain an environment where the criterion of humanity is constantly violated.[58] This means that while a perfectly covenantal relationship is unrealizable, even the Two Pillars paradigm faces limitations and difficulties. It will not be easy to implement the paradigm properly and to find a balance between covenant and contract. The Two Pillars paradigm provides a dialogical framework for participants to learn the covenantal way, cultivate covenantal norms, and continue to enact covenantal characteristics together with the contractual arrangement. The balancing point, interaction and implementation depend on a number of factors such as industry context, working environment, job nature, etc. There is no clear and simple solution to the arrangement because any attempt to capture humanizing covenantal characteristics distorts and reduces them to abstractions. With this in mind, I shall proceed to examine the approach and components of the Two Pillars paradigm when applied to employment arrangements.

57 Ibid., 85–6.

58 Siker quotes Barth's assertion on work as fundamentally 'a social act involving association and comradeship'. Competition may be unnecessary but is inevitable in modern capitalist economies. For an application of Barth's theology to work ethics, see Louke van Wensveen Siker, 'An Unlikely Dialogue: Barth and Business Ethicists on Human Work,' *Annual of the Society of Christian Ethics* (1989): 131–45.

5.5 The Two Pillars Paradigm on Employment Arrangements

The Approach

Modern employment arrangements are based on the legal contract. A written contract is often expected before the commencement of work. However, this written arrangement does not exclude the assumption of implicit employment terms. As shown in the above discussion on the development of implicit and relational contracts, legal practitioners are aware of observable but non-verifiable conditions of employment that are presupposed in the employment arrangement. These implicit elements characterize employment arrangements as they comprise significant relational concerns over and above their instrumental function. Besides observable conditions, the employer-employee relationship extends to unspoken understanding and contingencies that far exceed the contractual arrangement. The contract alone is insufficient to capture all of the components. An underlying covenantal awareness is necessary to act as the foundation and to interact with the written contract in sustaining a mutually beneficial employment relationship. To understand the role and interaction of covenant and contract within the Two Pillars paradigm, its various components need to be examined. The following discussion illustrates the Two Pillars approach to employment arrangements through a parallel assimilation of the conceptual components of contract and covenant as explained in chapter 4.2.

Form and Duration of Employment

The relatively short or fixed duration of a contract renders it insufficient in capturing a long-term cooperative relationship such as that of employment. A contract can be terminated upon satisfaction of the contractual terms or penalties. On the one hand, such exit arrangements provide safeguards from abuse and allow flexibility in job transfer and organizational change. It is therefore essential to commercial decisions or personal development.

On the other hand, the exit circumstances of a written contract can facilitate breakdown of relationships because the escape clause can be used as measureable means to undo the original commitment. Relying on contract terms alone may turn the highly valued attributes of commitment and promise into calculated assertions and expectation of rewards. When the perceived returns do not match expectations, the contract no longer acts to maintain a healthy employment relationship. The contractual mechanism does not contain in itself any motives to encourage self-giving attributes or long-term perspectives of trust. It is up to the participants to be aware of the underlying covenantal attributes that necessarily act together with the contract to enable a continuing employment arrangement.

The covenantal employment relationship is open-ended and long lasting. It captures the essence of a community working together towards mutually beneficial common goals. It is not based merely on calculated personal advantage. Performance measures and rewards need to be laid out and properly represented in a contract, but the covenantal elements of a continuing and open-ended relationship are essential to make the employment arrangement work. Through the employment covenant, the employee is bound to the organization's vision and shares this with other employees in an open-ended relationship of mutuality and loyalty. Contracts are in place to safeguard interests of the participants. Covenants implicitly grant participants their identities as trustworthy employees who belong to the organization. Each employee is personally involved in a covenantal organization. Their identity and trusting orientation provide the means for handling contingencies and working out difficulties. The contract ensures outcomes are fair and efficient, while the covenant calls for loyalty and care in the employment situation at hand. Both of these attributes must work together to promote a healthy and balanced workplace culture.

Structure and Intention of Employment

Employment originates from a society of cooperative servicing whereby participants contribute their specific skills for overall effectiveness and mutual benefits. Such intentions necessarily involve communal sharing and voluntary contributions. These covenant attributes must be retained in the employment situation as part of organizational norms to promote a healthy workplace. The written employment contract provides the possibility of eroding such personal participation into impersonal exchange of labour skill and hours. In many employment situations, working to the absolute conditions of rules and terms of the contract is one mild form of a strike. This means that in reality, employees do contribute their time and personal commitment to their job. Work attitude and personal dedication are important aspects of employment. The employment arrangement is obviously not entirely impersonal, and cannot be adequately represented through an impersonal market exchange model.

The Smithian notion of the division of labour regards the action and intentions of work as motivated by self-interest. The aggregate self-interested work contributions by individuals lead to cooperative outcomes. Smith sees this structure of working together as part of human nature and rational reason, not deriving from the contract but through accidental concurrence of individual passions. Therefore Smith offers us his famous saying, that 'it is not from the benevolence of the butcher, the brewer, or the baker, that we expect our dinner, but from their regard to their own interest'.[59] Smith's assertion presupposes a natural individual passion for different talents and occupations, through which every individual exerts their own effort in exchange for goods to care for themselves. In the employment arrangement, a similar division of labour occurs with respect to work nature within the organization. Employees obtain wages that are in turn used in the market to purchase daily necessities. Although Smith does not see the division of labour as originating from contractual arrangements, contracts act to enable and further enhance the notion. During his day and age, Smith lamented that the division of labour was limited by the extent of the market.[60] This limitation has been relaxed to a great extent by the

59 Adam Smith, *An Inquiry into the Nature and Causes of the Wealth of Nations* (Indianapolis: Liberty Press, 1981), I: 27.

60 Smith dedicated a chapter in his book to discuss the limitation of division of labour due to limits of the market. See Ibid., I: 30–6.

expansion of the market through the development of a contractual and commercial system that supports industrialization, modernization and globalization. The natural pursuit of self-interest is encouraged through the contractual mechanism, but remains inadequate to maintain the overall well-being of the individual and the common good of society. Covenant awareness points towards human spiritual needs on top of materialistic concerns. Impersonal and obligatory exchanges may serve material desires, but material desires cannot fully satisfy human needs. A covenantal working environment encourages voluntary sharing. It nurtures a culture that relies not only on rules but on caring and goodwill towards fellow workers. Division of labour under contracted processes and outcomes enhances efficiency and effectiveness. At the same time, an underlying awareness of covenantal elements promotes the overall well-being and integrity in the workplace. A well-balanced employment arrangement relies on both contractual and covenantal processes to complement each other.

Relational Aspects of Employment

As we have demonstrated in the previous chapter, social goods are as valuable to the individual as material goods. This is particularly important to the employees as the workplace is an environment where they spend much of their time on a daily basis. Employees work together in a community within the organization in relationship with each other. The quality of such relationships greatly affects job satisfaction and the well-being of the participants. Organizations in turn provide a platform of cooperation and interaction that is necessary to maintain the well-being of the self. The contractual nature of relationship focuses upon interests and gains, while the covenantal nature focuses upon mutuality and giving. These elements are not necessarily exclusive of each other. The covenantal characteristics of mutuality and giving are the foundation of harmony and voluntary cooperation, whereby interests and gains of the participants are protected and attained. As organizational goals and gains are achieved, individuals share mutually in the beneficial outcomes. Both contract and covenant are therefore necessary and advantageous in the employment relationship.

Many problems inherent in a purely contract-based employment relationship can be alleviated through covenantal assertions. An employment relationship based on calculative contractual terms alone focuses entirely upon self-interest and gives rise to a sense of insecurity. The resulting relationship is susceptible to imbalance of power, coercion and fear. These adverse conditions in turn affect the quality of the relationship and defeat the contractual purpose of safeguarding mutual interests. The covenant directs the participants' attention to the common good and loving relationships, providing the necessary relational elements of security and bonding. Although these qualities cannot be measured or quantified, they are vital to the well-being and proper functioning of both the individual and the organization. Good employment relationships result in synergies that benefit productivity and efficiency, leading to enhancement of the common interest. Employees who identify with an organization take pride in their work and dedicate themselves to achieve common organizational goals. While the contract generates respect for rules and standards, the covenant ensures respect for one another. While the contract promotes responsibility on a given task, the covenant calls for responsibility towards one another. These are all essential and beneficial characteristics in the workplace. Receiving and sharing interact in the Two Pillars paradigm to build a healthy community involving participants who work together in mutuality.

Authoritative Basis of Employment

Employer and employee are by definition within a hierarchical relationship that involves command and obedience. In the New Testament, the apostle Paul teaches respect, obedience and sincerity to the slave or employee; and similar reciprocity to the employer or master (Eph. 6:5–9). Whether under the contract or covenant, an authoritative basis is in place to mediate and arbitrate upon contingencies. In a purely covenantal situation, participants rely on the divine order and communal norms to govern relationships. This is not practicable given the inter-relations of believers and non-believers as equal counterparties in the modern working environment. Under the contractual arrangement, law and regulations are set out clearly to act as the authoritative guidance to individual behaviour and corporate decisions. Institutional rules and government authority serve to protect the societal order that embraces the employment structure. However, this does not mean that covenantal elements are neglected. The covenant aspects of employment present the employees as personal agents with responsibility for their own actions. As free agents to the employment arrangement, participants respect each other by acting with responsibility and integrity. The authoritative bases here are not power or coercion, but mutually binding relationships, commitment and trust. These are of the very essence of human integrity that must coexist with law and order to govern the employment relationship.

Process and Result of Employment

The contract-based labour market is formed upon commodification of work into labour hours, and the exchange of such labour hours for monetary rewards. The emergence of the labour market results in competition and the determination of the wage level as the price component for labour. Promise and commitment to common objectives during the employment process give way to obligation and bargaining. Depending on the contract alone hinders employment outcomes because the focus on cooperation and common purposes deteriorates into continuous bargaining and evaluation for self-interest and personal reward. The Two Pillars paradigm asserts that the covenant process is an essential complement to the contract in making the employment process meaningful to human life. The quality of work and workers' satisfaction depend not only upon work nature and tasks completed, but also the interpersonal relationships and team spirit among co-workers. In this regard, covenantal themes provide valuable insights in terms of balancing the employment process with humanizing qualities that in turn contribute to productivity.

The concept of the psychological contract in legal and business literature reminds us of the significance of the employment process in the mind of the individual. The covenant components of trust and promise align expectations of the employee and employer, and allow the pursuit of common objectives. On the other hand, a purely contractual approach based on benefit and reliance requires continuing evaluation of risks and rewards. Such calculative measures are detrimental to productivity and efficiency. For example, reliance on governance or audits to verify process effectiveness increases costs in both time and monetary terms. In an environment of covenantal foundation, resources allocated to these verification measures can be reduced or refocused to product quality or task enhancement.

Morality of Employment

In the organization, the employee is not merely something useful for production purposes. The employee participates freely, and continuously makes individual decisions that affect the overall benefit of the organization. The employer relies on employees to perform their duties diligently and effectively. These implicit requirements in the working environment presuppose moral integrity on the part of the employee. In return, the employee needs to have a certain level of trust in and reliance on, the morality of the employer and the organization to carry out business in an ethical manner. When the market views labour as a commodity, it loses its motive to promote ethical behaviour unless such ethical choices are directly tied to self-interested outcomes. The erosion of morality in behavioural decisions is detrimental to work relationships in many ways. For example, when trust and commitment is eroded, employee turnover rates may decrease productivity. As implicit ethical standards are lowered, the quality of services and goods produced may decrease. Additional costs may be required to safeguard morality in the workplace by establishing and enforcing written codes of conduct. Under the written contract or corporate governance, rules and standards take the place of individual judgement when making ethical decisions. To enhance the morality of organizations and therefore society as a whole, ethical awareness needs to be broadened to the communal level in a covenantal way. With a covenant awareness, organizations nurture an appropriate culture and ethical norms that enhance both the integrity of the individual employee and the organization as a whole.

The Implications

When applied to long-term employment arrangements, the Two Pillars paradigm asserts that contract and covenant work together to ensure a balanced employment arrangement that is mutually beneficial to all parties involved. Individual employees should have their needs protected and cared for, while they work in an environment that nurtures communal relationships and the well-being of the whole person. Employers are to entrust employees with the appropriate organization resources and objectives, while being rewarded with loyalty and commitment from the workforce. The organization as a whole not only strives towards productivity and profitability, but also retains a continuing healthy community of cooperation and harmony. To achieve a healthy balance between contract and covenant, it is necessary for management to focus resources on the covenantal components of the Two Pillars paradigm. This is because contractual arrangements involve written terms and quantifiable interests that naturally capture the attention of participants. The contract needs to be placed within a culture that promotes covenantal values to ensure implicit values are properly nurtured. This requires, first of all, top-down initiatives of covenantal leadership. Covenant characteristics are then related from the employer through management to the workers, forming a set of organizational norms that develop into a culture of the workplace. Further education and the increase in awareness encourage the participants to treasure covenantal values as the foundation of contractual interests.

The application of the covenant concept to society and business ethics is not new, but is often neglected. Pava asserts that covenantal organizations require covenantal leadership. By this, he means an emphasis on the characteristics of the covenant being open-ended, long-term in nature, and respectful of human integrity. Ambiguity is embraced as part of mutual responsibility by leaving the relationship open-ended rather than purely contractual. There is no time limit to the relationship. It protects the integrity, uniqueness and personhood of the participants by presupposing human freedom. At the same time, a background of relational order is nurtured in the employment environment to enable the exercise of human freedom.[61] Executives in the organization need to work together to promote a covenantal atmosphere that encourages openness, participation and mutual respect. The value of a positive working relationship and a sense of community in the workplace have long been noted in management approaches such as team-building concepts and workplace enhancement programmes. These tools should be developed to promote a solid covenantal foundation in the workplace.

Another example of communal awareness is the need for organizational governance to promote a healthy and ethical working environment. Caldwell and Karri present a conceptual framework based on stewardship theory characterized by covenantal relationships. They argue that organizational governance designed on a covenantal approach is more effective in building trust. Taking the covenantal relationship as a specialized form of relational contract, they argue that incentives and controls designed through contractual mechanisms can hardly build trust in the absence of covenantal relationships. They find the stewardship model ethically superior when compared with the agency model, because it honours the social obligations and duties to all stakeholders. The covenant approach to the stewardship model incorporates the ability to look internally within both the self and the organization, as well as towards the external environment in terms of organizational needs. This approach is consistent with the traditional management literature that recognizes organizational obligations as multi-dimensional, involving multiple aspects of economic and social performance. The covenant model supports a framework for managing change, promoting organizational culture and guiding moral development.[62]

61 Moses L. Pava, 'The Many Paths to Covenantal Leadership: Traditional Resources for Contemporary Business,' *Journal of Business Ethics* 29 (2001): 85–93.

62 Cam Caldwell and Ranjan Karri, 'Organizational Governance and Ethical Systems: A Covenantal Approach to Building Trust,' *Journal of Business Ethics* 58 (2005): 249–59.

The Two Pillars paradigm on employment arrangement implies a broadening of the meaning of work to embrace its rich and complex notions. Human work is instrumental, ontological, relational and more.[63] It is fundamental to the daily lives of all individuals. It supports the functioning of society as a whole. It can be paid or unpaid. Its process and outcome are both invaluable to the participant. As Meeks implies, the meaning of work should be expanded to embrace all aspects of activities within a covenantal society.

> The comprehensive meaning of work is active participation in the communal, social process. A new definition of work will have to go beyond the description of work as merely productive, wage earning, business, or professional. When we limit work to these definitions, the broader dimensions of work from which society actually lives remain invisible or repressed. Work is falsely defined unless we include reproductive or generative work. This includes all forms of familial and social service. The value of work has to do with increasing relationships among human beings and between human beings and God.[64]

63 In the Reformed theology of Barth, work takes on an even broader meaning in terms of human action. Within the freedom of human action in obedience to the Creator, the cosmos reveals the fact that it is upheld and governed by the order of creation both in its resourcefulness and limitation. In this cosmic sphere, human persons work to serve the coming of God's kingdom in the claim of their own existence as human creatures. Accordingly, human work is intended to be the fulfilment of the cosmic unity granted by the Creator. Rather than assisting in the Creator's work in any way, work is simply a form of obedience to God's command in creation. It reminds humankind of its creatureliness and relational nature. Through this essential activity, human persons cooperate in promoting their own existence. The basic motive of work is to earn our daily bread. This must be done in relationship with others, and must target genuine needs rather than superabundant desires and wants. There are other limitations in terms of specific needs, capabilities and circumstances. These mean that work is finite and must reside within boundaries such as the Sabbath command. At the same time, it is a positive affirmation of life. See Barth, *Church Dogmatics*, III/4: 516–51.

64 Meeks, *God the Economist: The Doctrine of God and Political Economy*, 154.

5.6 Further Applications and Insights

I have illustrated the mutual dependence and complementary interaction between covenant and contract by taking long-term employment arrangements as an example. My purpose of distinguishing between the two concepts is not to segregate them independently, but to reveal the characteristics and implications of each concept. It is thus demonstrated that total independence of covenant or contract is neither practical nor beneficial to the economy and society as a whole. The Two Pillars elements of fixed duration versus open-endedness, impersonal versus personal structures, self-interest versus the common good, institution rules versus personal agency, agreement versus commitment, individual ethics versus culture norms, etc., are in fact closely knitted together and interact continuously in dynamic ways under a given situation and changing economic circumstances. It is therefore vital that both covenant and contract are understood and enacted in economic activities such that there can be a healthy balance between objective functionality of economic transactions and subjective concerns over the well-being of the individual and of humankind.

The example in this chapter is limited to the overall application and insights offered by the Two Pillars paradigm to employment arrangements. In order to implement the Two Pillars in a given employment situation, we need to further investigate the specific circumstances of a give job. These may include specific industry, job nature, skills level, organizational structure, management style, wage structure, work environment, etc. In any given situation, an awareness and enactment of both covenant and contract characteristics would assist in deriving a well-balanced arrangement with a focus towards long-term relationships and mutual benefits. In particular, service industries that focus on the quality of human life benefit the most from the awareness and enactment of covenant characteristics.[65] These

65 For examples of how the covenant concept contributes to the study of ethics and care of patients in the medical profession, see Joseph J. Fins, 'From Contract to Covenant in Advance Care Planning,' *Journal of Law, Medicine and Ethics* 27 (1999):

may include medical and healthcare, education, social work, etc. In any typical organization, the covenant concept contributes to reflections over organization structure, management style and teamwork.

Further research is needed to examine alternate forms of employment arrangements in the modern market that may or may not be continuous in nature. These include nonstandard employment arrangements such as part-time, temporary and contract work.[66] Work arrangements that contain a short-term contractual focus and leave an open-ended renewal possibility may trigger additional issues in respect of job quality, employer-employee relationships, performance measurements, etc. Taking the situation one step further, the issues of employment redundancy and unemployment can also be examined through insights from the Two Pillars paradigm. In the modern context, employment redundancies may result from business relocation, changes in job nature, outsourcing, technological advancement, changes in ownership, business closure, etc. These may result in compulsory redundancies that force the early termination of contractual employment. Fundamental covenantal concerns re-emphasize the need for practical assistance and care both from the wider society and the employer concerned. Insights from covenant characteristics provide resources for further research into these redundancy situations and the related unemployment issues by pointing out the fundamental human need for work, the communal need for mutual caring and cooperation, and the possibility to work out transitional measures to help those in need of paid employment within the framework of covenantal relationship in the wider society.[67]

46–51; William F. May, 'Code, Covenant, Contract, or Philanthropy,' *The Hastings Center Report* 5, no. 6 (1975): 29–38; and Lesa W. Lawrence, et al., 'A Study of the Pharmacist–Patient Relationship: Covenant or Contract?,' *Journal of Pharmaceutical Marketing and Management* 9, no. 3 (1995): 21–40.

66 For a useful survey of sociological research on nonstandard employment relations, see Arne L. Kalleberg, 'Nonstandard Employment Relations: Part-time, Temporary and Contract Work,' *Annual Review of Sociology* 26 (2000): 341–65.

67 For studies on changing forms and relationships of employment, and the search for alternatives, see David Marsden, 'The "Network Economy" and Models of the Employment Contract,' *British Journal of Industrial Relations* 42 (2004): 659–84;

It calls for greater priority to be placed on the fundamental human needs such as work opportunities and mutual cooperation, over and above the human quest for efficiency and profits.

As we have seen, the Two Pillars paradigm presents an analytical tool that contributes to the observation and analysis of a given economic activity. The employment arrangement is only one of the many contract-based commercial market arrangements in modern society. Others may include property ownership, capital deployment, banking arrangements, financial exchange, commodity futures, international trade, etc. Contractual arrangements in all markets require covenantal assertions to provide a complementary balance. As illustrated through the employment arrangement, the employment contract alone does not embrace all essential elements that are vital to the well-being of the individual and the organization. The contract can safeguard and protect, yet it may also erode to coerce and exploit in the absence of covenantal integrity. Both the contract and covenant are there as tools and means to protect common interest and promote the common good.

A perfect economic order is not realizable on earth. Accordingly, the Two Pillars paradigm itself faces limitations and possibilities of distortion due to human sinfulness and finitude. Its effect is difficult to measure and involves many unquantifiable elements. Depending on the economic environment, context and issues at hand, the interaction between covenant and contract may differ and needs to be carefully worked out. Nevertheless, a proper Two Pillars structure reminds participants of the need to balance utility goals with humanizing elements for the well-being of the whole person. In particular, where modern markets and employment arrangements tend towards reliance on the contract, it is essential to cultivate the covenantal virtues and norms that complement the development of a humanized market. Using the Two Pillars paradigm as a framework for dialogue with the work of economists, I shall now turn to an exploration of fundamental market motif, assumption and approach.

---

and Kenneth R. Brousseau, et al., 'Career Pandemonium: Realigning Organizations and Individuals,' *Academy of Management Executives* 10, no. 4 (1996): 52–66.

CHAPTER 6

Theology and Economics in Dialogue

This chapter applies the Two Pillars paradigm in public dialogue with the work of economists, the economic approach and its assumptions. I will start by returning to the work of Adam Smith, the father of economics, to discuss and draw implications from his system that serves as the origin of economic theories. Moving from the original market motif to modern economics, I will then examine the assertions of Gary Becker, a renowned Nobel laureate who pioneered application of the economic approach to social behaviour. I will also draw upon the work of feminist economists who attempt to go beyond fundamental economic theory and econometrics to embrace an evaluation of the economic approach and its alternative use. The issues of market morality and government regulations are then discussed. In doing so, I place the Two Pillars paradigm in public discourse with a view to presenting ideas and alternatives that may illuminate the decisions and choices we make in the modern market.

I claim that the Smithian market motif originates from a worldview of spontaneous order that differs from the revelatory and relational order of the covenant. Accordingly, the motif is deficient in its presuppositions concerning humanity and community, these being based on impersonal contract rather than personal human qualities. At the same time, economic models that are applied beyond market exchanges to human behaviour degrade the value of nonmarket human activities. I argue that to rediscover and enact human qualities in the market, we must be aware of market limits and enact covenant characteristics to balance market activities. This extends to our understanding of morality and government policies. The maintenance of a healthy economic market is a continuous balancing act between the interaction and enactment of covenant and contract.

6.1 Market Motif: The Smithian System of Self-Interest and Sympathy

The modern market and its complexities are a result of gradual economic development throughout human history, affected by the intentional and unintentional decisions of society and market participants along the way. From Adam Smith's moral philosophy to contemporary mathematical models, the market continues to experience changes in response to the changing structure and needs of society. Yet its primary motivators remain the same. The market is driven by human needs and desires for economic activities, and therefore structured and formed by its participants. The market motif depends upon the enactment of human nature and its related values and worldviews. Theories about economics originate from the Smithian worldview of human nature that in itself has undergone continuous development in the form of new theories and interpretations. Where did we start and where are we heading? To find the answer to the underlying market motif of the original Smithian system, I examine its worldview and implications on the economic market. My argument is that the Smithian system sees economic activities as a natural, spontaneous order, leaving the market to develop naturally into its current contract-based structure. The resultant contract-based market structure is only a partial resolution of human need for economic activity and overall well-being. In contrast, the covenant concept presupposes a worldview based on revelation and divine providence. Its relational characteristics capture the essence of true humanity as persons in community with each other, and within the original intentional of the order of creation. Accordingly, covenantal concerns are essential parts of economic activities that must be rediscovered to promote human well-being in the market.

There is an underlying perception of the Deity in Smith's writings as he grew up in a Christian family and church environment. However, a closer look quickly reveals the tendency to stray from an authoritative Creator who actively participates in providential care, to an Author who created the natural order and left it in continuous natural evolution. Most scholars identify Smith as a deist, although a few question his commitment to belief in God, asserting that elements of the deity in his writing may have been there to avoid opposition from the church.[1] Although providence seems to have a part to play in his system, it takes place in a mysterious, hidden way widely known as the work of the 'invisible hand'.

> The all-wise Author of Nation has ... taught man to respect the sentiments and judgments of his brethren; to be more or less pleased when they approve of his conduct, and to be more or less hurt when they disapprove of it. He has made man ... the immediate judge of mankind; and has, in this respect, as in many others, created him after his own image, and appointed him his vicegerent upon earth, to superintend the behaviour of his brethren.[2]

The extent and nature of Providentialist underspinning of Smith's system is subject to wide debate, but its presupposition of a spontaneous order is evident.[3] This means that the origin of economics contains in

1 Deists generally refers to those who believe that God has created a natural order of reason and logic, without further revelation or intervention in human life. Deism is a vague term in itself with deists taking many types and forms under no consistent scheme. Byrne points out that deists have in common only their readiness to questions traditional revealed religions. Since Adam Smith has not mentioned religion and only hinted about his beliefs in his writings, his specific view of religion is subject to debate. Nevertheless, Smith's philosophical assertions clearly contain an evolutionary undertone that leads most to identify him with deism. For details about natural religion, natural theology and deism, see Peter Byrne, *Natural Religion and the Nature of Religion: The Legacy of Deism* (London: Routledge, 1989), 1–79.

2 Adam Smith, *The Theory of Moral Sentiments* (Indianapolis: Liberty Press, 1981), 128–30.

3 Scholars vary in their views about the religious assumptions in Smith's work, or what he means by the invisible hand. Niebuhr finds Smith's system embracing a divine order that seeks the well-being and happiness of all. Oswald describes Smith's system as one that presupposes a single grand mechanical system. Davis identifies the invisible hand as any classical god, a deceptive one hidden in the framework of law and government order. Rothschild interprets the invisible hand as a 'useful joke'. Hill suggests that Smith's model is teleological, extending it beyond a mere evolutionist concern. Evensky gives a good summary of Smith's moral philosophy in terms of its evolutionary vision and consideration of religious faith. A thorough discussion of

itself a tendency for a type of natural, spontaneous order that is distinct from revelation or the existence of a relational God. Because of this fundamental difference in worldview between Smith's spontaneous order versus a revelatory and relational order, the covenant concept has never been considered by Smith. The Smithian worldview largely promotes a self-regulatory economic order, whether its design is teleological or not. As we have seen in chapter 4, the general principles of contract law and contractual arrangements developed during the late seventeenth to eighteenth century, leading to the gradual formation of the contract-based market. Covenant characteristics based on creation, revelation, community and the regard for personal relationship are gradually eroded as markets lean towards a focus for a measurable, contractible exchange of goods and services.

The original Smithian system of human nature starts with 'sympathy', the non-experiential comprehension of others' feelings. According to Smith, there is an 'impartial spectator' within each individual that puts oneself in the situation of the other and forms an imaginary judgment of the situation. The impartial spectator's cognitive judgment provides feedback that triggers our feelings or emotions. This results in sympathy, allowing us to see pleasure or pain upon the fortune or misfortune of others. We therefore conceive other people's emotions although we do not experience them ourselves. The impartial spectator who approves or disapproves of a motive or action also becomes the basis for the moral standards of the

---

Smith's religious views and what the invisible hand means is beyond the scope of this book. It is sufficient for the purpose of my argument to establish a general presupposition of deistic, natural, spontaneous order underlying Smith's work. See H. Richard Niebuhr, 'The Religious Assumptions of Adam Smith,' *Journal of Theology for Southern Africa* 44 (2006): 6–22; Donald J. Oswald, 'Metaphysical Beliefs and the Foundations of Smithian Political Economy,' *History of Political Economy* 27 (1995): 449–76; J. Ronnie Davis, 'Adam Smith on the Providential Reconciliation of Individual and Social Interests: Is Man Led by an Invisible Hand or Misled by a Sleight of Hand?,' *History of Political Economy* 22 (1990): 341–52; Emma Rothschild, 'Adam Smith and the Invisible Hand,' *American Economic Review* 84, no. 2 (1994): 319–22. Hill, 'The Hidden Theology of Adam Smith,' 1–29; and Jerry Evensky, 'Adam Smith's Moral Philosophy: The Role of Religion and Its Relationship to Philosophy and Ethics in the Evolution of Society,' *History of Political Economy* 30 (1998): 17–42.

individual. As a result, the individual learns and develops from the feedback of surrounding people.

Contrary to common perceptions, Smith's view of human nature is not entirely egocentric.[4] He asserts that self-interest itself can become virtuous or evil depending on the consequential acts of the individuals. Smith sees rational self-interest as an unmitigated social good. This social good is beneficial for self and others because it is derived from the sympathetic feedback of others. It is supposed to be self-correcting as each individual seeks self-command by taking care of the 'good' of the self under sympathy with one another. Accordingly, the sympathetic concern for others balances the concern for oneself. This means that a person living in a community is not driven solely by self-interest but also considers sympathetic feedback from others. The communal aspect of human life acting as an essential balance to self-interest is a core element of Smith's system of human nature.

Smith places the role of morality within the self-interested mechanism. The virtue of self-interest in Smith's system is termed 'prudence'. Prudent individuals perform admirable acts for their own well-being. Smith finds that 'concern for our own happiness recommends to us the virtue of prudence: concern for that of other people, the virtues of justice and beneficence; of which, the one restrains us from hurting, the other prompts us to promote that happiness'.[5] To Smith, one always tends to sympathize with the benevolent affections, but at the same time needs to maintain a healthy self-interest based on a natural survival instinct. Society expects individuals to pursue their own self-interest, and admire those who strive to do so. He sees this as the natural and general order.

4 Werhane appropriately points out that 'according to Smith, human beings are not motivated merely by selfish passions or self-interest; both prudence and benevolence are virtues; and the basic virtue is not benevolence but justice'. See P.H. Werhane, *Adam Smith and His Legacy for Modern Capitalism* (Oxford: Oxford University Press, 1991), 23–4.

5 Smith, *The Theory of Moral Sentiments*, 262.

> The pursuit of the objects of private interest ... ought to flow rather from a regard to the general rules which prescribe such conduct, than from any passion for the objects themselves ... Even a tradesman is thought a poor-spirited fellow among his neighbours, who does not bestir himself to get what they call an extraordinary job, or some uncommon advantage. This spirit and keenness constitute the difference between the man of enterprise and the man of dull regularity.[6]

According to Smith, our natural tendency is to sympathize more with joy than sorrow, parade riches, and conceal poverty. Therefore our sentiment is to pursue riches and avoid poverty. We sympathize with the wealthy and powerful, and tend to protect their interests in disproportion to those of the poor. This is because rank and wealth represents human desires that we long for and tend to preserve. In our imagination, the pain associated with losses experienced by the wealthy is more agonizing than losses by those already in poverty. Accordingly, we tend to honour and respect those of higher social rank. To Smith, this natural sympathy helps to form the order of society.[7]

> The pleasures of wealth and greatness ... strike the imagination as something grand and beautiful and noble, of which the attainment is well worth all the toil and anxiety which are so apt to bestow upon it.[8]

This means that individual self-interest naturally prioritizes the pursuit of wealth and power not because of psychological security or self-interest alone, but due to our fundamental sentiment of sympathy. In Smith's system, this underlying sentiment for sympathy provides a natural order for preservation of humankind.

Having observed this system of natural order, Smith finds benevolence rather idealistic and unnatural in the face of self-interest and sympathy. This is because benevolence alone can neither lead to virtuous acts, nor can it become a primary motive for these acts. Rather than following our benevolence to help the poor, we sympathize with ranks and power in the

6 Ibid., 172–3.
7 Ibid., 50.
8 Ibid., 183.

pursuit of self-interest. This leads to his famous assertion of self-interest as the primary motive for merchants to provide their goods and services, as follows:[9]

> [M]an has almost constant occasion for the help of his brethren, and it is in vain for him to expect it from their benevolence only. He will be more likely to prevail if he can interest their self-love in his favour, and shew [*sic*] them that it is for their

9 I have moved from Smith's *The Theory of Moral Sentiments* ('TMS') to *An Inquiry into the Nature and Casues of the Wealth of Nations* ('WN') by taking a consistent view of his approach. In Germany during the late 1890s, economists questioned whether there had been contradictory concepts of human nature between TMS and WN. This started a long-standing debate known as 'das Adam Smith problem'. Economists from the German Historical School are of the opinion that TMS presents human beings as benevolent or altruistic creatures who are idealistically motivated to moral action through sympathy for others. In contrast, WN depicts human beings as egoistic and motivated exclusively by self-love and desires for material gain. Raphael and Macfie, the editors of the 1976 TMS, find that Smith himself provided the best evidence against the idea of a conflict between the two works by referring to WN in the advertisement to edition 6 of TMS. Smith saw WN as a continuation of TMS, and proposed to write another book on law and government, which never got published before his death. In terms of the consistency in content, Evensky argues that TMS is the voice of the moral philosopher while WN is a practical-prescriptive voice. Nieli treats self-interested acquisitiveness in economic relationships versus higher virtues of love and benevolence as different 'spheres of intimacy'. Ones ken takes the TMS as a regulating basis for economic behaviour in the WN. Teichgraeber points out that the originators of das Adam Smith Problem misconceived Smith's account of sympathy by equating it with benevolence alone, and then compared it with the disavowal of benevolence in the WN. The majority of scholars generally conclude that Smith is consistent in his approach from TMS to WN. See comments by D.D. Raphael and A.L. Macfie in the introductory chapter of Ibid., 20–5; Jerry Evensky, 'The Two Voices of Adam Smith: Moral Philosopher and Social Critic,' *History of Political Economy* 19 (1987): 447–68; Russell Nieli, 'Spheres of Intimacy and the Adam Smith Problem,' *Journal of the History of Ideas* 47 (1986): 611–24; August Oncken, 'The Consistency of Adam Smith,' *The Economic Journal* 7 (1897): 443–50; Richard F. Teichgraeber, 'Rethinking Das Adam Smith Problem,' *Journal of British Studies* 20 (1981): 106–23; and Leonidas Montes, 'Das Adam Smith Problem: Its Origins, the Stages of the Current Debate, and One Implication for Our Understanding of Sympathy,' *Journal of the History of Economic Thought* 25 (2003): 63–90.

> own advantage to do for him what he requires of them. Whoever offers to another a bargain of any kind, proposes to do this. Give me that which I want, and you shall have this which you want, is the meaning of every such offer; and it is in this manner that we obtain from one another the far greater part of those good offices which we stand in need of. It is not from the benevolence of the butcher, the brewer, or the baker, that we expect our dinner, but from their regard to their own interest. We address ourselves, not to their humanity but to their self-love, and never talk to them of our own necessities but of their advantages.[10]

According to Smith, the market is a self-correcting mechanism based on human nature, whereby economic agents compete to satisfy market demands for their own advantage. He finds this system self-constraining and mutually beneficial to everyone involved, not out of an egocentric self-interest based on greed, but a sympathetic self-interest for the preservation of humankind. Werhane asserts that the ideas of maximizing utility, narrow self-interest, individualism and the morally free invisible hand have all been erroneously attributed to Smith.[11] Smith is more a realist, developing the ideal of economic order in harmony with natural order.[12] He places the economic agent pursuing self-interest in the context of the need for cooperation. This means that people help one another so that they can care for themselves. Mutual dependence forms the basis of sympathetic self-interest in society.[13]

Smith admits that admiration and worship of wealth and power are corrupting, leading to neglect of the poor. Appearance and accomplishments become more admired than the inner virtues of a warrior. Underlying Smith's system is an evolutionary trend presupposing the preservation of humankind as the ultimate goal of human nature.

10 Smith, *An Inquiry into the Nature and Causes of the Wealth of Nations*, 26–7.

11 In the nineteenth-century, the 'invisible hand' becomes synonymous with the 'price mechanism' in economic analysis. For details about the modern debate between various schools of economic thoughts and new interpretations of the Smithian system, see Jan Peil, *Adam Smith and Economic Science: A Methodological Reinterpretation* (Cheltenham: Edward Elgar, 1999), 157–77.

12 Werhane, *Adam Smith and His Legacy for Modern Capitalism*, 5.

13 D.D. Raphael, *Adam Smith* (Oxford: Oxford University Press, 1985), 93–4.

> The self-love of man embraced … his body and all its different members, his mind and all its different faculties and powers, and desired the preservation and maintenance of them all in their best and most perfect condition. Whatever tended to support this state of existence was, therefore, by nature pointed out to him as fit to be chosen; and whatever tended to destroy it, as fit to be rejected.[14]

To Smith, nature is concerned primarily with the most effective and efficient means to ensure survival of the species and of social harmony. Each individual needs to be taken care of in the best way. The most effective and efficient means to do so is for each individual to look after himself or herself because a given individual does this better than looking after another individual.

> Every man is, no doubt, by nature, first and principally recommended to his own care; and as he is fitter to take care of himself than of any other person, it is fit and right that it should be so. Every man, therefore, is much more deeply interested in whatever immediately concerns himself, than in what concerns any other man.[15]

Smith's system is optimistic in the sense that prudence based on self-interest is seen as one of the virtues itself. In his system, the pursuit of self-interest by each individual in society will eventually work together and converge to cultivate a harmonious and efficient market. Against this is the pessimist's view that the market is viable only if self-interest is restrained by exogenous standards. To the pessimists, the market releases self-interest from moral restraints, erodes social ties, promotes individualistic advantages, substitutes cooperation by competition, and favours materialistic or hedonistic values.[16] Is the optimistic convergence of market sentiments towards an opulent economy possible? Paradoxically, the theological view of humankind is both pessimistic and optimistic. It is pessimistic in the sense that the human person whose nature of 'goodness' has been twisted by sinfulness cannot reach perfect goodness by itself. This assertion stands in direct contrast to the optimistic convergence of economic life based on

14 Smith, *The Theory of Moral Sentiments*, 272.

15 Ibid., 82–3.

16 Ian Maitland, 'Virtuous Markets,' *Business Ethics Quarterly* 7 (1997): 17–31.

natural evolution. At the same time, the theological worldview is optimistic in that there is providential order in this world and eschatological hope in the coming world. As such, it offers a positive outlook directed to the possibility of salvation upon seeking the truth. Taking a stance on natural evolution and relying on rational self-interest to evolve to an opulent market on its own is not feasible. To provide a solution for this deficiency, Smith relies on institutional measures to facilitate the market so that society will progress and converge into an ethical balance of sentiments, with self-command of the individual and a mature government to enforce justice.[17] Although Smith's system maintains a positive outlook, in reality the continuing striving for wealth and greatness leads to vanity or dead ends rather than the social harmony he proposes. The increase in wealth of a small minority does not add to the increase in wealth of the average individual, because of the problem of unjust distribution. The market does not naturally lead to an equitable distribution, as is evident from the increase in poverty and the disparity of wealth in rich and poor countries alike. On the other hand, institutional policies for re-distribution may hinder economic growth. The contemporary market seems to face a dead end and divergence of interests, rather than the convergence that Smith has predicted.

In Smith's system, instead of a moral sense of right and wrong, we use our passion and imagination to project what we are to others. Sympathy becomes the primary source of approval or disapproval. This system, whether truly naturalistic or not, is rather dangerous and arbitrary. Since there is no external standard or reference point for judgment except for our encounter with the other, one can act immorally or irrationally according to passionate inclinations. Smith's approach is to analyse the human passions in order to channel them to morally beneficial directions through social institutions.[18]

17 Evensky points out that this process is based on chances, circumstances, as well as international and unintentional consequences of individual actions. The ultimate outcome is general opulence. For a more detailed discussion, see Evensky, 'Adam Smith's Moral Philosophy: The Role of Religion and Its Relationship to Philosophy and Ethics in the Evolution of Society,' 10–72.

18 Muller observes that Smith's project is 'to take man as he is and to make him more like what he is capable of becoming, not by exerting government power and not

This worldview stands in direct contrast with the neo-Augustinian view that due to original sin, virtues cannot be derived entirely from the natural self, but must reside on the possibility of transcending sinful human nature through grace. Accordingly, no natural action is truly virtuous. Put in Smith's terms, the impartial spectator can never be impartial but must at least be partially influenced by self-interest and desires. The benevolent act, while already imperfect and unnatural under the system of sympathy, would never be truly benevolent. Approbation confirms the assertion that human nature only strives for the appearance of being virtuous, and that any such act can only be of apparent virtue.

Smith agrees that religion affords strong motivation for the practice of virtues.[19] Under his system, religious belief is part of the approbation and disapprobation process. Our motives depend on the natural agreeableness of sentiments and the precision of the rule imposed upon us in our system of belief. Smith's sense of the Deity is supported by the motive of self-interest, allowing the believer to strive towards the infinite goodness of his Creator.

> The sense of propriety too is here well supported by the strongest motives of self-interest. The idea that however we may escape the observation of man, or be placed above the reach of human punishment, yet we are always acting under the eye, and exposed to the punishment of God, the great avenger of injustice, is a motive capable of restraining the most headstrong passions, with those at least who, by constant reflection, have rendered it familiar to them.[20]

This suggests that according to Smith, the most important virtues of self-command, prudence, benevolence or justice are driven by fear of the Deity. Perhaps this represents Smith's awareness of the limitations or even sinfulness within human nature. Yet the mere negative passions of fear are not strong enough in themselves to uphold the basic virtues that

---

primarily by preaching, but by discovering the institutions that make man tolerably decent and may make them more so'. See Jerry Z. Muller, *Adam Smith in His Time and Ours* (New Jersey: Princeton University Press, 1993), 49–50.

19 Smith, *The Theory of Moral Sentiments*, 171.

20 Ibid., 170.

Smith proposes. Consequently, Smith himself seems to have given up on benevolence when he concludes that self-interest and sympathy within human nature are the major and overriding drivers of the market.

Self-love is acknowledged in the biblical commandment to 'love thy neighbour as thyself' (Lev. 19:18). We are commanded to love others as much as ourselves. Here, the virtue of loving the other is lifted to the level of loving oneself, presupposing that by nature one does love oneself predominately and to a great extent. Instead of moving from self-love to a relational notion of loving others, the Smithian system moves from an impartial spectator's judgement and a non-experiential sympathetic response to self-interest. Rather than the biblical, personal, relational concept of loving oneself and others, Smithian self-interest and sympathy remain impersonal. This is not to say that Smith's view is entirely wrong. His concept of self-interest is very much grounded in sinful human nature, much deeper than he would appear to admit himself. It captures the sinful finitude of humankind as the self continues its quest to further its own interest under approval of others. Unfortunately, this finite system does not promote awareness of human goodness. On the contrary, it directs attention towards the self, leaving room for neo-Smithian economists to derive egoistic and individualistic theories that Smith himself never proposed. In fact, Smith's system reminds us that within the order of creation, there can be an innate goodness in the human person that makes sympathetic self-interest beneficial to others. Such a positive, rational view of self-interest involves conducting oneself according to the 'goodness' of creation, taking care of oneself in a healthy and appropriate way, and putting oneself in the right place under the providential order of the Creator. Rather than continuing to direct such love and affection to oneself, we should re-direct our passions to others, working towards the virtues of benevolence and justice. Indeed self-interest is part of human nature. However, one of the many elements making humankind more than its mere creaturely counterparts is the presence of will or the ability to make choices, which makes possible transcendence of our mere animal selves.

In Smith's system, self-command plays an important role in deriving actions of benevolence and justice.[21] He asserts that the most perfect self-command, when exercised in a rational and unstressed manner, allows an individual to attend to the distress of others. This is embedded in a natural order that sustains itself in the form of providence. He argues that 'by acting according to the dictates of our moral faculties, we necessarily pursue the most effectual means for promoting the happiness of mankind, and may therefore be said, in some sense, to cooperate with the Deity, and to advance as far as in our power the plan of Providence'.[22] This providential self-reliance is in line with prudence, an important virtue based on Smith's concept of self-interest. However, prudence comes from the self, while the theological assertion of providence comes from the Creator God. Prudence is limited and weak in that it can only be as good as the natural 'goodness' of the human person. Providence involves the upholding of the universe, nature and all worldly creatures therein. Many religions preach the importance of self-command and good acts. Asian religions such as Hinduism and Buddhism teach ways to command the mind and soul through meditations and good deeds. In contrast, Christianity points out that the self, or the individual, does not have the innate strength to command perfect deeds. There is the need for a higher being, a reliance on God to reign over the self and to provide the strength for self-command. Good acts have to come naturally from a willing benevolence based on strength and obedience of the heart to God. Rather than following natural self-interest at all times, the will chooses to follow God and thereby opens up the arena of benevolence with the possibility of self-giving love. Smith's system is closed, with no exit from the tragedy that sinful human nature directs itself towards. His view of human nature may be somewhat optimistic, yet it is pessimistic in the options and possibilities open to the future of humankind.

21 Smith thinks that individuals 'of the most perfect virtue' join the 'most perfect command' of their own original and selfish feelings, to the 'most exquisite sensibility both to the original and sympathetic feelings of others'. See Ibid., 152.

22 Ibid., 166.

Smith is acutely aware of the 'helplessness' within human nature. Recognizing the innate inclination of human nature, Smith asserts that the impartial spectator takes only a partial view before and after action. He thinks that 'when we are about to act, the eagerness of passion will seldom allow us to consider what we are doing, with the candour of an indifferent person.'[23] Moreover, Smith has anticipated a continuous dynamic change in the standards of the impartial spectator, and hence society in general.

> The man of to-day is no longer agitated by the same passions which distracted the man of yesterday: and when the paroxysm of emotion, in the same manner as when the paroxysm of distress, is fairly over, we can identify ourselves … with the severe eyes of the most impartial spectator. But our judgments now are often of little importance in comparison of what they were before; and can frequently produce nothing but vain regret and unavailing repentance; without always securing us from the like errors in time to come.[24]

Although Smith recognizes this deficiency, he is not able to provide any solution. His argument for convergence and natural evolution does not appear to be fulfilled. In Smith's system, justice is served through law and order, under which individuals are driven by fear and sympathy for the ranks. The future of humankind faces a dead end of fear and chaotic divergence. To Smith, conscience is rooted in self-interest and sympathy. To be a worthy individual entails looking after ourselves and following our sympathetic passions to strive towards shared social standards to attain self-approbation and harmonious mutual opulence. Economic development throughout history and the state of the contemporary market point to the fact that Smith's ideology of convergence appears unrealizable. Instead of harmony and opulence, we are confronted with poverty, inequality and distribution problems. Technology and globalization bring new controversies that point towards divergence rather than convergence. The modern individual is driven more and more by market forces that lead towards negative manifestations of egocentric self-interest rather than the rational self-interest that Smith portrays. Reconsideration of the market needs to

23 Ibid., 157.

24 Ibid., 157–8.

start from reconsideration and redirection of human strivings, rather than leaving it to a natural, spontaneous order.

6.2 Market Limits: The Economic Approach to Human Behaviour

While the spontaneous development of the market falls short of promoting the overall well-being of economic participants, the problem is coupled by the attempt to apply the economic approach to nonmarket human behaviour. The modern human person cannot avoid being a market participant at the same time. We depend on the cooperative exchange of goods and services through the economic market to provide for our daily needs. When economic activities increasingly drive the daily lives of market participants, market boundaries become increasingly blurred. Some economists have begun to extend the economic approach to nonmarket activities and human behaviour. Is there a limit to the scope and content of the market exchange? I shall examine this through the work of the renowned economist Gary Becker.[25]

Becker received the Nobel Prize in economics in 1992, for his contribution in applying the economic approach to human behaviour and interaction. His work involves capturing nonmarket variables such as human capital, economic discrimination, household and family, crime and punishment, etc. in microeconomic analysis. Such analyses attempt to reveal the role of economic variables that more realistically reflect reality, and provide insights for policy decisions. At the same time, his approach moves beyond the more fundamental economic assumptions

25 Together with esteemed economists such as Frank Knight, Theodore Schultz, George Stigler, Milton Friedman and many others, Gary Becker belongs to the 'Chicago school' of economics that claims Adam Smith as one of its own. See Evensky, '"Chicago Smith" versus "Kirkaldy Smith"', 197–203.

of a perfect market and rational human behaviour to include imperfect information and irrational decisions. Becker's definition of human capital involves indirect household activities that influence the market, such as time invested in care of children, training to improve work skills, resources put into education, etc. For example, his model of the family asserts that fertility decisions are made by taking families as productive units and children as 'durable consumer goods'.[26] Accordingly, the value of children is quantified in terms of their qualities and costs as defined by resource investment and future income potential. Although the awareness and attempt to consider human behaviour in economic analysis appear helpful and essential in the first instance, Becker's approach is problematic in the way these tools are deployed. Rather than considering how human behaviour can affect economic models, Becker approaches the question from an opposite direction, using the economic approach to model human behaviour. This method unduly reduces human behaviour to presupposed economic acts. The reduction of families to production units and children to durable goods imposes a set of calculated norms to family life.[27] This approach shows an extreme use of the contract-based model, whereby human persons become priced and contractible. I will argue that such an approach also defeats its own purpose of concrete scientific analysis because the resulting models become abstractions that do not reflect the reality of human living.

26 Gary S. Becker, *The Economic Approach to Human Behavior* (Chicago: The University of Chicago Press, 1976), 169.

27 Becker's theory of fertility assumes that parents benefit from contemplating their children's happiness. Such happiness depends on their standard of living, inheritance of capital, and the rate of return on that capital. Accordingly, Becker concludes that fertility depends solely on the degree of 'altruism' defined as the benefit to the self arising from the increase in benefit of the others, and the rate of interest in terms of return on inheritance of capital. This approach is vastly simplistic, leaving out significant considerations such as contraception, abortion, biological facts, moral considerations, religious beliefs and values, social and family relations, etc. See Barbara R. Bergmann, 'Becker's Theory of the Family: Preposterous Conclusions,' *Challenge* Jan–Feb (1996): 12.

To study how Becker derives his approach, we first examine his definition of economics and the market. Becker derives his definition of economics by comparing the scopes of various options. He finds a focus on allocation of material goods to satisfy material wants too narrow because both tangible and intangible goods are involved in economic activities. A further step is then taken to define economics in terms of the market sector.[28] Similar to that proposed by the Two Pillars paradigm, this definition places economics within the scope of production and distribution of resources through the economic market. However, Becker finds this too limiting also. Instead, he broadens the scope of economics by extending 'the allocation of scarce means to satisfy competing ends' beyond the market sector to embrace all resources including political decisions and family activities.[29] This definition allows him to extend economics beyond the market sector to embrace scarcity and choice that characterize all resources including political decisions and family activities. Becker asserts that the unique power of economics is in its approach to integrate human behaviour.[30]

According to Becker, public goods such as welfare, healthcare, education and family marriage can all be captured in the economic model through a series of tautologies. For example, the decision to marry is made when expected utility from marriage exceeds the alternatives of remaining single or continuing to search for a suitable mate. Family activities such as work decisions, education and child custody all fall within the variables of a market in marriages. Becker contends that such a marriage market naturally places people with similar background, intelligence, race, education and other factors together. Demand and supply observed during such a market

28 Becker obtains this definition from the work of A.C. Pigou, who defines economic activities as those conducted directly or indirectly through monetary exchange.

29 Becker, *The Economic Approach to Human Behavior*, 3.

30 'The economic approach assumes the existence of markets that with varying degrees of efficiency coordinate the actions of different participants – individuals, firms, even nations – so that their behavior becomes mutually consistent.' This is, as Becker points out, coordinated through prices and other market instruments that constrain the desires of participants. See Ibid., 5.

process in turn supply data necessary for decisions on government funding.[31] Becker asserts that all human behaviour involves utility maximization that results from a stable set of preferences, an optimal amount of information accumulated, and other market inputs. Accordingly, he advocates the use of the economic approach as a unified framework for understanding human behaviour.[32] Not all economists agree with Becker's approach to human behaviour and his use of economic modelling. Nevertheless, his recognition by the discipline of economics and the Nobel Prize awarded clearly indicate the pursuit towards the recognition of economics as a science that embraces all human activities.

In contrast to the survey data used in sociological analysis, Becker's sociological economic approach uses market data to capture social interactions within a market paradigm. Instead of moving from hypothesis and empirical survey to derive observed outcomes and phenomena, the economic approach starts with a market paradigm and attempt to capture social interaction through modelling of market data. Feminist economist Barbara Bergmann points out that this type of 'observation-less' theorizing is the most common way economists seek to advance the science.[33] Since the method does not start from empirical observation but from a model that abstracts data to substantiate it, the result is an abstraction that may not represent reality. If economics is a science, it should model reality in order to further study of the subject. However, Becker's economic approach puts the subject in service of the axioms and methods by expanding its scope without contributing to our knowledge of the family or other human behaviour. Such an economic approach is more rigorous than alternative methods for modelling human behaviour, but not necessarily more authentic.[34]

31 Ibid., 1–11.

32 Ibid., 14.

33 Barbara R. Bergmann, 'Needed: A New Empiricism,' *Economists' Voice* 4, no. 2 (2007): 1–4.

34 Julie A. Nelson, *Feminism, Objectivity and Economics* (London: Routledge, 1996), 66.

The market paradigm and economic modelling are helpful in understanding and analysing market behaviour. However, when these tools are extended to nonmarket human behaviour, they lead to abstractions and distortions of reality. As discussed in chapter 4, the modern market has emerged from the development of the legal contract that enables its expansion. The contract serves to safeguard and regulate the market exchange through monetary units and agreed-upon terms and conditions. When these contractual relationships are captured through the economic approach, it implies a presupposition of contractual legality, prioritization in the form of monetary value, and abstraction of human qualities. This means that all goods and services must take on a price when entering the economic model because of the necessity to translate these into monetary units. When this method is extended to nonmarket variables, all sorts of human behaviour are forced to fall into a contractual mode, and tagged with a highly abstract price that reflects a social value derived by economic constraints.

In modern times, the market is continuing to expand globally. It is increasingly important to govern the scope of application of market exchanges and their related economic analysis, so that they continue to serve human persons, rather than vice versa. The role of markets must be critically scrutinized and continuously evaluated as the market expands and becomes globalized. To establish the scope and role of the market and to give it appropriate boundaries are vital and worthwhile tasks for economists. The Two Pillars paradigm continuously reminds us that relationships must not be reduced to contractual terms. Human relationships must remain covenantal. In this regard, the covenant is a heuristic tool that calls for society to acknowledge the need for genuine human relationships that are not price driven but based on loving, caring and gifting. At the same time, human behaviour in the market is a Two Pillars process involving both contractual exchange and covenantal care. The economic approach is useful, but its assumptions and limitations must be considered when deriving conclusions and making policy decisions. More importantly, economic values should not be exclusively imposed on human lives during the process.

6.3 Market Assumptions: Economic Models and Utility Maximization

After establishing the market limits, I now turn to a review of the market itself. I contend that economic methods are useful analytical tools for the contract-based exchange, but as with all methods, its underlying assumptions need to be continuously re-examined and improved upon. The market is often considered the most effective device known for generating human goods for material well-being. However, this emphasis on efficiency and effectiveness does not equate to total human well-being. Consumption is indeed essential to physical life, but it is not final and ultimate. Material or bodily needs serve the very basic requirements for sustaining human life, the essential intermediaries to total human well-being. Yet these intermediaries alone do not ensure well-being.

Utility theory in economics presupposes utility maximization, efficiency and, in many models, perpetual growth. In this regard, Becker sees the core elements of the economic approach as 'the combined assumptions of maximizing behavior, market equilibrium, and stable preference, used relentlessly and unflinchingly'.[35] He asserts that the economic approach does not assume self-interested individuals, but is merely a method of analysis. At the same time, he admits that the analysis assumes that individuals consistently maximize their own perceived welfare, whether they are selfish or altruistic. Such behaviour is forward-looking but rooted in past experiences. The maximizing process occurs within the contracts that quantify income, time, resources, social interactions, etc.[36] Are these economic assumptions

35 Becker, *The Economic Approach to Human Behavior*, 5. In Becker's later publications, he no longer regards stable preferences as a foundational assumption of the economic approach. For a detailed analysis on Becker's elimination of stable preferences from his foundational economic assumptions, see Robert A. Pollak, 'Gary Becker's Contributions to Family and Household Economics,' *Review of Economics of the Household* 1 (2003): 116–20.

36 Gary S. Becker, *Accounting for Tastes* (Massachusetts: Harvard University Press, 1996), 139.

really neutral, serving merely as analytical tools? The answer is negative. All maximizing acts necessarily involve maximizing among objectives, whether or not these are the same among different individuals. When these maximizing processes are placed within the context of contractual human activities, they become bounded by the monetary pricing mechanism that underlies the contracts involved. Non-contractible considerations such as caring and charity are abstracted when they are turned into contractible monetary units. When this economic approach is applied to human behaviour, the market equilibrium structure and maximizing assumptions are superimposed on human life.

A closer look at these core economic assumptions further reveals the problem of diversified interests in their practical application. For example, while companies work to maximize profits, individual members do not maximize the companies' profits. They maximize their own interest in terms of external goods and individual circumstances. Therefore the problem is not the maximization of the 'content' of individual interests, but the narrow conception of this as income. There are other interests such as community, excellence, loyalty, cooperation, etc. that individuals wish to satisfy. How do we define and measure values within such a wider variety of different interests and utilities? Economic models use different utility functions to capture these diversities and derive market equilibrium. They also attempt to find equilibrium points in utility functions to observe the aggregate, rationalized outcome of these diversities. This is done by a generalization and abstraction based on presupposed market objectives in monetary and contractual terms.[37] Market participants are thus led

37 Ferber and Birnbaum assert that the construction of these behavioural economic models is honourable in the development of theory, but the complex reality of the world is ignored in these simple abstractions that do not reflect reality. They point out that rather than imposing an economic imperialism across all human behaviour, the expansion in the scope of economics should move from the observation and analysis of economics, to the provision of choices that will be instrumental in modifying existing behaviour. Economic tools should not be used to impose economic values and judgement on decision making. Instead, economists should offer information to enable people to make more realistic decisions based on their own

back to the simple motivator that governs market behaviour – the notion of self-interest. While the utility function may take into account motives other then self-interest, such qualities tend to lose their personal value to a unique human person who does not align with the typical circumstances envisaged in the model.[38]

Becker includes social interactions in economic analysis by defining them as 'social income'. Social income is the sum of the individual's income and the monetary value of the social environment of the individual. This means that human relationships in Becker's economic models are defined by monetary earnings of the self, plus the monetary value of others to the self. For instance, the monetary value assigned to a give social environment is higher if social relationships within such an environment are more intimate. In a higher-valued social environment, income redistributed to the common good is of a higher value than that in a lower-valued social environment. This is because what benefits the others also benefits the self. Examples of such transfers of value can be seen through parental care for their children, concern for welfare of members in a community, or environmental care for the future generation. Through these social interactions, the family or wider community maximizes a consistent and transitive utility function subject to the given constraints. At the same time, the utility transfer and redistribution mechanism ensure participants are taken care of through the maximizing of social income.[39]

In Becker's models, the social environment is taken as an argument in a stable utility function. This means that the normal utility function $V = V(x, y)$, becomes $U = U(x, y, S)$. In this function, x and y are goods and

values and judgement. See Marianne A. Ferber and Bonnie G. Birnbaum, 'The "New Home Economics:" Retrospects and Prospects,' *The Journal of Consumer Research* 4 (1977): 19–28.

38 Lawson points out that Becker's models focus on the effective convergence of multiple utility functions across individuals, rather than allow differing utility functions to explain individual differences. He argues that these models are deterministic and ignore individual preferences. See Daniel Lawson, 'Gary Becker and the Quest for the Theory of Everything,' *University of Notre Dame* (2004): 1–18.

39 Becker, *The Economic Approach to Human Behavior*, 280–1.

services. The variable *S* represents social influences on utility measured in terms of 'social capital'. These social influences affect the probability of a given choice, and are considered complementary to the goods and services.[40] For example, the utility from consuming beer at a given time may be affected by the social companion or environment. The variable *S* is strongest when participants are forced to conform to social norms. Accordingly, social capital directly enters as a preference factor in the economic model. The variable *S* can then be extended to include behaviour habits, time specification, or summation of other factors. The marginal utilities or optimal points can thus be further analysed. Observing these economic models in action reveals the limitations of the economic approach. While the models are useful in analyzing market situations by scientifically isolating certain variables and studying their interaction under a given set of assumptions, the models do not capture all human irrationalities and life elements. They represent abstractions of reality within their own assumptions and limitations. There can always be features and externalities missing in or misrepresented by the variable *S* that will overwhelmingly affect outcome. In addition, social relationships are dynamic and reflect the personal values and choices of the individual at a given time and context. They can differ significantly among persons, families and cultures. For example, the core feature of love among family members refutes any representation as a variable *S* in the economic function because its transcendent potential is infinite. On the one hand, egocentric assumptions can render its value to a minimal. On the other hand, a perfectly self-giving and sacrificial covenantal love yields an infinite value. The social environment presents a wide range of relational elements, human potentials and possible irrationalities that cannot be adequately represented by mathematical variables alone.

Becker finds altruism to be a major factor when tying together family interests. For example, he finds that if children are expected to help their parents in old age, even non-loving parents would save less and invest more in the children's human capital. On the other hand, altruistic parents prefer

40 Gary S. Becker and Kevin M. Murphy, *Social Economics: Market Behavior in a Social Environment* (Massachusetts: Belknap Press, 2000), 8–11.

increases in their old age consumption to equal increases in their children's. Such parents always under-invest in their children's human capital if they have made their children feel guilty in terms of their obligation to provide for their parents. This is because when they suspect that their children provide for them only because of guilt, their expectation of their children's actual willingness to help is lowered. They then lower their investment in their children to balance this expectation. Therefore, Becker concludes that guilt is an inefficient cost. To Becker, what he terms as 'so-called family values' of obligation, duty and love, are greatly affected by public policies and economic conditions. He believes that heads of families who do not plan to leave bequests try to create a warm atmosphere in order that members are willing to assist those experiencing financial difficulties. Therefore social security helping the elderly will cause family members to drift apart. The incentive to invest in creating close relationships reduces when the related future economic motives decrease.[41]

Imposing Becker's economic worldview on all human behaviour brings about a set of economic priorities to human life based on economic assumptions. When individuals and communities are all perceived to maximize their own utilities and take full advantage of given opportunities in monetary terms, all items are given an economic value that can be difficult to determine. The notions of value and fairness thus become abstract and arbitrary. Human goodness, morality and conscience are allocated a value of null when altruistic acts, family bonds, social relationships and pursuit of the common good all require justification in terms of economic benefits. This worldview reduces all aspects of human life to contractible units that are quantifiable and exchangeable, and all human relationships to contractual arrangements that contain their own terms and conditions. Becker's economic approach to the family has been praised for its policy-relevance and 'researchability'. Unfortunately, by adopting a researchable and scientific approach that suits the mathematical model, the very essence of the family unit is diminished to a set of economic abstractions. The family is observed as if it is a mechanical consumption and reproduction

41 Becker, *Accounting for Tastes*, 154–5.

unit.[42] Relying on these underlying assumptions to derive policy decisions is highly detrimental.

In the economic family models described by Becker, families no longer retain the set of human values that are characterized by self-giving love, responsibility and trust. Human bonding is not considered except in the form of quantified abstraction. Taking this one step further, it is easy to conclude that the family structure is no longer necessarily the best structure for an investment market in child bearing and human capital manufacturing. If this is the case, individuals have in fact lost their true essence of being human persons. Bergmann criticizes Becker's theory of the family for its fatally simplistic and misleading assumptions that lead to preposterous conclusions. The use of economic analytical tools on family functions fails to appreciate the actual problems by ignoring essential elements of moral, relational and emotional natures. For example, Becker 'proves' that women benefit from polygamy over monogamy because they get a higher 'price' from selling themselves into polygamy marriages. This is based on the assumption that women are willing to supply themselves to men when they enjoy a higher value consumption bundle than that outside a marriage. The consumption bundle is in turn defined as the monetary purchasing power and utilities from such purchases.[43] Nelson appropriately points out Becker's misplaced labelling and misplaced concreteness.[44] For example, children should not be taken as commodities within a parental utility function. Within Becker's approach, concepts such as altruism are defined merely in terms of monetary and contractible returns.[45] The organic ele-

42 For a specific critique on Becker's economic approach to family and fertility, see Judith Blake, 'Are Babies Consumer Durables: A Critique of the Economic Theory of Reproductive Motivation,' *Population Studies* 22 (1968): 5–25.

43 Bergmann, 'Becker's Theory of the Family: Preposterous Conclusions,' 9–12.

44 Nelson, *Feminism, Objectivity and Economics*, 74–5.

45 Bergmann points out that Becker's altruistic individual is defined as one who derives positive utility from the increase in another's consumption. See Bergmann, 'Becker's Theory of the Family: Preposterous Conclusions,' 11. This economic labelling conveniently twists the moral natural of altruism by fitting it into the utility paradigm that assigns ultimate benefits to the egocentric self. Accordingly, the head of a given family unit can be altruistic by focusing on the target to consume more without regard

ments of human life are therefore isolated from the economic models. Seemingly concrete definitions of notions such as marital bargaining and divorce threats receive a misplaced concreteness that misrepresents reality. It is an extreme misuse of scientific requirements to derive narrow and restrictive assumptions.[46]

Economics concerns human life. Its assumptions and methods should always include a concern for human qualities and communal connections. In the original Smithian system, sympathy works within the human person and leads to actions for others. However, sympathy alone is inadequate. Sen distinguishes between sympathy and commitment. Sympathy is a concern for others when the situation affects one's own welfare. When one is affected personally by the other, it is a case of sympathy. If one is not personally worse off but acts in the view of right and wrong, it is a case of commitment. Therefore sympathy is essentially egocentric, whereby one's own utility can be increased by sympathetic action. In contrast, action based on commitment is non-egocentric. Sympathetic acts are easier to measure because utility is involved. However, when the choice based on sympathy happens to coincide with that of commitment, their relative value and priority are more difficult to ascertain. The presence of uncertainties and judgement further complicates the matter. Sympathy may complicate a Pareto optimum and upset the competitive equilibrium. Nevertheless, the revised economic model will still apply. Commitment destroys the model because of the possibility of counter-preferential choices, requiring a total revamp of the entire model.[47] For example, in a repeated game such as the

---

for separate wills and interests of individual family members. The love and kindness of companionate marriage are obviously ignored in the economic approach.

46 Pollak interprets Becker's altruist model as an ultimatum game that involves a fixed sum of money. Commitment is essential to these one-shot non-cooperative ultimatum games because the game ends if the responder rejects the offer. Accordingly, the altruist in Becker's model attains a most preferred point within the constraint of offering the minimal amount adequate for keeping someone in the family. This description offers another way of presenting the egocentric self-interest maximizing nature of Becker's altruist family model. See Pollak, 'Gary Becker's Contributions to Family and Household Economics,' 126.

47 Sen, *Choice, Welfare and Measurement*, 91–3.

Prisoner's Dilemma described in chapter 5.3, motives based on sympathy and commitment interact to derive different outcomes. The same decision made by two different parties does not necessary result from the same motive. If total commitment is assumed, the model becomes empty because no alternate outcomes are possible other than the seemingly irrational choice of committing to the other party regardless of potential reward.

The approach used by Sen is one that draws upon both the usefulness and limitations of economic modelling to analyse market activities. It does not superimpose an economic imperialism to human behaviour, but assesses the interaction and impact of nonmarket human variables on economic models. This results in a more in-depth understanding of economic activities, and a new direction for policies and decision-making. A paradigm shift for the economic model needs to involve the expertise of economists in analysing and deriving these modelling assumptions and techniques, as well as the continuous awareness and reflection on market limitations and nonmarket human concerns in conducting economic activities. The latter mission is one that is taken up through the Two Pillars paradigm. The former task, together with a concern for the latter, relies on the continuing efforts of economists.

6.4 Market Morality: Ethics and the Common Good

Perhaps the most easily understood set of market variables that is subject to abstraction in the economic models is morality. The contract alone is inadequate to safeguard the ethical standards and to promote the common good that are essential to a well-balanced and harmonious society. In a modern pluralistic society, moral and ethical standards become increasingly unclear. Tradition or common consensus does not necessarily promote morality. The application of economic models to moral concerns is another area open to debate. For example, a paper by Becker and Elísa argues for offering monetary incentives to increase the supply of organs for medical transplantation. This appears to be an easy and obvious market solution to satisfy the supply shortage, if all moral and related concerns can be put aside. To price the value of organs donation, Becker and Elísa take into account the risk factor and time lost during recovery from surgical procedures. The variables considered in assessing the elasticity of demand include: waiting time, availability and access to the black market. Becker and Elísa argue that the seeming commodification of body parts is similar to the use of another woman's womb for surrogating, because paying to save lives is no different morally than paying to create lives. They also assert that since the workplace compensates workers taking higher physical risks with higher pay, physical risks are already priced in the market. For the financially deprived individuals who are more likely to sell their organs, Becker and Elísa argue that they should not be deprived of the revenue they can get from wealthy individuals.[48] From a theological point of view, the buying and selling of living organs present a problem grounded in the creation of humankind as unique persons in the image of God. The unique value and significance of each human life is received as a gift from the Creator, and therefore cannot be price-tagged. Even for the non-believer, ethical issues such as the value of human life, the priority of organ transplants, etc., should be considered rather than merely focusing on economic benefits and market demand. The covenant reminds market participants of morality issues such as caring for workers taking high risk jobs, urging employers to ensure safety measures are upheld, and ensuring workers are not exploited. It calls for the wider community to help improve the overall well-being of those living in poverty, rather than setting up markets to exploit what is left of them. The economic model should not impose its priorities to human life, but examine and set the appropriate market boundaries based on an awareness of covenant concerns.

The market has a natural tendency to erode morality because of the corrosive effect of individualistic self-interest. This self-interest concept

48 Gary S. Becker and Julio Jorge Elísa, 'Introducing Incentives in the Market for Live and Cadaveric Organ Donations,' *Journal of Economic Perspectives* 21, no. 3 (2007): 3–24.

favours the wealthy individuals because its priorities are valued in monetary terms. Nevertheless, whether it is the original notion of Smithian self-interest or the later egocentrism that drives the market, the market relies on a basic level of morality that assumes the presence of fundamental values such as honesty and fairness. Nussbaum points out that modern economics presupposes *homo economicus* as a self-interested or utilitarian maximizer, and altruism as a type of egocentrism for enhancing individual reputation. Some economists, including Amartya Sen, actively argue that these assumptions are inadequate. Sen offers sympathy and commitment as independent sources of motivation. Nussbaum asserts that this is recently confirmed through striking empirical evidence during the times of the Holocaust, when a significant number of people risked life, family, comfort and reputation to rescue the Jews.[49] Ethical motivators provide courage for deliberate actions in light of the good. In this regard, the contract is inadequate to safeguard the transcendent moral norms and ideologies that are valuable parts of human life. Accordingly, human relationships must remain covenantal in essence even though contractual arrangements are entered into as means of exchange. The elimination of covenant elements from human relationships is not only a moral problem but affects the very essence of humanity.

Traditionally, morality has always been a core area of focus in Catholic social teachings. In July 2009, Pope Benedict XVI issued the encyclical titled *Caritas In Veritate*, pointing out the importance of truth in our understanding of charity and economics. Charity is the core of Catholic social teachings and must be grounded in the love and truth that give authentic substance to human relationships. Without truth, love becomes empty and arbitrary. Benedict XVI expresses truth in the *logos* that creates *dia-logos*, the communication and communion of values. This truth enables us to let go of subjective opinions and gather for the assessment of authentic substance of all things. It points us to the charity that resides in

49 Martha C. Nussbaum, 'Flawed Foundations: The Philosophical Critique of (a Particular Type of) Economics,' *The University of Chicago Law Review* 64 (1997): 1197–1214.

Christ, a charity of love as a gift, in acceptance and communion. Truth as the foundation of charity is therefore a convergence of faith and reason, of a love that demonstrates this truth.[50] Benedict XVI's call for the awareness and rediscovery of truth as the foundation of charity is highly relevant at a time of financial turmoil and global economic crisis.

Charity as one of the core elements of morality requires authenticity that is based on the truth. This truth resides in the teachings of Christ. Benedict XVI pronounces his assertions effectively to the believing community, especially on the importance of morality and truth in the modern market. However, mere assertions on moral matters require a broader framework to place them in perspective for better understanding and enactment, especially for the non-believing community. I assert that for the non-believer, the truth remains hidden but the concepts of covenant, conscience and economic agency serve as guidance towards the truth. The covenant process challenges the conscience of human persons as agents to the economic activities that in turn require morality for proper functioning. Indeed Benedict XVI discusses useful practical issues such as intellectual property rights, the role of the government, and ecological concerns in his encyclical.[51] To further assert a theological voice that is relevant and

50 Benedict XVI asserts that 'development, social well-being, the search for a satisfactory solution to the grave socio-economic problems besetting humanity, all need this truth.' See Pope Benedict XVI, 'Caritas In Veritate,' *Encyclical Letter* (2009): par. 5.

51 Phillips points out that the encyclical makes a rare and notable foray into the intellectual property issue, particularly in the healthcare area. Intellectual property abuses may have led to irresponsible conduct and licensing protection for the rich. Nevertheless, Phillips asserts that intellectual property protection helps to address fake and harmful products. The encyclical fails to provide a balanced thesis on the positive and negative aspects of different kinds of intellectual properties. See Jeremy Phillips, 'Caveat Caritas!,' *Journal of Intellectual Property Law and Practice* 4 (2009): 603. Indeed the contractual elements of intellectual property rights have merits of their own, yet a covenant foundation is necessary to prevent excessive legalism and proper use of these protective means. What Benedict XVI is presenting resides at the level of a general framework that can be strengthened and balanced through the description of the Two Pillars paradigm.

understandable to the wider public, a broader theological foundation is necessary.[52] The covenant concept serves as a heuristic tool in this regard, and further extends the universality of moral understanding to the overall economic framework through the Two Pillars paradigm.

Values are important in the market because they present the objective goals and standards that govern all market activities. These values that steer the direction of economic development must be based on the universal truth. Benedict XVI questions the complexity and definition of 'development' in modern times. Although the world is increasing its aggregate wealth, there are also increasing inequalities.[53] Economic activities continue to involve corruption and illegality in both rich and poor countries. Multinational companies sometimes fail to respect human rights and exploit the poor. International aid often fails to reach the needy. These prevailing economic problems reiterate that mere economic and technological progress is insufficient for society. Economic development must take into account the true needs of total well-being to avoid the negative consequences of growth marked by irregularities and imbalances. These market irregularities and imbalances pointed out by Benedict XVI coincidentally align with the Two Pillars paradigm's objective to balance the market.

One of the major objectives of the Two Pillars balancing mechanism is a re-focusing of economic activities on authentic human life and the morality of human persons. Benedict XVI strongly reminds us that the human person is the focus and aim of all economic and social life. He asserts that 'the primary capital to be safeguarded and valued is man, the

52 Novak points out that some sentences in the encyclical are 'almost impossible to parse in practical terms'. I think that it is not Benedict XVI's intention to address policy details or fully analyse economic issues. Rather, the encyclical is a call for a worldview that sees economics in the form of charity based on the foundation of truth. Nevertheless, I contend that a call for charity in truth falls short of a definitive framework that adds to the process of decision making. Practical solutions to specific economic issues need to be addressed separately, but a practical and relevant overview is needed to establish market balance. See Michael Novak, 'Pope Benedict XVI's *Caritas*,' available from <http://www.firstthings.com/onthesquare/2009/08/pope-benedict-xvis-caritas-1> (cited 17 August 2009).

53 Benedict XVI, 'Caritas In Veritate,' par. 22.

human person in his or her integrity'.[54] Accordingly, issues such as work, labour mobility, welfare, inequity, freedom, marginalization, etc., those that concern human economic life, are the primary concerns of government and institutions. Culture and education must help individuals to define themselves with a nature that transcends the self, carrying the truth and morality that are necessary to promote market integrity. This includes a respect for life, the universal right to food and water for all people, as well as the right to be freed from all discrimination.[55] The enactment of human morality is presented as fundamental to human development, an integral part of authentic human living. Unfortunately, modern society is driven more by monetary economic motives than such unquantifiable human qualities. These assertions about human morality are fundamental because they form the essence of human life and truth. They are part of covenantal living.

Benedict XVI points out that 'the market is the economic institution that permits encounter between persons, inasmuch as they are economic subjects who make use of contracts to regulate their relations as they exchange goods and services of equivalent value between them, in order to satisfy their needs and desires'.[56] He calls this 'commutative justice'. In contrast, he calls for distributive justice and social justice for the market economy, in recognition of the relational nature of the market. One month after its release, a group of sixty-eight evangelical Protestants jointly acknowledge their support for the encyclical *Caritas in Veritate*, inviting discussion and responses to its content. As they indicate, the encyclical sees humankind not as the victims of globalization or economic activities, but as protagonists who work for solidarity, justice and the common good. These are norms that transcend and transform the economic motives for

54 Ibid., par. 25.

55 Benedict XVI insists on the openness to life as the core of true development, openly condemning institutions that spread abortion, promote sterilization and permit euthanasia. See Ibid., par. 28.

56 Ibid., par. 35.

profits and perpetual growth.[57] I agree that solidarity and mutual trust are vital elements for proper functioning of the market. Furthermore, it is up to the market participants to work together to attain balanced and healthy economic activities. During this process, the contract is necessary to regulate economic functions, but the contract alone does not produce the social cohesion required for proper economic activities. A proper understanding and implementation of the covenant is essential in this regard.

While Protestant and Jewish traditions reflect upon the covenant concept, Catholic social teachings use the concept of the common good. My opinion is that these are two similar but fundamentally different notions. The common good focuses on community and public goods, representing the conditions or social assets that serve the good of all societal participants.[58] The covenant, on the other hand, is a broader concept that is fundamental to human life. It embraces the common good and moves beyond it to penetrate all human relationships. The common good serves alongside other value concepts such as justice, freedom, equality and morality that are essential to humanity. The covenant is a process and means of relating for attaining the values common to societal participants, while the common good represents one of the covenant characteristics or objectives. The covenant consists of a rich history that highlights connections and solemn promises, communal bonds and justice, as well as the possibilities of plurality and hierarchy. The covenant pillar of the Two Pillars market continuously reminds participants of the need to enhance human relationship, responsibility, morality and cooperation. It carries the common good as one of its many objectives, together with the quest for caring relationships, self-giving love and authentic human living.

The common good is recognized and advocated in the development of welfare economics. Lutz understands the common good as 'arguments

57 Sixty-eight Signatories, 'Doing the Truth in Love: An Evengelical Call for Response to *Caritas in Veritate*,' available from <http://www.firstthings.com/onthesquare/2009/08/doing-the-truth-in-love58-an-evangelical-call-for-response-to-caritas-in-veritate> (cited 18 August 2009).

58 The Vatican II definition of the common good and its theological characteristics are discussed in chapter 4.6.

of how to organize the social economy so as to allow its members to realize a common interest in the provision of certain basic goods to all members of the community'.[59] He points out that social economics recognizes a common good and makes room for a social dimension in economic analysis. Accordingly, it is a critical re-examination of the methodology and assumptions of the orthodox individualistic creed. Indeed not all strands of social economics fall into the problematic application of the economic approach to human behaviour. Welfare economics focuses on the volume and distribution of welfare in relation to national income. It works towards the common good through analysing societal issues such as unemployment, social costs and equality.[60] It recognizes the proposition that competitive equilibrium does not lead naturally to the common good. Welfare economics represents an important step towards the recognition of alternate economic paradigms, the need for humanizing the market, and the involvement of virtuous objectives such as justice, equity and the common good in economic analysis.[61]

Unfortunately, welfare economics and its assertions are often excluded from mainstream economic analysis. Sen laments the increasing gap between ethics and modern economics by pointing out that welfare economics has become increasingly dubious because of the suspicion of the

59 Mark A. Lutz, *Economics for the Common Good: Two Centuries of Social Economic Thought in the Humanistic Tradition* (London: Routledge, 1999), 3.

60 Welfare economics challenges normative utility-based economics and acknowledges the need for rights and freedom. One example is the capability approach advocated by Amartya Sen, discussed in chapter 4.3. These approaches presuppose the basic norms of material sufficiency and respect for human dignity. For a thorough discussion of the history of social and welfare economics, see Ibid., 104–45.

61 Welfare economics remains a specialization to be interpreted and developed. Nevertheless, its underlying criteria appear to be consistent with Scholastic moral philosophy and a view for the common good. As with all methodologies, it contains its own limitations and need for further research. For discussions about these limitations, see Amartya Sen, 'Personal Utilities and Public Judgements: Or What's Wrong With Welfare Economics,' *The Economic Journal* 89 (1979): 537–58; and Stephen Worland, 'Justice and Welfare Economics,' *Review of Social Economy* 63 (2005): 369–82.

use of ethics in economics. Welfare economic assertions are not allowed to influence predictive economics because predictive economics insists that human actions are based on self-interest only.[62] It is not my argument that the abstract economic models which exclude ethical elements are unproductive. Abstractions contain some relevance in themselves when applied appropriately to the market exchange. My argument is that to use these models positively, we need to analyse the results in light of covenant concerns that complement and balance our understanding of economic activities. This is because economic activities have their very fundamental concerns over the human person and persons in relationship with each other. As discussed in chapters 3 and 4, ethics and the common good are integral parts of covenant characteristics. The covenant concept goes beyond these moral concerns through its deep roots in human history and its rich content regarding human life and essential qualities for the well-being of the whole person. The awareness and rediscovery of covenant values can provide insights for the development of economic methodology and assumptions. These interdisciplinary dialogue and reflection are realized through advocating the Two Pillars paradigm to promote the covenant as an essential and complementary foundation to the existing market that is largely contract-based.

According to Benedict XVI, desiring the common good is a requirement of justice and charity.[63] He appropriately asserts that the market does not exist in the pure state but is shaped by the configurations that define it and give it direction.[64] Economics and financial instruments must be used to serve human life and the common good, not vice versa. In this regard, Catholic social teachings that are often seen as an endorsement of the market economy seek to place authentic human social relationships within economic activities. I contend that this notion is indeed an essen-

62 Amartya Sen, *On Ethics and Economics* (Oxford: Basil Blackwell, 1987), 27–57.

63 'To take a stand for the common good is on the one hand to be solicitous for, and on the other hand to avail oneself of, that complex of institutions that give structure to the life of society, juridically, civilly, politically and culturally, making it the *polis*, or "city".' See Benedict XVI, 'Caritas In Veritate,' par. 7.

64 Ibid., par. 36.

tial part of human living and can be positively beneficial when structured and carried out in a balanced and moral way. The covenant captures this notion of the common good and further extends it to present a relational process that is fundamental to creation and human nature. An awareness of the common good helps shift our focus from the benefit of the individual to the aggregate. An understanding of the covenant links this move for sharing and aggregate benefits to a pre-existing foundation of relationships, loyalty and commitment to community. While the common good takes us to the notions of sharing and common concerns, the covenant asserts that such sharing and concerns are based on a stronger cosmic bonding that ties creation together under the relational order fundamental to humankind. The covenant interacts with the contract in the Two Pillars paradigm to ensure a well-balanced economic market as advocated in Catholic social teaching.

The covenant concept that originates from the very beginning of Yahweh's relationship with the chosen people of Israel is thoroughly explored in the Jewish tradition. Sacks presents covenant as the politics of the common good, through which everyone gathers to ensure the dignity of each other. The concept of the common good gives meaning to a responsible society. For example, proper consumption habits take into consideration the common good of environmental protection. Covenantal concerns for the environment not only direct common resources to environmental protection, but also cultivate such responsibility in the daily lives of every citizen. Covenant binds people together in commitment to future interests, such that the related virtues become part of covenantal norms in the community.[65]

Covenant relationships are based on the integrity to preserve freedom and individuality. Therefore covenant necessarily allows for pluralities and differences. Sacks asserts that 'covenants exist because we are different and seek to preserve that difference, even as we come together to bring our several gifts to the common good'.[66] Despite its inadequacy to capture

65 Sacks, *The Home We Build Together: Recreating Society*, 152–3.
66 Sacks, *The Dignity of Difference: How to Avoid the Clash of Civilizations*, 203.

relational processes, the common good contributes to the understanding of the covenant. It enhances secular understanding of the covenant concept and serves to define one of the many targets of covenantal living.[67] Indeed human persons function within different levels or relational spheres ranging from kinship and social relationships, to commercial acquaintance and strangers on the streets. Nevertheless, communities share common relational objectives whether it is in the deepest level of intimacy and sharing, or the wider notion of living in justice and harmony. These basic covenantal spheres are common across time and cultures.

Morality needs to penetrate all aspects and levels of human life, from the individual to the communal, from the familial to the global. As Benedict XVI points out, purchasing is always an act beyond simple economics. It is a moral act through the decision of the moral and economic agent.[68] Social responsibility and other moral concerns present another important reason for establishing market limits. The Two Pillars paradigm actively promotes the awareness and necessity of morality in the market through its covenant pillar. The covenant that advocates self-giving love and mutual trust in turn interacts with the contract that ensures fairness and prevents exploitation. The market does not automatically look after the needs of those who do not have adequate purchasing power at a given time, e.g. children, the sick or disabled. It does not present equality in distributive allocation or consideration for public goods. More importantly, it neither promotes a natural concern for ethics in business, nor equips a standard of morality in individual participants. The presence of market imperfections means

67 When describing the universal sense of community, Mount asserts that 'affirmations about creation in the image of God and covenant with God are one way of enunciating such convictions, but plural religious communities may yet find common cause toward a common good from uncommon starting points'. See Mount, *Covenant, Community and the Common Good: An Interpretation of Christian Ethics*, 51.

68 'Hence the consumer has a specific social responsibility, which goes hand-in-hand with the social responsibility of the enterprise. Consumers should be continually educated regarding their daily role, which can be exercised with respect for moral principles without diminishing the intrinsic economic rationality of the act of purchasing.' See Benedict XVI, 'Caritas In Veritate,' par. 66.

that the economic method of organizing production and distribution in the market does not adequately promote equity or justice.[69] Indeed even perfectly functioning markets cannot ensure equity or justice. Therefore active education and enactment of covenant characteristics must be given high priorities and be developed in the form of economic norms.

The market cannot function properly without morality. Contracts set out the rules and terms of exchange so that participants in a given transaction have something to fall back on. This default mechanism acts as a passive enforcement of trust and increases trustworthiness of a stranger in the market. Consequently, the contract in turn enhances the covenant values of justice and responsibility. These moral measures reside with the parties entering into the transaction. It is up to the market participants, at both the individual and communal levels, to derive and enact moral standards and humanizing measures for market activities. There is a highly significant role for the government and regulators in this process.

6.5 Market Regulations: The Role and Policies of the Government

The scope and content of state intervention in the economic market has been a widely debated subject in politics, law, sociology and economics for many years. Even the original Smithian system recognizes the need for legislation in the market. Smith identifies three vital roles for the government: defence, justice and public works. Defence is for the protection and security of the commonwealth. Justice should be independent from executive powers because it requires full attention and should not be subject to intervention by politics. Public works means that institutions must be

69 Antonio Lattuada, 'A Positive Valuation of the Market in Ethical Perspective,' in *Outside The Market No Salvation?*, ed. Dietmar Mieth and Marciano Vidal (London: SCM Press, 1997), 79.

established to facilitate commerce through different means such as youth education, public instructions, religious teachings, etc. Accordingly, Smith's world of commerce is not an ideology or self-sufficient system, but one that requires institutional intervention to direct it towards positive ends.[70] Society has changed in many complex ways since the Smithian times. Proper governance and legislation in the market are not only important but require continuous refinements and updates in the dynamic modern market.

Sacks points out two institutions dominated society in the past half-century – the state and the market. The state refers to people as a nation. 'The market relates to us as individuals. We choose, we spend, we buy as we wish and can afford, and in so doing we think primarily of ourselves.'[71] The market undermines loyalties by directing an individual's attention towards personal monetary gain or the pursuit of power. It constantly introduces new products, better deals and more attractive options.[72] In the modern market, the Smithian notion of self-interest has been developed and twisted into egocentrism and individualism. The human person is confronted with an environment that rewards quantifiable gains and individualistic pleasures. Self-preservation and human relationships degenerate into self-protection and individual gains. The challenge to modern economists and policy makers is to re-introduce covenantal characteristics in the contractual market to derive a balanced platform for economic functions.

Sacks identifies the market, the state, and covenant as three different approaches to social life and the logic of association. The state forces people to act properly. The market pays people to do so. Both of these require

70 As Muller suggests, the thread that runs through all of Smith's work is 'how the market can be structured to make the pursuit of self-interest benefit consumers; how the passion for the approval of others can make us act more selflessly; how public institutions can be structured to ensure that they deliver the service they are mandated to provide; how other desires for sex and for progeny can be structured by the law to create family institutions that foster self-control; and how institutions concerned with defence and taxation can be structured to avoid unnecessary wars, while averting military defeat which had so often destroyed civilized societies in the past'. See Muller, *Adam Smith in His Time and Ours*, 6–7.

71 Sacks, *The Home We Build Together: Recreating Society*, 149.

72 Ibid., 154–5.

treating people with dignity and respect. In contrast, a moral relationship requires treating people as ends, not means. Covenants create cooperation through moral associations that turn 'you' and 'I' into 'We'. 'Covenant is a binding commitment, entered into by two or more parties, to work and care for one another while respecting the freedom, integrity and difference of each. Covenant is politics without power, economics without self-interest.'[73] I assert that while these are three different approaches to economic life, they need not conflict with each other. The question is how these approaches interact and work together in their respective spheres to promote authentic market activities contributing to positive economic life. The state protects human rights, enhances economic justice and educates the participants. The market provides a platform for free and independent exchange. The covenant creates moral associations, promotes trust and enhances human bonding. In the Two Pillars paradigm, the state takes on a vital role to educate, protect and regulate. It re-iterates the need for a covenantal approach to balance the contractual arrangement, and monitors the contribution to social capital and common good within the market structure.

How and how much should government intervene in market activities? Here we turn again to the work of some economists who attempt to build indirect variables into their models. Becker recognizes the importance of culture, norms, social structure and other indirect factors affecting economic behaviour, but asserts that the techniques and approaches used by other disciplines are not powerful enough to analyse social influence on behaviour. Lifestyles, trends, traditions and cultural norms greatly influence behaviour and choices. Becker's solution is for parents, schools, religions, governments and other institutions to mould the preferences of the next generation. This is done through social markets that capture social forces and factors affecting formation of social groups.[74] I agree that positive norms and preferences need to be educated and cultivated in the society.

73 Ibid., 151.

74 Becker and Murphy, *Social Economics: Market Behavior in a Social Environment*, 4–5.

However, I must add that it is not a matter of blind moulding, but a primary concern for educators and institutions to promote the morality and covenant characteristics that are vital to a well-balanced market and proper understanding of human relationships.

I have already demonstrated how the valuable tool of economics takes on a negative turn when it exceeds market limits. Similar problems start to arise when Becker applies his approach to analyse matters of public concern such as the legitimacy of government spending on terminal care. In a study by Becker, Murphy and Philipson, the value of terminal care is found to be much higher than anticipated, and higher than the marginal value of life, by redefining the economic variables involved. First, the patient's 'willingness to pay' is taken to increase non-linearly towards the end of life. Second, the social value of a life is assumed to be greater than its private value where the extension of a given life has positive external effects on others.[75] Third, the 'hope of living' component that is often ignored on end-of-life care is added to the model. Fourth, the value of life-extension is taken to be independent of the quality of life of the patient. A mathematical model is then constructed based on these assumptions and variables, taking into account other factors such as insurance and medical technologies. The results of this study show that there is a high consumer demand for longevity. This leads to the conclusion that high spending on medical care at the end of life is rational. Based on an economic definition of value, the demand for medical technologies and expensive terminal care therefore presents a huge potential market for investment purposes.[76]

This study of terminal care presents a few points for reflection. First, the concern from funders and policy makers about the 'value' of terminal medical care is not only an economic one. It also involves family values, moral considerations and philosophical worldviews. The economic approach presented involves a great degree of abstraction and finitude in its observa-

75 These positive effects include the concerns of family members, as well as interest groups benefiting from the public provision of care.

76 Gary S. Becker, Kevin M. Murphy and Tomas Philipson, 'The Value of Life Near Its End and Terminal Care,' *National Bureau of Economic Research* 13333 (2007): 1–21.

tions and policy recommendations. Second, the need for re-defining the variables involved in the model represents a previously missing awareness of covenant values in family and society. With the covenant assertions of the Two Pillars paradigm, these missing variables and alternate assumptions should be easily identifiable. Third, the econometrics involved in the analysis has its own limitations in terms of isolating dependent valuables for analysis one at a time. Consequently, it is difficult to consider all variables in aggregate and to observe how they interact. This is a limitation common to many social science methodologies. Fourth, following on the previous point, the problem is not only how these variables are studied, but their definitions that in turn fulfil the 'requirements' of the models in deriving a given set of results.[77] For example, the value of hope is defined as the 'current utility of future survival' in economic terms. The value of life is then found to be an increasing function of hope in a function that denotes the marginal value of life. The positive relationship between hope and marginal value of life is therefore placed in the form of mathematical language in the model based on definition of the variables and their relationship. The result appears intuitive regardless of the economic language. Fifth, although the paper concludes by pointing towards the social value of life and the importance of hope, these life values are affirmed only because of their economic and monetary potential. Incentives for larger spending in terminal care exceed the value of life estimates in the empirical data, making the value of life towards its end higher than expected. The element of hope is thus monetarized, legitimating the allocation of resources into

77 Ferber argues that the most serious problem with the neoclassical model is the crucial assumption that all people are rational, without a clear definition of rationality. She points out that while Becker's model attempts to maximize utility, utility can be defined as whatever is being maximized, and people are assumed to be rational as long as they maximize such utility. This means that the behavioural economic models can be constructed to achieve a predetermined set of results by defining the assumptions and variables to satisfy certain presuppositions. See Marianne A. Ferber, 'A Feminist Critique of the Neoclassical Theory of the Family,' in *Women, Family and Work: Writings on the Economics of Gender*, ed. Karine S. Moe (Massachusetts: Wiley Blackwell, 2003), 13.

terminal care. Insurance and government policies for enhancing terminal care are found necessary because of the inelasticity of demand in this market. Following this trend of thought is dangerous because human life cannot be commodified in monetary terms. The reasons for enhancing terminal care must be derived from a covenantal love that cares for and preserves human life and values.

Taking points four and five together, the economic approach to terminal care is therefore a discussion of the observed reasons for a high demand for terminal care services, and an assertion for placing human qualities such as willingness, hope and social value in economic terms. A monetary value can then be attached to each of these elements for empirical purposes. During this process, human qualities are abstracted and observed based on an assigned meaning. The economic task is to observe, analyse and enhance the efficiency and effectiveness of the caring process, rather than making a judgement of its necessity based upon monetary returns. The question of distribution and allocation of resources needs to consider not only the economic value to the individual and to society as a whole, but also covenantal values such as respect for life and loving care for the others. As a result of abstractions and assumptions, economic analyses of social behaviour disregard transcendent life values and can lead to detrimental implications for policy making.[78] The value of terminal care for wealthy families able to pay for medical care may be higher in economic terms than those in poverty. This does not mean that there are differences in the value of human life.

Benedict XVI appropriately points out the importance of laws and regulations and their proper uses, as follows:

> Economic life undoubtedly requires contracts, in order to regulate relations of exchange between goods of equivalent value. But it also needs just laws and forms of redistribution governed by politics, and what is more, it needs works redolent of the spirit of gift. The economy in the global era seems to privilege the former logic,

78 One example of such abstraction is the discussion on the feasibility of a human organs market detailed in section 6.4 above. Relying on the economic model alone leaves moral considerations out of the decision making process.

> that of contractual exchange, but directly or indirectly it also demonstrates its need for the other two: political logic, and the logic of the unconditional gift.[79]

Political logic and economic functions are closely knitted together in modern society.[80] Results of monetary policies and the ability to promote economic growth significantly influence the result of elections. The direction and basis for government decisions on the economy therefore becomes increasingly important. The times for blind faith in a *laissez-faire* market have passed with the observable increases of inequity and failure of the financial markets.[81] For example the resources for higher education are fixed and regulated. Concerns over social capital and public goods are the primary focus of redistribution. This need has resulted from a lack of awareness in the covenantal characteristics that must work to balance the contractual motives in the economic market.

79 Benedict XVI, 'Caritas In Veritate,' par. 37.

80 Some may misread Benedict XVI's encyclical as one in favour of a world government. In fact, the primary concern of the encyclical is in the underlying anthropological and moral spirit of economic activities. For information about the role of government and institutions discussed in the encyclical, see Douglas A. Sylva, 'Is Benedict in Favor of World Government?,' available from <http://www.firstthings.com/onthesquare/2009/08/is-benedict-in-favor-of-world-government> (cited 20 August 2009). As Kenneally points out, the encyclical does not advocate any specific institutional program or economic policy. It focuses on integral human development in truth and calls for deeper reflection on the economy and its goals. See Kenneally, 'Benedict XVI, Economist,' available from <http://www.firstthings.com/onthesquare/2009/08/pope-benedict-xvi-economist> (cited 21 August 2009).

81 As Atiyah points out, the government is actively involved in the allocation of resources both in developing and developed countries. 'Governments directly control, for instance, the resources to be invested in the nationalized industries, and in all the public goods and services directly supplied by the State or by other public bodies. Governments also effectively manipulate the market, by price controls, wage controls, and other legal and fiscal arrangements which depress demand for this product or stimulate demand for that one. And within the public system itself, the process of decision-making on resource allocation is delegated to Committees or corporate bodies who do not function by market methods.' See Atiyah, *The Rise and Fall of Freedom of Contract*, 717.

6.6 Market as a Continuous Balancing Act between Two Pillars

In an economic experiment called the 'Ultimatum Game', two people are asked to share a sum of money. One person proposes a way of splitting it while the other decides whether to accept. If the second person decides to accept, they split the money accordingly. If the second person does not accept the money, both walk away without any money. According to the self-interest maximizing model, the second person should accept any proposed split that gives the second person a positive amount by the first person. Even a 9:1 split will benefit both parties. However, results of the experiment show that the further away the deal is from a 5:5 split, the more likely for the deal to be rejected. When the first person proposes a split that is perceived to be unfair or exploitative, the second person is likely to reject the deal so that both persons walk away empty-handed.[82] This interesting experiment points towards a reality that transcends a simple self-interested motif for economic activities. Economic relationships always take place within a social context. This places the motives of economic agents beyond mere financial interests. The economic market must become a platform that supports both the reciprocity in exchange activities, and the human characteristics of relationships and gifting. A humanized economic market involves a continuous balancing act of contractual arrangements and covenantal concerns.

Contract is an instrument of economic order and protection. Covenant is a relational process. Formal or written parts of contractual relationships are in fact constitutions establishing legislative and administrative processes for the relationships involved.[83] Examples of these are collective bargaining agreements and corporate charters. Macneil asserts that these formulations

82 Julie A. Nelson, *Economics for Humans* (Chicago: University of Chicago Press, 2006), 73–5.

83 As Ian R. Macneil points out, this view is supported by other legal scholars including Fuller, Cox, and Shulman.

contain dangers of hierarchical misuse and coercion. This is because reliance on such formal constitutional terms reduces patterns of communications and behaviour to a dysfunctional neoclassicism.[84] Participants may suffer from the imbalance of power or imperfect information within the contractual arrangement. Discrete and defined legalism does not promote a continuing and balanced relational exchange. A proper balance between the contract and covenant is therefore vital to the market. Contracts define boundaries with legal authority while covenant establishes the values within. Covenant denotes a process of gifting while contract requires reciprocity. Contract and covenant interact not to exclude the other, but to establish a mutual bond that promotes cooperation in the acts of gifting and receiving. The covenant process does not require reciprocity while the recipient reacts in gratitude and thanksgiving. The act of reciprocity is thus carried out in trust and caring, taking place as a form of communication that transcends a simple transactional exchange.

Some free-market advocates see the economy as a self-regulating machine that can be scientifically analysed through mathematical modelling. This metaphor is an abstraction that does not reflect reality. Nelson finds this metaphor damaging because it encourages irresponsible neoliberal pro-business policies, as well as the development of impractical anti-market alternatives. When the economy is taken as an automatic machine, it is left to run naturally under presupposed self-interest. Nelson asserts that the economy should not take on the metaphor of a machine, but a living organ that is simultaneously a symbol of bodily functioning and a symbol of moral and spiritual life. The 'body' of this living organ involves the economic activities of production, employment, financial responsibility, growth and opportunities for the enjoyment of life. The 'soul' of this living organ denotes the ethical aspects of spiritual development, emotionally healthy relationships, mutual respect, care for the weak and needy, as well as ecological sustainability. A body that lacks the soul leads to an exclusive

84 Ian R. Macneil, 'Contracts: Adjustment of Long-Term Economic Relations under Classical, Neoclassical, and Relational Contract Law,' *Northwestern University Law Review* 72 (1977): 894.

focus on short-term profit, oppressive and alienating work relationships, and a fixation on growth and consumerism. A soul that lacks the body becomes passive about the provision of goods and services, neglect of practical needs and constraints, financial irresponsibility, and fear of money and power.[85] To Nelson, the solution for injecting life into the body of economics is to re-introduce the human soul and ethical concerns into economic activities. This paradigm recognizes the need for the economy to accommodate the reality of human life, i.e. human persons as relational beings that have ethical and spiritual needs. In order for the economic market to support the reality of human living, it must contain the vital characteristics of spiritual and ethical concerns. These are fully and more appropriately captured in the covenant assertions of the Two Pillars paradigm.

While self-love may include both individual needs and wants, community is a basic human need that is unquantifiable in economics and neglected within the market. When human persons form communities that relate to each other under the covenant, both quantifiable and unquantifiable needs are optimized. On the other hand, when persons become individualistic and self-protecting in the market under contractual terms, the powerful persons dominate with their wants at the expense of most other people's needs. Stackhouse identifies 'power' as a realistic factor in all relationships. As a more powerful party enters into relationship with a weaker party, the question of domination is inevitable. Within a covenant, each party becomes bonded into one another's destiny, fully committing under mutually binding principles.[86] Instead of the dehumanizing and impersonal ways of the contract-based market, humanity needs to rediscover the covenantal way that is fundamental to human nature. The relationship between the contract and covenant in the Two Pillars market is a continuously balancing act that supports the reality of authentic human living.

85 Nelson, *Economics for Humans*, 52–61.

86 The covenant is 'an unveiling of the potential for covenantal life given in creation, the promise of God's preservative care for the whole of creation invoked after the neglect of God's ways brought destruction to the earth and after spiritually pretentious humanity brought about the scattering of cultures that fractured any sense of the common good'. See Stackhouse, *Globalization and Grace*, 162.

Identifying the limits of economics and market functions does not reduce the value of economic analysis and expertise. On the contrary, my findings point to a better deployment of economic methods and their significance in analysing market activities as well as providing vital information for policy decisions. At the same time, economic analysis should retain its focus on contractual market variables while maintaining an acute awareness of organic human activities contained in the covenant. The covenant continues to remind us of the need for morality and concern for the common good. An analysis of the Smithian notions of self-interest, benevolence and sympathy reveals that the origin of economics does not presuppose egocentric self-interest or a self-sufficient free market. In fact, Smith emphasizes efficiency and cooperation in the division of labour, and the need for government enactment of defence, justice and public works. What differs between Smithian economics and theology is the former's deistic reliance on the natural evolution of the market. This worldview shows a positive reliance upon human nature and the underlying self-sustaining mechanism conducted through the 'invisible hand'. Theological anthropology questions these presuppositions. A total dependence on human striving and natural evolution cause the market to become increasingly contract-based, eroding covenant characteristics and dehumanizing economic activities to impersonal contractual exchanges. The Two Pillars paradigm is a continuous balancing act that upholds a balanced market for both efficient cooperation and the well-being of the whole person.

CHAPTER 7

Conclusion

7.1 The Quest to Humanize the Market

In this book I have argued for the Two Pillars paradigm, whereby the covenant concept acts and interacts with the contract arrangement to uphold a well-balanced economic market. The preceding chapters present and illustrate a theological response to economics that places theology in public discourse and dialogue. My formulation of this theological response starts from exploring the federal or covenantal foundation of society that humankind has originally been equipped with. The covenant concept has been applied to political society in the past and forms the basis of the original federal political structure. The covenantal federalism of Johannes Althusius provides insights for the application of covenant to society and the economic order. It points towards the historical significance of the covenant concept, as well as its deep roots in the formation of political structures. At the same time, Althusius' description of the polity and its consociations provides a blueprint for human relationships and the economic order. It shows that human relationships transcend material functionalities and can be facilitated by a covenantal social structure to promote covenant values and norms. Economic order is embedded in a covenantal system of codependence and cooperation that not only procures the material necessities of life, but also upholds the rights and equality that are vital to harmonious living and individual well-being.

After identifying the covenant concept as a theological response to society and the economic order, I have proceeded to examine the foundation of the modern market by exploring the economic assumptions about human nature and the Smithian origin of the discipline of economics.

Presuppositions concerning the human nature of self-interest, sympathy and benevolence lead to an economic worldview for the natural evolution of the market. This development is in turn promoted and enhanced by the development of contract arrangements and contract law. The result is a market mechanism that is increasingly contract-based. This mechanism carries its own priorities including maximization of individual utilities, independent freedom of choice, and efficiency in production. It sets rules and boundaries that require measurement in monetary terms and fairness in transactions. The contract-based market contains a tendency for relatively short or fixed exchanges, as well as impersonal and obligatory relationships. Contracts present some benefits such as enabling positive competition, expanding scope and horizon of cooperative exchange, protecting against exploitation, and providing for third-party mediation and arbitration of disputes. In a contract-based market, morality and ethics are upheld through personal decisions and expectations about future benefits or penalties.

Analysis of the positive and negative aspects of contractual arrangements shows that contracts are useful means of market exchange but must be balanced through an alternative measure that captures the organic human aspects of cooperative economic activities. The theological concept of the covenant is identified as the original means of relational exchange put forth by the divine Creator when He seeks to re-establish an everlasting, loving relationship with His people. Characteristics of the covenant such as love, sharing, trust, cooperation, justice, etc., have been embedded in the human heart since creation. The theological task is to rediscover and re-introduce this authentic means of relational exchange to the modern economic market. The covenant does not replace the contract, and should not be confused with the contract. It promotes an open-ended, long-lasting relationship that is communal. Participants in the covenant enter willingly into a sharing relationship with trust, love and commitment. The covenant embraces a view for social bonding, communal ethics and the common good.

Modern economics carries a set of presuppositions including utilities maximization and rational behaviour. However, utilities and profits maximization are not the sole objectives of individuals and corporations. In a living and changing society of human persons, objectives are necessarily multiple and dynamic in nature. Individuals not only maximize utilities but also consider overall well-being, social bonding, family needs and community interests. Corporations attempt to maximize profits while continuing to run their business as going concerns. They aim to develop their business in the long-run, and to protect the interests of multiple participants including shareholders, consumers, suppliers and employees. Economic activities are at the same time balancing acts within a complex multitude of individual, family, social and community considerations. Competition stimulates productivity and efficiency. A perfect market coordinates an optimal allocation of resources. Unfortunately, no market is perfect and its imperfections or defects are highly detrimental to human life. Following the self-regulating route of natural market development presents an increasing over-reliance on the contractual arrangement and monetary mechanism. Moreover, even the market in its perfect form fails to account for the social capital and the common good that are essential to communal living. Cooperation and community must take on covenantal characteristics to enable authentic human living.

I have shown that some economists such as Amartya Sen, feminist economists and others are aware of the limitations of the modern economic paradigm. They show that a paradigm shift is not only necessary but possible by questioning fundamental assumptions in econometrics, or introducing alternative concepts such as the capabilities approach. Such a paradigm shift needs to be actively promoted for the formation of a set of healthy and balanced market norms that recognize both the need for market efficiency and human morality. In response to the need for alternative economic paradigms, I have introduced the theological concept of the covenant, analysed its contents and its relationship with the contract, and illustrated how it can interact positively with the contract to ensure a well-balanced economic market. A market that overly relies on the contract as a means of transaction leads to detrimental effects such as individualism, commodification and dehumanization. A perfect covenantal market of gifting and sharing can only reside in the end of time. I argue for a Two Pillars paradigm whereby covenant and contract act and interact simultaneously to uphold the economic market. The practical application of this paradigm has been illustrated through an examination of the relational contract and long-term employment arrangement in chapter 5. Although relational contracts and game theory serve an alternate view of observing economic activities and attempt to present the relational aspects of economic activities, they fall short of fully capturing certain covenant characteristics that are essential to an employment arrangement. The covenant reminds us that trust, respect, loyalty, integrity, identity and commitment, among others, must be present. These characteristics interact with the contract that protects fairness and equality in the workplace.

The covenantal way of life is strongly rooted in every aspect of the complexities that make up human life and its multiple spheres of social interaction. It embraces an origin dating back to the anthropology of creation, a historical process from the very beginning of Israel as a people of God, and a continuing significance as the very foundation of human relationships. It is a process that enables the continuing quest of humankind in its search for the truth and relational well-being. In covenantal economic relationships human persons finally set aside all fear and doubt to share and cooperate for mutual enjoyment of the gifts from creation. This ultimate economy of grace and gifting presents an eschatological hope that is the longing of every human heart. A perfectly covenantal market is an economy of sharing, gift and grace that can only be realized in the eschaton. The economy of grace requires no contract or legality. It thereby exerts a particular freedom that can be understood as freedom from obligations and necessities. In voluntary giving, the provider gives freely out of love and care while the receiver receives in gratitude and thanksgiving. The participants are free from the burden of reciprocity, sharing in the abundance of resources and communal relationship that underlie the acts of giving and receiving. A true gift does not demand a gift in return. It is a voluntary exertion of a loving act.

A shift from the contract-based approach to the Two Pillars paradigm requires an understanding of the covenant characteristics and development of covenant norms through promotion and education. To promote a paradigm shift by balancing contractual inclinations with relevant covenantal elements, egocentric self-interest must be redirected to relational needs and common interest. Efficiency and competition are balanced with sharing and cooperation. Private rights and ownerships need to take into account social capital and the common good. The market should embrace both the universality and particularity of individual and communal participants. Both personal agency and legal regulations are required as part of the authoritative measures of economic order. Freedom in the market does not involve freedom of choice alone, but also freedom in obedience to authoritative measures, and freedom in terms of caring and sharing. Finally, our quest for perpetual economic growth can be balanced with the covenantal elements of satisfaction, security and thanksgiving. Presentation of the covenant characteristics and the paradigm shift reveals an alternate worldview to the market that at the same time remains feasible and realistic.

The economic market provides a platform of interaction and interdependence for human persons to communicate and cooperate. It serves a positive and important function in society. However, the market also tends to create unintended consequences when left unattended. Distorted human nature causes a natural erosion of human goodness and creates individualistic, coercive or unethical misuse of market functions. A healthy market relies on individuals to act in trust and good faith with a concern for the common good and overall human well-being. These covenant characteristics cannot be discarded in the name of efficiency and economic modelling. Under a purely contractual arrangement, love is reduced to material exchange based on human feelings and will. Losing its transcendent form, pleasure or pain becomes the sole measure of love. Material gains and losses take over as the measurements for relationships, down to those within the family and marital relations.[1] The satisfaction of human needs and wants form the basis of the economic market. The contract that involves consent from the parties involved entering into a mutually agreed upon arrangement appears similar to a covenant, yet without any external normative structure. The human experience involved in such commercial dealings is

1 Stackhouse describes a marriage under contract to be 'a perspective in which the satisfaction of the felt needs of individuals is sovereign, with doubt as to whether any normative order exists for such relationships'. See Stackhouse, *Covenant and Commitments: Faith, Family, and Economic Life*, 32.

based on egocentric self-interest where the interests or value of external entities do not enter into the model for maximization of personal gains. To the modern economist and social contract advocates, the motivator is self-interest. To the covenanters, the motivator is the realization of the need for bonding. The covenant connects the individual to fellow human persons to create mutual dependence based on trust and cooperation. The covenant concept lifts the individual's horizons above and beyond the contractual market to an economic order based on concern for others rather than interest for oneself.

Covenantal communities are bonded in forms of covenantal love rather than transactions of power as in politics, or of wealth.[2] Sacks sees human relationship with God residing in human hearts, while the relationship between two human persons necessitates enactment. Therefore loving kindness need to be practised. He asserts that 'we must love strangers as well as neighbours, in the simple sense of human solidarity, and in a national context, from the covenant of citizenship.'[3] This assertion reminds the economic agent not to forget the morality and kindness that should always be practised even when dealing with strangers in the market. Contract-based transactions should still be grounded upon a covenant undertone of ethical dealings. Rather than the contract being a partial covenant that loses its covenantal essence, the covenant embraces the contract as part of a simple encounter with neighbours even when it is with a stranger in a possibly one-off market transaction.

Brueggemann identifies 'covenant' as a subversive paradigm highly relevant to contemporary living. He asserts that 'the central affirmations of covenant stand against and subvert the dominant forms, patterns and presuppositions of our culture and of cultural Christianity ... the covenant theme offers an alternative perception of how things are in heaven and how

2 Sacks describes these as 'places where we learn the intimate grammar of reciprocity, the delicate choreography of ethical intelligence, the knowledge that love given is not given in vain, and that by sharing our vulnerabilities we discover strength'. See Sacks, *To Heal a Fractured World: The Ethics of Responsibility*, 54.

3 Sacks, *The Home We Build Together: Recreating Society*, 180.

they could be on earth'.[4] The concept of covenant reminds us of renewal and community. It points towards a new ecclesiology and solidarity in a culture of division and isolation. Lamenting the failure of sociology in providing possibilities of community, Brueggemann proclaims the most unlikely thing of a community of solidarity on earth, simply because God moves towards solidarity in heaven. Therefore solidarity is possible on earth, through human covenanting, making all things new.[5] The covenant is one of the major forms of providential ordering. It institutionalizes the scriptural models presented in the relationship between God and human persons, providing a model for the formation of civil societies.[6] The covenant concept rides above other patterns of human relationships because it embeds the purposes of the divine order, will and care. The Jewish community is one that has a strong tradition of the covenantal way of life. Human beings have an inherent propensity for contractual relationships that protect the interests of the relevant parties, whether from a standpoint of self-interest or mutual interests. These mutually agreed upon contracts can include a covenantal dimension, or a gradation of covenantalism.[7]

Stackhouse points out that the modern person is confounded with multiple vocations to multiple covenants. Everybody faces their own sets of complex experiences within areas of work, family, economics, education, recreation, politics, religious commitments, etc. In order to retain integrity through these mazes, we must recognize our authentic nature in the image of God, and the covenantal nature of our vocations in the pluralisms of life. We must hold tight to a sense of calling and empowerment by God in our service, so that the kingdom of God can be enacted starting from within

4 Brueggemann, 'Covenant as a Subversive Paradigm,' 1094.

5 Ibid., 1096.

6 Stackhouse, *Globalization and Grace*, 163.

7 The Jewish political scientist Daniel J. Elazar puts forth the idea of 'gradations of covenantalism' from a tendency of human persons to carry out contractual transactions based on mutual agreement. These gradations are to be found in between the concepts of covenant and contract. See Daniel J. Elazar, *Covenant & Commonwealth: From Christian Separation through the Protestant Reformation* (New Brunswick: Transaction Publishers, 1996), 8.

ourselves. The doctrine of vocation was extended and applied to all believers during the Reformation. This converges with the concept of covenant in all the arenas of life, including material market exchanges. The covenant concept stands over and above impersonal contractual dealings to provide meaningful human relationships. Covenants ought to be seen as means of grace and service that start from the self-giving love of Christians who act to realize their authentic human nature in the image of God. These are Christians who understand the calling to live rich and full lives in each of the complex areas of human life, taking them as possible means of grace. These areas can and may breakdown, be distorted, fail, and even become destructive. Nevertheless, Christians must hold tight to the faith that these destructive trends are reversible and reconcilable upon God's redemptive power in Christ.[8] As such, it is the task of the community of faith to seek covenantal renewals in all aspects of life on earth. Being one of the most fundamental desires of human nature, the material aspects of economics remain at the very forefront of this battlefield between the self-interested, impersonal contract, and the self-giving moral covenant.

7.2 Further Research, Dialogue and Limitations

The covenantal polity is deeply rooted in the historical development of political structures. As discussed in chapter 3, the covenant is known to humankind as part of human nature in the order of creation. Covenant characteristics are embedded in human goodness and are revealed through the human quest for truth. The covenant is not a new invention, but a rediscovery of the original intention of creation and relational order. It marks the process and means of relationship between humankind and the Divine, as well as among human persons. Through the quest for knowledge and truth, we can discover and apply humanistic alternatives to the market that reflect

8 Stackhouse, *Covenant and Commitments: Faith, Family, and Economic Life*, 155–7.

human goodness and promote total well-being. Interdisciplinary dialogue contributes significantly to this quest. The analysis of fundamental worldviews, discussion of alternate approaches, and openness in the exchange of knowledge, all help to contribute to this purpose.

Modern society consists of a multitude of communal spheres, each with its own covenantal objectives and contractual rules. The Two Pillars paradigm does not offer a perfect solution to economic problems. In fact, even the perfect market cannot ensure perfect solutions because of the finitude and sinful tendency within human nature. The Two Pillars paradigm offers a frame of reference in order to observe, analyse and reflect upon economic situations. It promotes the need for humanizing the market for overall well-being, and presents this possibility through the enactment of covenant values. It contributes to the awareness and understanding of the interdependence and necessary interactions between contractual legalities and covenantal characteristics in the market. Based on this framework, individual market participants are constantly reminded of the importance of both contract and covenant in economic activities. The market in aggregate is reminded of the need for a balanced set of values and norms to enhance overall human well-being.

The Two Pillars paradigm is only a starting point. Its application and relevance have been demonstrated in chapter 5. Similar to the employment arrangements and relational contracts discussed in chapter 5, the framework can be further applied to analyse other similar topics such as property purchase or rental arrangement, debts and financial instruments, wealth and monetary units, welfare and public goods, ecological concerns, education and healthcare, etc. It is a starting point for further application to specific economic issues as they arise. The strength of this paradigm lies both in its practical applicability to economic issues, as well as its universality and relevance for both believers and non-believers alike. It serves as a continuous reminder that covenant characteristics are valuable and vital to human life, while the contract serves a parallel and equally important role in the modern market exchange.

The Two Pillars paradigm follows the ethical-practical theological approach presented by Herman Bavinck. This approach places the Two Pillars paradigm in the arena of public theology in response to society. Since economic life resides within the context of the political and sociological environment, we can be facing a number of different issues at the same time during the attempt to regulate economic life, making the situation highly complex and rather unpredictable. Political problems such as government instability, terrorism and international strife are highly detrimental to economic activities. Attempts to control these effects involve dealing with different worldviews, interest groups and cultures beyond the capability of an economic paradigm alone. Other issues such as global climate change or ecological preservation involve both political and economic decisions that require covenantal cooperation among different nations. These are all big issues that challenge the application of both covenant values and contractual legalities through complicated processes of negotiation. For example, climate and ecology are areas more fundamental to human life then political and economic interests. They concern the place and responsibility of humanity within the cosmic creation, as well as the ontological existence of the whole cosmos. Covenant awareness contributes to reflection on these issues by pointing out the theological worldview and by calling for the pursuit of the divine order embedded in creation. The Two Pillars paradigm remains far from providing easy solutions to these complex economic issues, but serves to remind decision-makers about the need for enactment of covenant values.

As a theological response to the market, the scope of this book is limited to a fundamental reflection on the underlying economic worldview, assumptions and approach. The notions of covenant and contract explored are limited to the scriptural and theological covenants, and the legal and economic contracts. It does not explore alternate views on human nature and development of the social contract. Since economic order necessarily resides within the context of political structures, the organization of society and the mechanism of coordination among communities and individuals have a significant impact on economic activities. The role of the state and institutions, societal structures, social welfare considerations and the influence of the constitutional political economy are further areas of research suggested by the Two Pillars paradigm in its context within the polis.

My study on the behavioural economics of Gary Becker shows that market and nonmarket activities must be segregated and treated appropriately according to their genuine nature. Commodification of nonmarket human qualities induces distortions and unintended negative consequences. A proper worldview starts with a thorough understanding of and reflection upon human nature, rather than an attempt to impose the worldview of economics into all walks of life. Economic security and equality result from a concern for community life, love and sharing. In Scripture, such qualities result from a dependence on the Creator, giver of all life and material abundance. In the human community, these same qualities result from a communal effort to enact the covenant principles of loving, sharing and gifting.

Economics is a discipline that necessarily involves debates regarding fundamental values, political decisions, sociological concerns and psychological responses. It affects so many aspects of human life at both the individual and societal levels that warrant not only interdisciplinary, but multidisciplinary exchange of information and insights. There is a close relationship between economics and politics, especially in modern times when financial policies and economic outcomes greatly influence public votes. Indeed the market is a vital part of human life, serving as a means for cooperation and codependence. The close relationship of economics, politics and society further reiterates the importance of upholding covenantal values through education and development of social norms. As the market broadens its scope to become globalized, understanding and enactment of covenant characteristics are increasingly significant since these characteristics remain fundamental and essential to the overall well-being of both individuals and communities.

My critique of the economic approach and behavioural models does not suggest a diminished role for economists. Contrary to this, I find the discipline of economics increasingly important in the modern world when markets expand globally and economic activities continue to flourish. The economists of this age carry the vital mission of research and reflection on the means and ends in promoting healthy economic activities that support cooperation, moral and harmonious living. Young economists should be equipped not only with the science of econometrics, but a broader worldview of sharing, caring, trust and cooperation necessary for societal living. The importance of economic philosophy that marks the roots and origin of the discipline should not be overlooked. Econometric models need to be enhanced through new mathematical approaches, as well as supplemented by philosophical reflections. The rapidly changing modern times call for continuous re-examination of basic economic approaches and assumptions, and challenges the economists to derive methods tailored to the age of globalization and dynamic change.

The Two Pillars paradigm puts forth a motion that draws upon the missing covenantal characteristic essential to human nature in order to balance the contractual inclination of the market exchange. The role of the government and institutions is equally important in the modern economy. The market can serve as an efficient and effective means of exchange, but it must contain the proper standards and limits. There are also nonmarket aspects of human life that need to be addressed as such. These include the activities of family units, social welfare, public goods and societal norms. Theology provides fragments of fundamental truth to facilitate reflection and development of individuals as well as of human society. Economists are the experts in observing and analyzing market information. Government and institutions serve to deploy the findings of the experts and enact the regulations and common interest that serves society as a whole.

From a wider perspective, this book presents an interdisciplinary study between theology and the humanities, in particular the discipline of economics. It extends towards a multidiscipline essence as the study also draws upon the work of sociologists and legal scholars where appropriate. It offers a comprehensive paradigm in contrast to the traditional piecemeal discussion of ethical issues in economics. The paradigm is realistic and relevant rather than ideological in nature. To understand the complex human person and the dynamic economic activities in modern times, it is necessary to integrate the variety of knowledge and resources offered across academic disciplines. Such integrative analysis can provide results and recommendations that are not attainable from a single academic discipline alone.

Modern economic problems and the financial crisis remind us of the need for a deeper understanding of human nature and the human situation with greater humility and open-mindedness. This understanding can be further promoted through an integration of knowledge and input from multiple disciplines. In this regard, theological anthropology and the Christian worldview present valuable insights. The economic issues confronting us today are multiple and complex. The Two Pillars paradigm asserts a covenant balance that contributes to observations, analysis and decision-making both at the individual and communal levels. This does not mean that problems become easily resolved. In reality, covenant concerns add to the complexity of economic models and may complicate the decision-making process. This is because if only a monetary, impersonal and egocentric focus is maintained, our models and decisions can be abstracted and simplified. The covenant values of charity, love, commitment, etc. carry risks and undesirable consequences. Within human finitude and sinfulness, free gifting may induce disappointment and loss. At the same time, it is only through the exertion of covenant values that humankind may find its identity, truth, and the goodness of human life.

It is neither implied, not is it necessary that all parties to a covenant are converted believers. The existential importance of the covenant in Christian experience is that believers reside in the hope of God's people, with the virtues, strength and eschatological context of living a life of faith. The promise of perfect agape love is given to the believer, who is protected and empowered to act accordingly.[9] Covenant is about narratives and renewal. The story-telling nature of covenantal narratives allows persons in community to form societies with memory and identity. A society of free persons enters into covenantal relationships to work together for a gracious, just and compassionate world. Such a society is moral, future-oriented and goal-directed, with each person being a participant on a journey towards a destination. A covenantal society democratizes responsibility, allows pluralistic freedom, and empowers its citizens.[10] This covenantal way of living is risky because one does not enter into covenants on the basis that others are trustworthy. As Cronin points out, we are always engaged in the process of putting ourselves in the hands of others – doctors, car mechanics,

9 Horton, *Covenant and Eschatology: The Divine Drama*, 17–18.
10 Sacks, *The Home We Build Together: Recreating Society*, 120–5.

teachers, parents, etc. Accordingly, what is most often conveyed in human relationships is a sense of responsibility rather than gift, although the gift or grace element remains in the background. Through participation in covenantal relationships, the human person expresses participation in the inclusive covenant that embraces all humanity. Covenant takes the notion of human nature as the image of God from its metaphysical discussion to concrete interpersonal relationships. In this light, the Torah of Israel is not merely law and order, but loving guidance that enacts the biblical teachings of justice, kindness and humility before God.[11]

7.3 The Call for Covenantal Living

I have drawn upon the covenant concept and covenant theology from the Protestant tradition and as a scriptural theme in this book. In line with this Protestant approach, I have deployed a theological notion of human nature that follows the Calvinist tradition. On certain occasions, I have engaged with Catholic social teachings to illustrate the particular concepts of labour and morality. The starting point of my argument is that economics begins from assumptions about human nature. In formulating a theological response to the modern economic market, I have drawn from theological sources as well as multiple disciplines including economics, law and sociology. I sympathize with the Christian personalism approach that engages with the existing human situation, acknowledges the need for an economic system to satisfy human needs, and advocates the need for development of the human person. This approach recognizes liberty in terms of authentic value and in the context of community with others. At the same time, my covenant standpoint differs from Christian personalism in that it places a higher priority on the relationship between God and humanity. I find Christian personalism overly optimistic about human

11 Cronin, *Rights and Christian Ethics*, 210–16.

morality and the capacity to know the Creator. Accordingly, an economy of sharing and personal responsibility is an ultimate goodness that one strives for but remains partially unrealizable for the moment. The contract serves an interim purpose of governance and protection in this regard. In the modern world where a multitude of different value systems claim allegiance, Christian covenantal living serves to witness the presence of the kingdom of God in an already-but-not-yet manner. At the same time, the boundaries between spiritual and secular may not be as concrete as advocated in the past. The Creator God remains the God of providence whose sovereignty embraces the natural and the secular while injecting fragments of truth in the self-giving love that He reveals to humankind.

A covenantal culture of trust, cooperation and community life is vital to genuine human life. The covenant pillar of the Two Pillars paradigm continuously reminds us of the need to protect morality, foster communal life, and to act as good stewards to all creation. It reminds us that proper concepts of freedom and morality must be educated and communicated. The contract necessitates and enables commodities to take on a common monetary value. The covenant acknowledges the values of gifting and sharing. A relational contract binds the participants to the voluntary legal obligations concerned. A covenantal relationship transcends the formal agreement to embody implicit human qualities of caring and sharing. The covenant provides for intimacy and bonding while the contract protects again exploitation.

To the Christian who is residing in this already-but-not-yet life on earth, all human persons are fully submerged in market activities and economic life. To live the full Christian life includes taking up the covenantal responsibilities and stewardship of economic pursuits. As earthly economic agents, we abide by the rules of the contract and the legal regulations of the market. At the same time, we must remain fully aware of the covenant characteristics that we exert through a deep longing of the spiritual in our hearts. Covenant and contract serve together to uphold market activities for authentic human living that treats persons as organic individuals and communal beings who act in relation to each other. In this regard, it is up to the Christians in all walks of life to carry the mission of Christ in witnessing and demonstrating the love of God through covenantal living.

The Christian community is called to act as 'light of the world' in every aspect of daily living. Dealing primarily with the allocation of material resources, economics appears to be the least significant area when it comes to spiritual concerns. Perhaps this is partly the reason for its neglect by Christian scholars throughout the ages. Paradoxically, economics is also the most influential sphere of life affecting both believers and non-believers whether they are concerned with the spiritual or not. It is indeed the very frontline of the battlefield for issues affecting contemporary living. Nowadays, economic concerns have extended beyond trade and commerce to penetrate areas such as healthcare, education, welfare services, etc. The modern day Christian is finding it harder to uphold Christian values when confronted with economic priorities. In light of such difficulties, a covenantal paradigm provides energy and courage afresh for Christian mission. As Brueggemann suggests, 'the world is intended by God to be a community that covenants, that distributes its produce equally, that values all its members, and that brings the strong and the weak together in common work and common joy'.[12] It is the mission of the believing community to articulate, anticipate and practise this covenantal renewal and transformation.

To the non-Christian who naturally resides in economic market, we must understand and be aware of the market values that in turn affect our overall well-being. The covenant concept is a basic fundamental paradigm for human relationships and community life. It embraces the morality, responsibility and commitment that have been eroded in modern society. A rediscovery and renewal of the covenant way of living is essential not only to economic order, but to all spheres of society. As Niebuhr asserts, 'the world has this fundamental moral structure of a covenant society and that what is possible and required in the political realm is the affirmation and reaffirmation of man's responsibility as a promise-maker, promise-keeper, a covenanter in universal community.'[13]

12 Brueggemann, 'Covenant as a Subversive Paradigm,' 1097.

13 Niebuhr, 'The Idea of Covenant and American Democracy,' 135.

An understanding of the significance, characteristics and interactions of the contract and covenant is only a starting point. It is the first step towards balancing market activities within the Two Pillars paradigm. Social sciences can present mega theories and models that analyse societal living. Theology can suggest fragments of truth to provide insights and reflections. However, it is up to each and every individual economic agent to decide and enact human values that transcend mere contractual or monetary concerns. The covenant is the mean that helps us achieve this end together. It is the essential tool to attain a well-balanced economy, a tool that is known to humankind from the beginning of time but gradually eroded as we over-rely on contract-based activities.

The call for covenantal living is a redemptive call for rediscovery of and return to an authentic human life in relation to the Divine, other human persons, and the whole cosmos. It draws the participants to a transcendent truth that embraces the goodness of creation and the ability to enjoy the abundance received as gift. It asserts that genuine morality should be nurtured in the human heart so that it becomes an intrinsic motivator for the economic agent to carry out moral acts. The terms of the covenant echo the requirement of a contractual arrangement. However, it is not a mere contract of exchange. It is a covenantal contract in which a reciprocity of justice, compassion and humility is called for not in obligation, but in gratitude to the steadfast love of God as the prophet Micah proclaims, 'He has showed you, O man, what is good; and what does the Lord require of you but to do justice, and to love kindness, and to walk humbly with your God?' (Micah 6:8)

Bibliography

Agus, Jacob B. 'The Covenant Concept – Particularistic, Pluralistic, or Futuristic,' *Journal of Ecumenical Studies* 18 (1981): 217–30.

Allen, Joseph L. *Love and Conflict: A Covenantal Model of Christian Ethics*. Nashville: Abingdon Press, 1984.

Althusius, Johannes. *Politica*. Indianapolis: Liberty Fund, 1995.

Arce, M., Daniel, G. and Sandler, Todd. 'The Dilemma of the Prisoners' Dilemmas,' *Kyklos* 58 (2005): 3–24.

Atherton, John. *Transfiguring Capitalism*. London: SCM Press, 2008.

Atiyah, P.S. *The Rise and Fall of Freedom of Contract*. Oxford: Clarendon Press, 1979.

Axelrod, Robert. *The Evolution of Cooperation*. London: Penguin, 1990.

Bader-Saye, Scott. 'The Freedom of Faithfulness,' *Pro Ecclesia* 8 (1999): 437–58.

Baker, George, Gibbons, Robert and Murphy, Kevin J. 'Relational Contracts and the Theory of the Firm,' *The Quarterly Journal of Economics* 117 (2002): 39–84.

Baker, J. Wayne. 'Faces of Federalism: From Bullinger to Jefferson,' *Publius* 30, no. 4 (2000): 25–41.

Barnett, Tim and Schubert, Elizabeth. 'Perceptions of the Ethical Work Climate and Covenantal Relationships,' *Journal of Business Ethics* 36 (2002): 279–90.

Barth, Karl. *Church Dogmatics*. Edinburgh: T. & T. Clark, 1958.

Bavinck, Herman. *Reformed Dogmatics, vol. 1: Prolegomena*. Grand Rapids: Baker Academic, 2003.

Bavinck, Herman. *Reformed Dogmatics, vol. 2: God and Creation*. Grand Rapids: Baker Academic, 2004.

Bavinck, Herman. *Reformed Dogmatics, vol. 3: Sin and Salvation in Christ*. Grand Rapids: Baker Academic, 2006.

Bavinck, Herman. *Reformed Dogmatics, vol. 4: Holy Spirit, Church, and New Creation*. Grand Rapids: Baker Academic, 2008.

Becker, Gary S. *Accounting for Tastes*. Massachusetts: Harvard University Press, 1996.

Becker, Gary S. *The Economic Approach to Human Behavior*. Chicago: The University of Chicago Press, 1976.

Becker, Gary S. and Elísa, Julio Jorge. 'Introducing Incentives in the Market for Live and Cadaveric Organ Donations,' *Journal of Economic Perspectives* 21, no. 3 (2007): 3–24.
Becker, Gary S. and Murphy, Kevin M. *Social Economics: Market Behavior in a Social Environment*. Massachusetts: Belknap Press, 2000.
Becker, Gary S., Murphy, Kevin M. and Philipson, Tomas. 'The Value of Life Near Its End and Terminal Care,' *National Bureau of Economic Research* 13333 (2007): 1–21.
Benedict XVI, Pope. 'Caritas In Veritate,' *Encyclical Letter* (2009).
Bergmann, Barbara R. 'Becker's Theory of the Family: Preposterous Conclusions,' *Challenge* Jan–Feb (1996): 9–12.
Bergmann, Barbara R. 'Needed: A New Empiricism,' *Economists' Voice* 4, no. 2 (2007): 1–4.
Berman, Harold J. 'The Religious Sources of General Contract Law: An Historical Perspective,' *Journal of Law and Religion* 4 (1986): 103–24.
Bernheim, B. Douglas and Whinston, Michael D. 'Incomplete Contracts and Stategic Ambiguity,' *American Economic Review* 88 (1998): 902–32.
Bird, Robert C. 'Employment as a Relational Contract,' *University of Pennsylvania Journal of Labor and Employment Law* 8 (2005): 149–217.
Blake, Judith. 'Are Babies Consumer Durables: A Critique of the Economic Theory of Reproductive Motivation,' *Population Studies* 22 (1968): 5–25.
Blau, Judith R. *Social Contracts and Economic Markets*. New York: Plenum Press, 1993.
Booth, Philip, ed. *Catholic Social Teaching and the Market Economy*. London: Institute of Economic Affairs, 2007.
Botman, H. Russel. 'Covenantal Anthropology: Integrating Three Contemporary Discourses of Human Dignity.' In *God and Human Dignity*, ed. Soulen, R. Kendall and Linda Woodhead, 72–86. Grand Rapids: Eerdmans, 2006.
Bratt, James D., ed. *Abraham Kuyper: A Centennial Reader*. Grand Rapids: Eerdmans, 1998.
Bright, John. *Covenant and Promise*. London: SCM Press, 1977.
Bromley, David G. and Busching, Bruce C. 'Understanding the Structure of Contractual and Covenantal Social Relations: Implications for the Sociology of Religion,' *Sociological Analysis* 49 (1988): 15–32.
Brousseau, Kenneth R., Driver, Michael, J., Eneroth, Kristina and Larsson, Rikard. 'Career Pandemonium: Realigning Organizations and Individuals,' *Academy of Management Executives* 10, no. 4 (1996): 52–66.
Brueggemann, Walter. 'Covenant as a Subversive Paradigm,' *Christian Century* 97 (1980): 1094–9.

Brueggemann, Walter. 'Covenanting as Human Vocation: A Discussion of the Relation of Bible and Pastoral Care,' *Interpretation* 33 (1979): 115–29.

Bull, Clive. 'The Existence of Self-Enforcing Implicit Contracts,' *The Quarterly Journal of Economics* 102 (1987): 147–60.

Byrne, Peter. *Natural Religion and the Nature of Religion: The Legacy of Deism* London: Routledge, 1989.

Caldwell, Cam and Karri, Ranjan. 'Organizational Governance and Ethical Systems: A Covenantal Approach to Building Trust,' *Journal of Business Ethics* 58 (2005): 249–59.

Carlyle, R.W. and Carlyle, A.J. *A History of Mediaeval Political Theory in the West*. London: William Blackwood & Sons, 1936.

Carney, Frederick S. 'Association Thought in Early Calvinism.' In *Voluntary Associations: A Study of Groups in Free Societies*, ed. Robertson, D.B., 39–53. Richmond: Westminster John Knox Press, 1966.

Chaplin, Jonathan. 'Suspended Communities or Covenanted Communities? Reformed Reflections on the Social Thought of Radical Orthodoxy.' In *Radical Orthodoxy and the Reformed Tradition*, ed. Smith, James K.A. and James H. Olthuis, Grand Rapids: Baker Academics, 2005.

Congdon, Tim. 'The Law: Freedom or Merit?,' *Ecoonomic Affairs* 14, no. 2 (1994): 41.

Cortina, Adela. *Covenant and Contract: Politics, Ethics and Religion*. Leuven: Peeters, 2003.

Cosden, Darrell. *A Theology of Work: Work and the New Creation*. Cumbria: Paternoster, 2004.

Craswell, Richard. 'Contract Law, Default Rules, and the Philosophy of Promising,' *Michigan Law Review* 88 (1989–1990): 489–529.

Cronin, Kieran. *Rights and Christian Ethics*. Cambridge: Cambridge University Press, 1992.

Daly, Herman E. and Cobb, John B., Jr. *For the Common Good: Redirecting the Economy Toward Community, the Enviornment, and a Sustainable Future*. Boston: Beacon Press, 1989.

Davis, J. Ronnie. 'Adam Smith on the Providential Reconciliation of Individual and Social Interests: Is Man Led by an Invisible Hand or Misled by a Sleight of Hand?,' *History of Political Economy* 22 (1990): 341–52.

Dayton-Johnson, Jeff. 'Knitted Warmth: The Simple Analytics of Social Cohesion,' *The Journal of Socio-Economics* 32 (2003): 623–45.

Elazar, Daniel J. 'Althusius and Federalism as Grand Design'. Available from <http://www.jcpa.org/dje/articles2/althus-fed.htm> (cited 15 February 2008).

Elazar, Daniel J. *Covenant & Commonwealth: From Christian Separation through the Protestant Reformation*. New Brunswick: Transaction Publishers, 1996.

Elazar, Daniel J. *Covenant & Polity in Biblical Israel: Biblical Foundations & Jewish Expressions*. New Brunswick: Transaction, 1998.

Elazar, Daniel J. and Kincard, John, ed. *The Covenant Connection: From Federal Theology to Modern Federalism*. New York: Lexington, 2000.

Evensky, Jerry. 'Adam Smith's Moral Philosophy: The Role of Religion and Its Relationship to Philosophy and Ethics in the Evolution of Society,' *History of Political Economy* 30 (1998): 17–42.

Evensky, Jerry. '"Chicago Smith" versus "Kirkaldy Smith",' *History of Political Economy* 37 (2005): 197–203.

Evensky, Jerry. 'The Two Voices of Adam Smith: Moral Philosopher and Social Critic,' *History of Political Economy* 19 (1987): 447–68.

Everett, William Johnson. 'Contract and Covenant in Human Community,' *Emory Law Journal* 36 (1987): 557–68.

Feinman, Jay M. 'Critical Approaches to Contract Law,' *UCLA Law Review* 30 (1982): 829–60.

Feinman, Jay M. 'Significance of Contract Theory,' *University of Cincinnati Law Review* 58 (1990): 1283–318.

Ferber, Marianne A. 'A Feminist Critique of the Neoclassical Theory of the Family.' In *Women, Family and Work: Writings on the Economics of Gender*, ed. Moe, Karine S., Massachusetts: Wiley Blackwell, 2003.

Ferber, Marianne A. and Birnbaum, Bonnie G. 'The "New Home Economics:" Retrospects and Prospects,' *The Journal of Consumer Research* 4 (1977): 19–28.

Figgis, John Neville. *From Gerson to Grotius*. Cambridge: Cambridge University Press, 1916.

Figgis, John Neville. 'Political Thought in the Sixteenth Century.' In *The Cambridge Modern History*, ed. Ward, A.W., G.W. Prothero and S. Leathes, Cambridge: Cambridge University Press, 1905.

Fins, Joseph J. 'From Contract to Covenant in Advance Care Planning,' *Journal of Law, Medicine and Ethics* 27 (1999): 46–51.

Forrester, Duncan B. *Christian Justice and Public Policy*. Cambridge: Cambridge University Press, 1997.

Forrester, Duncan B. *On Human Worth: A Christian Vindication of Equality*. London: SCM Press, 2001.

Forrester, Duncan B. *Theological Fragments: Explorations in Unsystematic Theology*. New York: T & T Clark, 2005.

Forrester, Duncan B. and Skene, Danus. *Just Sharing: A Christian Approach to the Distribution of Wealth, Income and Benefits*. London: Epworth Press, 1988.

Forrester, W.R. *Christian Vocation: Studies in Faith and Work*. London: Lutterworth, 1951.

Fox, Alan. *Beyond Contract: Work, Power and Trust Relations*. London: Faber, 1974.

Frank, Robert H. 'Beyond Self-Interest,' *Challenge* Mar–Apr (1989): 4–13.

Friedman, Lawrence M. *Contract Law in America: A Social and Economic Case Study*. Wisconsin: University of Wisconsin Press, 1965.

Friedrich, Carl J. *The Age of the Baroque*. New York: Harper & Row, 1952.

Gardner, E. Clinton. *Justice and Christian Ethics*. Cambridge: Cambridge University Press, 1995.

Gasper, Des. 'Is Sen's Capability Approach an Adequate Basis for Considering Human Development?,' *Review of Political Economy* 14 (2002): 435–61.

Gierke, Otto von. *The Development of Political Theory*. New York: Howard Fertig, 1966.

Gilbert, Daniel R. Jr. 'The Prisoner's Dilemma and the Prisoners of the Prisoner's Dilemma,' *Business Ethics Quarterly* 6 (1996): 165–78.

Goldberg, Victor P. 'A Relational Exchange Perspective on the Employment Relationship.' In *Firms, Organization and Labour: Approaches to the Economics of Work Organization*, ed. Stephen, Frank H., 127–45. London: Macmillian, 1984.

Goldingay, John. *Old Testament Theology Vol. I: Israel's Gospel*. Illinois: InterVasity Press, 2003.

Gooch, George P. *English Democratic Ideas in the Seventeenth Century*. Cambridge: Cambridge University Press, 1927.

Gorski, Philip S. 'Calvinism and Revolution: The Walzer Thesis Reconsidered.' In *Meaning and Modernity*, ed. Madsen, Richard, 78–104. Berkeley: University of California Press, 2002.

Gorsky, Jonathan. 'Beyond inclusivism: Richard Harries, Jonathan Sacks and The Dignity of Difference,' *Scottish Journal of Theology* 57 (2004): 366–76.

Gough, J.W. *The Social Contract: A Critical Study of Its Development*. Oxford: Clarendon Press, 1957.

Grau, Marion. *Of Divine Economy: Refinancing Redemption*. New York: T & T Clark, 2005.

Harper, Ian R. and Gregg, Samuel, ed. *Christian Theology and Market Economics*. Cheltenham: Edward Elgar, 2008.

Hartropp, Andy. 'Christianity and Economics: An Annotated Bibliography by Andy Hartropp', *Journal of the Association of Christian Economists* special issue (December 1997): 1–36.

Hay, Donald A. *Economics Today: A Christian Critique*. Vancouver: Regent College Publishing, 2001.

Herman, Stewart W. *Durable Goods: A Covenantal Ethic for Management and Employees*. Notre Dame: University of Notre Dame Press, 1997.

Hill, Lisa. 'The Hidden Theology of Adam Smith,' *The European Journal of the History of Economic Thought* 8 (2001): 1–29.

Hill, Peter J. and Lunn, John. 'Markets and Morality: Things Ethicists Should Consider When Evaluating Market Exchange,' *Journal of Religious Ethics* 35, no. 4 (2007): 627–53.

Hollenbach, David. *The Common Good and Christian Ethics*. Cambridge: Cambridge University Press, 2002.

Horton, Michael S. *Covenant and Eschatology: The Divine Drama*. Louisville: Westminster John Knox Press, 2002.

Horsley, Richard A. *Covenant Economics: A Biblical Vision of Justice for All*. Louisville: Westminster John Knox Press, 2009.

Hübner, Hans. 'Covenant.' In *The Encyclopedia of Christianity*, ed. Fahlbusch, Erwin, Jan Milic Lochman, John Mibiti, Jaroslav Pelikan and Lukas Vischer, 710–13. Grand Rapids: Eerdmans, 1999.

Hueglin, Thomas O. 'Covenant and Federalism in the Politics of Althusius.' In *The Covenant Connection: From Federal Theolgoy to Modern Federalism*, ed. Elazar, Daniel J. and John Kincard, New York: Lexington, 2000.

Hueglin, Thomas O. *Early Modern Concepts for a Late Modern World: Althusius on Community and Federalism*. Waterloo: Wilfrid Laurier University Press, 1999.

Hueglin, Thomas O. 'Johannes Althusius: Medieval Constitutionalist or Modern Federalist?,' *Publius* 9, no. 4 (1979): 9–41.

Hueglin, Thomas O. and Fenna, Alan. *Comparative Federalism*. Toronto: Broadview Press, 2006.

Hviid, Morten. 'Long-Term Contracts and Relational Contracts.' In *Encyclopedia of Law and Economics*, ed. Bouckaert, Boudewijn and Gerrit de Geest, 46–72. Cheltenham: 2000.

Hviid, Morten. 'Relational Contracts, Repeated Interaction and Contract Modification,' *European Journal of Law and Economics* 5 (1998): 179–94.

Iannaccone, Laurence R. 'Economics of Religion: Debating the Costs and Benefits of a New Field,' *The Economics of Religion: A Symposium* (2005).

Jenkins, Willis. *Ecologies of Grace: Environmental Ethics and Christian Theology*. New York: Oxford University Press, 2008.

John Paul II, Pope. 'Laborem Exercens,' *Encyclical Letter* (1981).

Kalleberg, Arne L. 'Nonstandard Employment Relations: Part-time, Temporary and Contract Work,' *Annual Review of Sociology* 26 (2000): 341–65.

Karlberg, Mark W. *Covenant Theology in Reformed Perspective*. Oregon: Wipf and Stock Publishers, 2000.

Kenneally. 'Benedict XVI, Economist'. Available from <http://www.firstthings.com/onthesquare/2009/08/pope-benedict-xvi-economist> (cited 21 August 2009).

Kessler, Friedrich. 'Contracts of Adhesion – Some Thoughts about Freedom of Contract,' *Columbia Law Review* 43 (1943): 629–42.

Klempa, William. 'The Concept of the Covenant in 16th and 17th Century Continental and British Reformed Theology.' In *A Covenant Challenge to Our Broken World*, ed. Miller, Allen O., 130–47. Atlanta: Darby Printing, 1982.

Kraus, Hans J. 'God's Covenant: Old and New Testaments.' In *A Covenant Challenge to Our Broken World*, ed. Miller, Allen O., 79–83. Atlanta: Darby Printing, 1982.

Lattuada, Antonio. 'A Positive Valuation of the Market in Ethical Perspective.' In *Outside The Market No Salvation?*, ed. Mieth, Dietmar and Marciano Vidal, 77–84. London: SCM Press, 1997.

Lawrence, Lesa W., Rappaport, Harvey M., Feldhaus, Joseph B., Bethke, Art L. and Stevens, Robert E. 'A Study of the Pharmacist–Patient Relationship: Covenant or Contract?,' *Journal of Pharmaceutical Marketing and Management* 9, no. 3 (1995): 21–40.

Lawson, Daniel. 'Gary Becker and the Quest for the Theory of Everything,' *University of Notre Dame* (2004).

Leibenstein, Harvey. 'The Prisoners' Dilemma in the Invisible Hand: An Analysis of Intrafirm Productivity,' *American Economic Review* 72, no. 2 (1982): 92–7.

Leo XIII, Pope. 'Rerum Novarum,' *Encyclical Letter* (1891).

Levin, Jonathan. 'Multilateral Contracting and the Employment Relationship,' *The Quarterly Journal of Economics* 117 (2002): 1075–103.

Long, D. Stephen. *Divine Economy: Theology and the Market*. London: Routledge, 2000.

Long, D. Stephen and Fox, Nancy R. *Calculated Futures: Theology, Ethics, and Economics*. Texas: Baylor University Press, 2007.

Lovin, Robin W. 'Equality and Covenant Theology,' *Journal of Law and Religion* 2 (1984): 241–62.

Loy, David R. 'The Religion of the Market,' *Journal of the American Academy of Religion* 65 (1997): 275–90.

Lutz, Mark A. *Economics for the Common Good: Two Centuries of Social Economic Thought in the Humanistic Tradition*. London: Routledge, 1999.

MacLeod, W. Bentley and Malcomson, James M. 'Implicit Contracts, Incentive Compatibility, and Involuntary Unemployment,' *Econometrica* 57 (1989): 447–80.

Macneil, Ian R. 'Contracts: Adjustment of Long-Term Economic Relations under Classical, Neoclassical, and Relational Contract Law,' *Northwestern University Law Review* 72 (1977): 854–905.

Macneil, Ian R. *The New Social Contract: An Inquiry into Modern Contractual Relations*. New Haven: Yale University Press, 1980.

Maitland, Ian. 'Virtuous Markets,' *Business Ethics Quarterly* 7 (1997): 17–31.

Marsden, David. 'The "Network Economy" and Models of the Employment Contract,' *British Journal of Industrial Relations* 42 (2004): 659–84.

May, William F. 'Code, Covenant, Contract, or Philanthropy,' *The Hastings Center Report* 5, no. 6 (1975): 29–38.

McCoy, Charles S. and Baker, J. Wayne. *Fountainhead of Federalism*. Louisville: Westminster John Knox Press, 1991.

Meeks, M. Douglas. 'Being Human in the Market Society,' *Quarterly Review* 21 (2001): 254–65.

Meeks, M. Douglas. 'The Economy of Grace: Human Dignity in the Market System.' In *God and Human Dignity*, ed. Soulen, R. Kendall and Linda Woodhead, 196–214. Grand Rapids: Eerdmans, 2006.

Meeks, M. Douglas. *God the Economist: The Doctrine of God and Political Economy*. Minneapolis: Fortress Press, 1989.

Meilaender, Gilbert. 'A View from Somewhere: The Political Thought of Michael Walzer,' *Religious Studies Review* (1990): 197–201.

Mieth, Dietmar and Vidal, Marciano, ed. *Outside the Market No Salvation?* London: SCM Press, 1997.

Miller, Allen O., ed. *A Covenant Challenge to Our Broken World*. Atlanta: Darby Printing, 1982.

Moe, Karine S., ed. *Women, Family, and Work: Writings on the Economics of Gender*. Massachusetts: Wiley Blackwell, 2003.

Moltmann-Wendel, Elisabeth and Moltmann, Jürgen. *Humanity in God*. London: SCM Press, 1983.

Moltmann, Jürgen. *The Church in the Power of the Spirit*. London: SCM Press, 1977.

Moltmann, Jürgen. *Creating a Just Future: The Politics of Peace and the Ethics of Creation in a Threatened World*. London: SCM Press, 1989.

Moltmann, Jürgen. *God for a Secular Society: The Public Relevance of Theology*. London: SCM Press, 1999.

Moltmann, Jürgen. *God in Creation: An Ecological Doctrine of Creation*. London: SCM Press, 1985.

Moltmann, Jürgen. *Man: Christian Anthropology in the Conflicts of the Present*. Philadelphia: Fortress Press, 1971.

Moltmann, Jürgen. *The Trinity and the Kingdom of God: The Doctrine of God.* London: SCM Press, 1981.

Moltmann, Jürgen. *The Way of Jesus Christ: Christology in Messianic Dimensions.* London: SCM Press, 1990.

Montes, Leonidas. 'Das Adam Smith Problem: Its Origins, the Stages of the Current Debate, and One Implication for Our Understanding of Sympathy,' *Journal of the History of Economic Thought* 25 (2003): 63–90.

Moser, Paul K. 'Human Persons: Their Nature, Faith, and Function,' *Ex Auditu* 13 (1997): 17–36.

Mount, Eric Jr. *Covenant, Community and the Common Good: An Interpretation of Christian Ethics.* Cleveland: The Pilgrim Press, 1999.

Mulcahy, Linda and Tillotson, John. *Contract Law in Perspective.* London: Cavendish Publishing, 2004.

Muller, Jerry Z. *Adam Smith in His Time and Ours.* New Jersey: Princeton University Press, 1993.

Nell, Edd S. 'A Reformed Approach to Economics: Christian Reconstructionism,' *Journal of the Association of Christian Economists* (1993): 6–20.

Nelson, Julie A. *Economics for Humans.* Chicago: University of Chicago Press, 2006.

Nelson, Julie A. *Feminism, Objectivity and Economics.* London: Routledge, 1996.

Nelson, Robert H. *Economics as Religion: From Samuelson to Chicago and Beyond.* Pennsylvania: Pennsylvania State University Press, 2001.

Nelson, Robert H. 'What is "Economic Theology"?' Second Abraham Kuyper Consultation on 'Theology and Economic Life: Exploring Hidden Links' Princeton Theological Seminary, Princeton, New Jersey, 22 March 2003.

Newman, Louis E. 'Covenant and Contract: A Framework for the Analysis of Jewish Ethics,' *Journal of Law and Religion* 9 (1991): 89–112.

Niebuhr, H. Richard. 'The Idea of Covenant and American Democracy,' *Church History* 23 (1954): 126–35.

Niebuhr, H. Richard. 'The Religious Assumptions of Adam Smith,' *Journal of Theology for Southern Africa* 44 (2006): 6–22.

Nieli, Russell. 'Spheres of Intimacy and the Adam Smith Problem,' *Journal of the History of Ideas* 47 (1986): 611–24.

Novak, Michael. 'Pope Benedict XVI's *Caritas*.' Available from <http://www.firstthings.com/onthesquare/2009/08/pope-benedict-xvis-caritas-1> (cited 17 August 2009).

Nussbaum, Martha C. 'Flawed Foundations: The Philosophical Critique of (a Particular Type of) Economics,' *The University of Chicago Law Review* 64 (1997): 1197–1214.

O'Hara, Erin Ann. 'Trustworthiness and Contract.' In *Moral Markets: The Critical Role of Values in the Economy*, ed. Zak, Paul J., New Jersey: Princeton University Press, 2008.

O'Neill, Onora. *A Question of Trust*. Cambridge: Cambridge University Press, 2002.

Ogletree, Thomas W. *Hospitality to the Stranger: Dimensions of Moral Understanding*. Louisville: Westminster John Knox Press, 2003.

Oncken, August. 'The Consistency of Adam Smith,' *The Economic Journal* 7 (1897): 443–50.

Oslington, Paul. 'A Theological Economics,' *International Journal of Social Economics* 27 (2000): 32–44.

Oswald, Donald J. 'Metaphysical Beliefs and the Foundations of Smithian Political Economy,' *History of Political Economy* 27 (1995): 449–76.

Paul, Ellen Frankel, Miller, Fred D. Jr. and Paul, Jeffrey, ed. *Ethics and Economics*. Oxford: Basil Blackwell, 1985.

Pava, Moses L. 'The Many Paths to Covenantal Leadership: Traditional Resources for Contemporary Business,' *Journal of Business Ethics* 29 (2001): 85–93.

Pearce, David G. and Stacchetti, Ennio. 'The Interaction of Implicit and Explicit Contracts in Repeated Agency,' *Games and Economic Behavior* 23 (1998): 75–96.

Peil, Jan. *Adam Smith and Economic Science: A Methodological Reinterpretation*. Cheltenham: Edward Elgar, 1999.

Phillips, Jeremy. 'Caveat Caritas!,' *Journal of Intellectual Property Law and Practice* 4 (2009): 603.

Polanyi, Karl. *The Great Transformation: The Political and Economic Origins of Our Time*. Boston: Beacon Press, 1957.

Pollak, Robert A. 'Gary Becker's Contributions to Family and Household Economics,' *Review of Economics of the Household* 1 (2003): 111–41.

Pressman, Steven and Summerfield, Gale. 'Sen and Capabilities,' *Review of Political Economy* 14 (2002): 429–34.

Preston, Ronald H. *Religion and the Ambiguities of Capitalism*. London: SCM Press, 1991.

Rae, John. *Life of Adam Smith*. London: Macmillan, 1895.

Raphael, D.D. *Adam Smith*. Oxford: Oxford University Press, 1985.

Rendtorff, Rolf. '"Covenant" as a Structuring Concept in Genesis and Exodus,' *Journal of Biblical Literature* 108 (1989): 385–93.

Richardson, J. David. 'Frontiers in Economics and Christian Scholarship,' *Christian Scholar's Review* 17, no. 4 (1988): 1–20.

Rieger, Joerg. *No Rising Tide: Theology, Economics and the Future*. Minneapolis: Fortress Press, 2009.

Riley, Patrick. 'Three 17th Century German Theorists of Federalism: Althusius, Hugo and Leibniz,' *Publius* 6, no. 3 (1976): 7–41.

Robertson, D.B., ed. *Voluntary Associations: A Study of Groups in Free Societies*. Richmond: Westminster John Knox Press, 1966.

Rothman, Rozann. 'The Impact of Covenant and Contract Theories on Conceptions of the U.S Constitution,' *Publius* 10, no. 4 (1980): 149–63.

Rothschild, Emma. 'Adam Smith and the Invisible Hand,' *American Economic Review* 84, no. 2 (1994): 319–22.

Rousseau, Denise M. 'Psychological and Implied Contracts in Organizations,' *Employee Responsibilities and Rights Journal* 2 (1989): 121–39.

Sacks, Jonathan. *The Dignity of Difference: How to Avoid the Clash of Civilizations*. London: Continuum, 2003.

Sacks, Jonathan. *The Home We Build Together: Recreating Society*. London: Continuum, 2007.

Sacks, Jonathan. 'Markets and Morals,' *First Things* 105 (2000): 23–8.

Sacks, Jonathan. *To Heal a Fractured World: The Ethics of Responsibility*. London: Continuum, 2005.

Salmon, J.H.M. *The French Religious Wars in English Political Thought*. Oxford: Clarendon Press, 1959.

Sauer, James B. 'Christian Faith, Economy, and Economics: What Do Christian Ethics Contribute to Understanding Economies?,' *Journal of the Association of Christian Economists* 42 (2003): 17–25.

Sen, Amartya. *Choice, Welfare and Measurement*. Oxford: Basil Blackwell, 1982.

Sen, Amartya. *Development as Freedom*. Oxford: Oxford University Press, 1999.

Sen, Amartya. *Moral Codes and Economic Success*. London: London School of Economics, 1993.

Sen, Amartya. 'The Moral Standing of the Market.' In *Ethics and Economics*, ed. Paul, Ellen Frankel, Fred D. Jr. Miller and Jeffrey Paul, 1–19. Oxford: Basil Blackwell, 1985.

Sen, Amartya. *On Ethics and Economics*. Oxford: Basil Blackwell, 1987.

Sen, Amartya. 'Personal Utilities and Public Judgements: Or What's Wrong With Welfare Economics,' *The Economic Journal* 89 (1979): 537–58.

Sen, Amartya. *Resources, Values and Development*. Oxford: Basil Blackwell, 1984.

Sen, Amartya. *The Standard of Living*. Cambridge: Cambridge University Press, 1985.

Signatories, Sixty-eight. 'Doing the Truth in Love: An Evengelical Call for Response to *Caritas in Veritate*.' Available from <http://www.firstthings.com/onthesquare/

2009/08/doing-the-truth-in-love58-an-evangelical-call-for-response-to-caritas-in-veritate> (cited 18 August 2009).
Siker, Louke van Wensveen. 'An Unlikely Dialogue: Barth and Business Ethicists on Human Work,' *Annual of the Society of Christian Ethics* (1989): 131–45.
Skillen, James W. 'From Covenant of Grace to Equitable Public Pluralism: The Dutch Calvinist Contribution,' *Calvin Theological Journal* 31 (2006): 67–96.
Skinner, Quentin. *The Foundations of Modern Political Thought*. Cambridge: Cambridge University Press, 1978.
Skinner, Quentin. *Visions of Politics*. Cambridge: Cambridge University Press, 2002.
Smith, Adam. *An Inquiry into the Nature and Causes of the Wealth of Nations*. Indianapolis: Liberty Press, 1981.
Smith, Adam. *Lectures on Jurisprudence*. Indianapolis: Liberty Press, 1982.
Smith, Adam. *The Theory of Moral Sentiments*. Indianapolis: Liberty Press, 1981.
Smith, James K.A. and Olthuis, James H., ed. *Radical Orthodoxy and the Reformed Tradition*. Grand Rapids: Baker Academic, 2005.
Smith, Timothy L. 'Work and Human Worth,' *Christian Century* 84 (1967): 1094–7.
Soulen, R. Kendall and Woodhead, Linda, ed. *God and Human Dignity*. Grand Rapids: Eerdmans, 2006.
Stackhouse, Max L. *Covenant and Commitments: Faith, Family, and Economic Life*. Louisville: Westminster John Knox Press, 1997.
Stackhouse, Max L. *Globalization and Grace*. New York: Continuum, 2007.
Stackhouse, Max L. 'The Moral Meanings of Covenant,' *Annual of the Society of Christian Ethics* (1996): 249–64.
Stackhouse, Max L. *Public Theology and Political Economy: Christian Stewardship in Modern Society*. Grad Rapids: Eerdmans, 1987.
Stackhouse, Max L., McCann, Dennis and Roels, Shirley J., ed. *On Moral Business: Classical and Contemporary Resources for Ethics in Economic Life*. Grand Rapids: Eerdmans, 1995.
Stephen, Frank H., ed. *Firms, Organization and Labour: Approaches to the Economics of Work Organization*. London: Macmillian, 1984.
Sylva, Douglas A. 'Is Benedict in Favor of World Government?' Available from <http://www.firstthings.com/onthesquare/2009/08/is-benedict-in-favor-of-world-government> (cited 20 August 2009).
Tanner, Kathryn. *Economy of Grace*. Minneapolis: Fortress Press, 2005.
Tawney, Ronald H. *Religion and the Rise of Capitalism*. London: John Murray, 1948.

Teichgraeber, Richard F. 'Rethinking Das Adam Smith Problem,' *Journal of British Studies* 20 (1981): 106–23.

Tiemstra, John P. 'Christianity and Economics: A Review of the Recent Literature,' *Christian Scholar's Review* 22 (1993): 227–47.

Tiemstra, John P., ed. *Reforming Economics: Calvinist Studies on Methods and Institutions*. New York: Edwin Mellen Press, 1990.

Torrance, Alan J. 'On Deriving "Ought" from "Is": Christology, Covenant and *Koinonia*.' In *The Doctrine of God and Theological Ethics*, ed. Torrance, Alan J. and Michael Banner, London: T & T Clark, 2006.

Torrance, Alan J. and Banner, Michael, ed. *The Doctrine of God and Theological Ethics*. London: T & T Clark, 2006.

Torrance, James B. 'The Covenant Concept in Scottish Theology and Politics and Its Legacy,' *Scottish Journal of Theology* 34 (1981): 225–43.

Trebilcock, Michael J. *The Limits of Freedom of Contract*. London: Harvard University Press, 1993.

Trimiew, Darryl M. 'The Renewal of Covenant and the Problem of Economic Rights: The Contributions of Daniel Elazar,' *Annual of the Society of Christian Ethics* 20 (2000): 105–9.

Tucker, Gene M. 'Covenant Forms and Contract Forms,' *Vetus Testamentum* 15 (1965): 487–503.

Tullock, Gordon. 'Adam Smith and the Prisoners' Dilemma,' *The Quarterly Journal of Economics* 100 (1985): 1073–81.

Waldman, Don E. *Microeconomics*. Boston: Pearson Addison Wesley, 2004.

Walzer, Michael. *The Revolution of the Saints: A Study in the Origins of Radical Politics*. London: Weidenfeld and Nicolson, 1966.

Ward, A.W., Prothero, G.W. and Leathes, S., ed. *The Cambridge Modern History*. Cambridge: Cambridge University Press, 1905.

Warsh, David. 'How Selfish Are People – Really?,' *Harvard Business Review* May–Jun (1989): 26–34.

Waterman, Anthony Michael C. 'Economists on the Relation Between Political Economy and Christian Theology: A Preliminary Survey,' *International Journal of Social Economics* 14 (1987): 46–68.

Wehberg, Hans. 'Pacta Sunt Servanda,' *The American Journal of International Law* 53 (1959): 775–86.

Weingartner, Robert J. review of *Economy of Grace*, by Tanner, Kathryn, *Missiology*, 34 (2006): 262–4.

Weir, David A. *The Origins of the Federal Theology in Sixteenth-Century Reformation Thought*. Oxford: Clarendon Press, 1990.

Werhane, P.H. *Adam Smith and His Legacy for Modern Capitalism*. Oxford: Oxford University Press, 1991.

Wogaman, J. Philip. review of *God the Economist: The Doctrine of God and Political Economy*, *Theology Today*, 47 (1990): 198–202.

Worland, Stephen. 'Justice and Welfare Economics,' *Review of Social Economy* 63 (2005): 369–82.

Zak, Paul J., ed. *Moral Markets: The Critical Role of Values in the Economy*. New Jersey: Princeton University Press, 2008.

Index

STUDIES IN THEOLOGY SOCIETY AND CULTURE

Religious and theological reflection has often been confined to the realm of the private, the personal or the Church. In Europe this restriction of religion and theology can be traced back to the Enlightenment and has had long-lasting and pernicious consequences for the understanding of religious faith and society. On the one hand, there has been a rise in religious fundamentalisms around the globe, while, on the other hand, so-called advanced societies are constructed mainly along economic, pragmatic and rationalistic lines. Added to this is the reality that religious faith is increasingly lived out in pluralistic and multi-faith contexts with all the challenges and opportunities this offers to denominational religion.

This series explores what it means to be 'religious' in such contexts. It invites scholarly contributions to themes including patterns of secularisation, postmodern challenges to religion, and the relation of faith and culture. From a theological perspective it seeks constructive re-interpretations of traditional Christian topics – including God, creation, salvation, Christology, ecclesiology, etc. – in a way that makes them more credible for today. It also welcomes studies on religion and science, and on theology and the arts.

The series publishes monographs, comparative studies, interdisciplinary projects, conference proceedings and edited books. It attracts well-researched, especially interdisciplinary, studies which open new approaches to religion or focus on interesting case studies. The language of the series is English. Book proposals should be emailed to any, or all, of the following:

Series Editors:

- Dr Declan Marmion, Milltown Institute of Theology and Philosophy, Sandford Road, Dublin 6, Ireland (dmarmion@milltown-institute.ie)
- Dr Gesa Thiessen, Milltown Institute of Theology and Philosophy, Sandford Road, Dublin 6, Ireland (gthiessen@milltown-institute.ie)
- Dr Norbert Hintersteiner, Irish School of Ecumenics, Bea House, Milltown Park, Dublin 6, Ireland (norbert.hintersteiner@tcd.ie)

Vol. 1 Patrick Claffey and Joe Egan (eds):
Movement or Moment? Assessing Liberation Theology Forty Years after Medellín.
276 pages. 2009. ISBN 978-3-03911-991-2.

Vol. 2 Declan Marmion and Gesa Thiessen (eds):
Trinity and Salvation: Theological, Spiritual and Aesthetic Perspectives.
197 pages. 2009. ISBN 978-3-03911-969-1.

Vol. 3 Pádraic Conway and Fáinche Ryan (eds):
Karl Rahner: Theologian for the Twenty-first Century.
265 pages. 2010. ISBN 978-3-0343-0127-5.

Vol. 4 Declan O'Byrne:
Spirit Christology and Trinity in the Theology of David Coffey.
274 pages. 2010. ISBN 978-3-0343-0191-6.

Vol. 5 Joe Egan:
From Misery to Hope: Encountering God in the Abyss of Suffering.
384 pages. 2010. ISBN 978-3-0343-0234-0.

Vol. 6 Forthcoming

Vol. 7 Jean Lee:
The Two Pillars of the Market: A Paradigm for Dialogue between Theology and Economics.
301 pages. 2011. ISBN 978-3-0343-0700-0.